# Slavery and Freedom in the Mid-Hudson Valley

SUNY SERIES, AN AMERICAN REGION:
STUDIES IN THE HUDSON VALLEY

THOMAS S. WERMUTH, EDITOR

# Slavery and Freedom in the Mid-Hudson Valley

Michael E. Groth

SUNY PRESS

Published by State University of New York Press, Albany



Printed in the United States of America



For information, contact State University of New York Press, Albany, NY
www.sunypress.edu

Production, Ryan Morris
Marketing, Fran Keneston

Library of Congress Cataloging-in-Publication Data

Names: Groth, Michael E., 1965- author.
Title: Slavery and freedom in the Mid-Hudson Valley / Michael E. Groth.
Description: Albany, NY : State University of New York Press, [2017] | Series: SUNY series, An American region: studies in the Hudson Valley | Includes bibliographical references and index.
Identifiers: LCCN 2016031418 (print) | LCCN 2016045943 (ebook) | ISBN 9781438464572 (hardcover : alk. paper) | ISBN 9781438464565 (pbk. : alk. paper) | ISBN 9781438464589 (ebook)
Subjects: LCSH: African Americans--Hudson River Valley (N.Y and N.J.)--History. | African Americans--New York--Dutchess County--History. | African Americans--Hudson River Valley (N.Y. and N.J.)--Race identity. | Slavery--New York (State)--Dutchess County--History. | Slaves--Emancipation--New York (State) | Antislavery movements--New York (State)--History. | Hudson River Valley (N.Y. and N.J.)--History. | Dutchess County--History.
Classification: LCC F127.H8 G88 2017 (print) | LCC F127.H8 (ebook) | DDC 306.3/620974733--dc23
LC record available at https://lccn.loc.gov/201603141

10 9 8 7 6 5 4 3 2 1

# Contents

# Tables and Illustrations

# Acknowledgments

This volume is probably too many years in the making. I owe significant debts to many. I must begin by expressing appreciation to Thomas Dublin, under whose thoughtful mentorship this project began as a dissertation at Binghamton University more than two decades ago. Other historians at Binghamton at the time who contributed to my doctoral work in some way include Richard Dalfiume, Melvyn Dubofsky, Sarah Elbert, Paul Finkelman, David McBride, and Brendan McConville. Colleagues at Dutchess County colleges proved especially helpful in this project's early stages. Clyde Griffen of Vassar generously shared the research he and his wife Sally completed years ago for their study of mid-nineteenth-century Poughkeepsie. It was always a pleasure to work with Richard Wiles at Bard College, who very generously shared his expertise in local and regional history. His colleague Frank Oja instructed me in SPSS.

I have had several opportunities over the years to rethink my original dissertation in the form of conference papers, professional articles, book chapters, and public lectures. Stefan Bielinski, Thomas J. Davis, Douglas Egerton, Graham Hodges, Andor Skotnes, Nikki Taylor, Margaret Washington, Shane White, and Donald Wright provided criticism and advice as panel chairs, commentators, and conference participants. Richard Wiles and Wendell Tripp provided valuable editorial direction for early articles on manumission and the freedom struggle in the Mid-Hudson Valley. I must also thank Thomas Wermuth and the staff at the *Hudson River Valley Review*. Joseph Tiedemann, Eugene Fingerhut, and Robert Venables served as editors for an earlier version of chapter 2 that appeared in *The Other Loyalists*. Fergus Bordewich shared thoughts about the Underground Railroad in the Hudson Valley region. I am particularly grateful to colleagues who have joined me in exploring the black experience in the Hudson Valley. A. J. Williams-Myers first pointed to the richness of the regional African American experience decades ago. Myra Young Armstead and Edythe Ann Quinn have provided advice and encouragement throughout this long process. I got to know each of them when this project was in its infancy. An earlier version of chapter 3 appeared in Myra's collection *Mighty Change, Tall Within*. I am especially thankful to Myra for providing the final push to get me to complete this book once and for all.

This volume would not have been possible without the indispensable assistance of many librarians, archivists, and state and local historians. The local history collection at Adriance Memorial Library in Poughkeepsie is extraordinarily rich, and the assistance Myra Morales and her staff provided many years ago proved invaluable. The Office of the Dutchess County Historian and different individuals associated with the Dutchess County Historical Society have been very helpful over the years. Eileen Hayden provided valuable assistance during the preliminary stages of this project. Lorraine Roberts and the founding members of the black history committee posed provocative questions and provided encouragement. Sheila Webb at the Church of Jesus Christ of Latter-day Saints in Poughkeepsie provided a wealth of historical and genealogical knowledge. I must also thank archivists, librarians, and staff at Bard College, Binghamton University, Cornell University, the Dutchess County Archives, the Dutchess County Surrogate's Court, the Franklin Delano Roosevelt Library in Hyde Park, the Manuscript and Records Division at the New York Public Library, the New-York Historical Society, the New York State Archives and Library in Albany, the New York State Historical Association in Cooperstown, the Pleasant Valley Historical Society, the Rhinebeck Historical Society, the Schomburg Center for Research in Black Culture, the Stanford Public Library, the Starr Library in Rhinebeck, Vassar College, and Wells College. The Poughkeepsie City School District graciously shared early school records. Reverend McLaughlin, pastor of Poughkeepsie's Smith Metropolitan AMEZ Church in the early 1990s, provided information on early church history.

Teaching obligations and administrative responsibilities at a very small liberal arts college have delayed the completion of this project, but I would like to think that more than two decades as a faculty member at Wells College have enriched the volume in other ways. Teaching a wide variety of courses in US history has allowed me to appreciate the complexity of the American experience. Thoughtful questions and perceptive observations from many Wells students over the years have allowed me to perceive issues and questions through their eyes. I must also thank my colleagues at Wells, whose provocative questions at different Faculty Club presentations over the years forced me to think about my work from different disciplinary perspectives. A sabbatical leave enabled me to complete the manuscript.

Several individuals have assisted me in the final stages of this project. I thank the anonymous readers of the preliminary manuscript for their perceptive observations and criticisms. SUNY Press acquisitions editor Amanda Lanne-Camilli helped to usher me through the preliminary stages of the publication process. I am especially grateful to Jessica Kirschner, who promptly and patiently answered my many questions. Ryan Morris guided me through the final stages of the production process. Lisa Hoff in the Wells College library helped to track down obscure citations. David Foote at Wells College, Patricia Moore at the Dutchess County Historical Society, and Dyan Wapnick at Saint James Episcopal Church in Hyde Park helped to identify and improve digital images.

I owe the greatest debt to those closest to me. Sandy, Michaela, Monica, Jonathan, and Daniel played no direct roles in the production of this volume. In fact, they probably share at least some blame for the long delay in its completion. For that—for consistently reminding me about what is most important—I'm eternally grateful. Finally, I must thank my parents, Ed and Lorraine, whose unconditional love and unfailing encouragement made all the difference in the world. I dedicate this book to them.

# Introduction

SLAVERY WAS HARDLY A SOUTHERN PHENOMENON. It became the American South's "peculiar institution" only after it ended in most other parts of the Americas during the late eighteenth and early nineteenth centuries. Over the past decades, historians have exposed the largely forgotten history of slavery in the North and its aftermath. The slave system was never as integral to the development of the Middle Colonies and New England as it was in the mainland South or West Indies, and the northern slave population remained comparatively small. However, the increasing importance of black labor during the seventeenth and eighteenth centuries transformed the northern colonies into full-fledged slave societies by the eve of the Revolution. Not only did slaves assume important economic roles, but the institution also deeply embedded itself into the political, social, and cultural fabric of northern life.[1] The "racialization" of slavery—the association of bondage with black skin and the hardening of boundaries between freedom and slavery—left an indelible and lasting impact. Slavery in New York and other parts of the North ended only after a painfully long process, and its legacy cast a long shadow. During the early decades of the republic, race remained central to the construction of nationalism, economic growth, the emergence of middle-class culture, and the popularization of politics. Race assumed inordinate importance in the wake of northern emancipation, as intensifying racial prejudice and discrimination provided anxious whites a semblance of security and order amid rapid and convulsive change. Although a courageous abolitionist minority valiantly defied the intensifying negrophobia of the antebellum period, a majority of white Americans by the mid-nineteenth century had constructed a racially exclusive definition of citizenship that equated freedom with whiteness and set people of color apart as a decidedly inferior caste. Ultimately, the experience of slavery in the North, the ordeal of northern emancipation, and the emergence of white supremacy in the nominally Free States are as vital to understanding racial formation in the United States before the Civil War as the expansion of slavery across the Lower South.[2]

Explorations into the history of race in the North have focused heavily on the experiences of emancipated slaves and free people of color before the Civil War. Although black northerners represented only a small fraction of the nation's African American population and comprised no more than two percent of the population of the Free States, their lives provide valuable insights into the nature of race, citizenship, and democracy in the American experience. A small minority, free blacks remained a troubling anomaly in a nation that recognized slavery and defined citizenship in racial terms. In many respects, black Northerners lived on society's margins, largely excluded from skilled trades and professions, denied educational opportunities and avenues of advancement, subjected to popular contempt and ridicule, and disqualified from the rights and privileges of full citizenship. For the most part, however, the thrust of scholarship on the free black experience has cast African Americans not as passive victims but as actors who demonstrated agency, creativity, and resilience. A few decades ago, Ira Berlin identified the Revolutionary Era as a transformative moment when men and women liberated from bondage laid the foundations of free black life.[3] Scholars in the generations since have demonstrated that racial oppression and economic adversity served as catalysts for the formation of dynamic communities that adapted creatively to hostile environments. Free blacks in the North established independent households, churches, educational institutions, fraternal societies, and benevolent associations that nurtured a collective consciousness and provided a wellspring of political activism and protest. Throughout the Early Republic and antebellum period, black abolitionists waged a relentless crusade against slavery in the South and racial discrimination in the North, thereby composing an eloquent and powerful counternarrative to proslavery thought and the ideology of white supremacy.[4]

Having demonstrated the vibrancy of black life in the Early Republic, historians have begun to delve deeper for more sophisticated and nuanced understandings of community and African American identity.

The contours of black life varied across both time and space. African American culture was incredibly dynamic and adaptive, evolving and changing over time. There was never a single "free black experience." Northern communities differed from those in the Slave South and Midwest; free people of color in seaports led lives different from those in interior regions. Even in the Free States, regional cultural differences distinguished black Bostonians, Cincinnatians, New Yorkers, and Philadelphians from each other. Moreover, the very concept of a free black community itself can be problematic. Free African Americans, most of whom were native-born, were simply too few to create institutions that were fully separate or formulate a cultural worldview fundamentally different from that of the overwhelming white majority. "Community" is a highly ambiguous term. A product of sentiment as well as a function of personal networks and social institutions, the "free black community" was in part a romanticized ideological construct that can obscure as much as it reveals. As Billy Smith has pointed out, "community" had little practical meaning for many working people preoccupied with the daily struggle for survival.[5] Leslie Harris has suggested that a community can be better understood not as a static entity but as a fluid and dynamic *process* of intersections among different people, forces, and contested ideas.[6] Individual communities were hardly homogeneous; members differed according to nativity, cultural heritage, color, age, class, gender, education, religious belief, and political ideology. Failure to acknowledge divisions and even discord would only romanticize a mythical free African American experience and ignore the genuine devastation wrought by slavery and racism. Ultimately, only an honest assessment that exposes conflict as well as consensus, victimization as well as agency, and failure as well as triumph can fully humanize those who lived in the past.[7]

Whatever their differences, all people of color occupied a unique social space in the United States. Common ancestry and the shared experience of oppression united all Americans of African descent in the generations before the Civil War.[8] All free blacks ultimately confronted the most agonizing questions about their place in American life. The forging of an independent community life after emancipation should be understood not only as an exercise of freedom but also as an attempt to define individual and collective identity. Over the course of many generations, Euro-Americans had come to associate liberty with whiteness and equate slavery with black skin. Was there a place for emancipated slaves in a white republic? What did it mean to be a free person of color in a nation that countenanced slavery and excluded nonwhites from equal citizenship? At the dawn of the twentieth century, the African American scholar W. E. B. Du Bois famously described the fundamental question as the painful dilemma of "dual-consciousness."[9] Could people of color in the United States be both "African" and "American"? Did assuming one identity necessitate the renunciation of the other? Did inclusion into free society require the repudiation of one's racial identity and cultural heritage?

Answers to such questions could be complicated and convoluted. Identity was fluid and amorphous, continually shifting and evolving. It was both chosen and influenced from without by others. At different moments in time some free people of color consciously attempted to distance themselves from their ancestral past by deliberately immersing themselves into white bourgeois culture. Other black Americans proudly embraced their color and consciously identified with their African roots. In religious sermons, political oratory, the printed word, and public commemorations in the streets, black nationalists constructed an imagined Pan-African nation that united black Americans in the United States with peoples of color across the wider African Diaspora. Scholars, however, have struggled to decipher the deeper meaning of black nationalism preceding the Civil War. Did such expressions emanate principally from a common cultural heritage? African cultural forms not only survived the traumatic Middle Passage but also proved remarkably resilient in the New World. Historians such as Craig Wilder and Leslie Alexander have argued that African conceptions of kinship, gender, work, and religion lay at the very foundation of free black community institutions.[10] Other scholars have deemphasized the cultural origins of black nationalism. How enduring could African cultural influences have been over time, as the passing of African-born slaves slowly severed direct links to the African continent? Historians such as Elizabeth Rauh Bethel and Patrick Rael have argued that black racial consciousness in the generation preceding the Civil War was largely an American creation. The "African" identity free blacks celebrated was largely an imagined and romanticized historical construction fashioned to meet the psychological, social, and political needs of native-born black Americans in an increasingly hostile environment. Rather than look to foreign ideas and values for inspiration, black abolitionists drew heavily upon American republican thought and constructed a militant racial nationalism not to separate themselves from their fellow Americans but to assert their humanity and demand the rights of equal citizenship.[11]

Given the complexity of the free African American experience and the complicated nature of identity, scholars must historicize their analysis by placing their subjects in specific times and places. Scholarship on slavery and free black life in the North has focused heavily on the urban experience.[12] Such attention is warranted given the availability of source material and the propensity of many African Americans in rural areas to migrate to towns and cities in the wake of emancipation. However, inordinate focus on urban centers ignores a significant number of free blacks who remained in the countryside or resided in smaller rural villages—particularly in New York. Slavery in the northern colonies was largely an urban phenomenon, but the Hudson River Valley presented a notable exception. During the eighteenth century, the exceptionally fertile region between Albany and New York City emerged as the agricultural heartland of the province. Foodstuffs and other commodities not sold or exchanged in local markets made their way downriver to New York City and beyond. Unable to recruit a sufficient number of free workers and indentured servants, regional producers turned to enslaved laborers. By the end of the eighteenth century, New York contained the largest number of slaves in the North—three-fifths of whom lived and worked in the Hudson Valley.[13]

The African American experience in rural regions differed from that in urban communities, and those differences raise important questions about community formation and the construction of black identity before the Civil War. Conceivably, people of color in the countryside experienced the painful dilemma of dual-consciousness even more acutely than black city dwellers. The lives of slaves and free African Americans in rural regions were more intertwined with those of white masters, employers, and neighbors than was the case for urban residents. People of color in the countryside could not escape into the anonymity of the city to become "unrecognized" and "unrecognizable" among many other black, brown, and yellow faces.[14] What impact did spatial intimacy with whites, relative isolation from other people of color, and dispersed settlement have on rural black life? African Americans in rural environments lacked access to those institutional resources—separate black churches, benevolent societies, fraternal associations, and other community organizations—that solidified communal bonds and nurtured black consciousness in an urban setting. Did the absence of such institutions impoverish rural black residents and inhibit the formation of a collective identity? Constraints on black life in the countryside extended beyond simple demography. Dispelling traditional assumptions about the end of slavery in the North, historians have documented entrenched resistance to emancipation among many white residents. The political battles over abolition were especially contentious in larger slave states like New York, which adopted an exceptionally conservative scheme of emancipation.[15] What were the practical consequences of gradual abolition for black life in the countryside? Did the conservatism of emancipation and the legacy of bondage—persistent racial prejudice and rural poverty—prevent the establishment of independent black institutions and inhibit the formation of autonomous black communities? Did political conservatism and racial hostility stifle black political activism? How did African Americans in the countryside and black residents of rural villages define themselves and conceive of their place among those around them?

This volume addresses these questions by examining the African American experience in Dutchess County and the Mid-Hudson Valley between the colonial period and the mid-nineteenth century, when the intensifying sectional crisis brought the nation closer to the precipice of civil war. Located roughly equidistant between Albany and New York City, Dutchess County is bordered by the Hudson River to the west, Connecticut to the east, Columbia County to the north, and Putnam and Westchester Counties to the south.[16] After rather inauspicious beginnings, Dutchess rose rapidly to become one of the wealthiest counties in the province and state. The county contained one of the largest black populations outside of the New York City region prior to the Civil War. The long freedom struggle waged by black residents of Dutchess and the central Hudson region proved especially arduous. Dispersed settlement and the small size of slaveholdings rendered bondage in the countryside more oppressive than slavery in an urban environment. Resistance to emancipation in New York was nowhere more pronounced than in the Hudson Valley, and the gradualism of abolition took a formidable toll on black life in Dutchess County during the post-revolutionary period. Moreover, the legacy of bondage cast a long shadow after emancipation; the Hudson Valley remained among the most politically and socially conservative regions in the state, and free black residents struggled to achieve upward mobility in a rapidly changing economy. Nevertheless, however oppressive, the experience of slavery and its devastating legacy failed to derail the African American freedom struggle in Dutchess County. By the mid-nineteenth century, local black residents had established small but dynamic communities and had constructed a vibrant racial consciousness. However, the protracted freedom struggle and the agonizing transition from slavery to freedom in Dutchess County suggest that black residents in the rural Hudson Valley experienced more profoundly than their urban counterparts the trials and tribulations of exercising freedom and constructing identity in a white republic.

# 1
# Slaves and Slavery in the Mid-Hudson Valley

Bob was one of many colonists whose strength and ingenuity helped to settle the eighteenth-century Hudson Valley. A young man in his mid-twenties at the time of the Revolution who stood a full six feet tall, Bob was literate, highly skilled, and exceptionally versatile. Not only did he perform the myriad tasks associated with farming in the region, but he also labored as a gifted craftsman. An accomplished carpenter, Bob could also "turn, [and] make shoes" as a cobbler and even work with "mortar in a doctor's shop." Simply put, the man was a "mechanical genius."[1] Bob readily conforms to the popular image of the enterprising and rugged Early American pioneer in all but one very important respect. For Bob was a slave, one of several thousand Africans and African Americans whose muscle, sweat, intelligence—and sometimes blood—proved indispensable to the development of the Mid-Hudson Valley. As elsewhere in the Americas, colonists in the region turned to enslaved workers to meet an insatiable demand for labor in an expanding economy. By the time of the Revolution, Africans and African Americans were a visible presence in local fields, homes, mills, and shops and on the region's roads and riverfront landings. Enslaved men and women in the central Hudson Valley shared much with slaves who toiled downriver in New York City, but their experience differed from those in colonial seaports in important respects. Bondage in Dutchess County could be brutal and violent, and household slavery in the countryside could be extraordinarily oppressive. Low population density and dispersed settlement isolated many black residents from one another, and slaves in rural regions lacked those social and cultural supports available in urban centers. In the midst of such a stultifying environment, however, slaves in the Mid-Hudson region carved out a small degree of personal and communal autonomy that afforded a means of psychological and cultural resistance.[2]

The African presence in early New York predated European settlement of the central Hudson Valley. Slave labor proved vital to the development of New Netherland. Uninterested in promoting extensive settlement but unable to recruit a sufficient labor force, the Dutch West India Company relied on involuntary bound labor to establish a permanent presence in North America during the first part of the seventeenth century. Company slaves cleared land, constructed buildings, erected fortifications, laid out roads, and performed other heavy labor in New Amsterdam and fledgling settlements in the lower and upper Hudson Valley. Dutch slavery was largely a New World creation. The institution did not exist in the United Provinces. Bondage in early New Netherland was neither codified nor systematic, and people of African descent held an ambiguous legal status. Relationships between masters and slaves were ad hoc and familiar, and bound laborers in the Dutch province enjoyed privileges that later generations of slaves would not. Blacks worked their own plots, engaged in independent economic activity, served in the militia, and even represented themselves in court. Under a system of "half-freedom," slaves enjoyed full liberty to live and work for themselves in exchange for annual payments and a promise to perform labor when called upon by the Dutch West India Company. "Half-freedom" was not inheritable, but several slaves in the province managed to negotiate their own manumission. Although their cultural origins and position as bound laborers clearly set slaves apart from free white colonists, people of color in New Netherland did not constitute a distinct racial caste. Emancipated slaves enjoyed the same rights and privileges as other free colonists; several became freeholders. Coming from many different parts of the wider Atlantic World, blacks in New Netherland were intimately familiar with different European, African, and American ways. They retained a strong African identity but also fused and adapted other cultural forms. Although denied full church membership, for example, some people of African descent attended Christian religious services; a few black couples in New Amsterdam even solemnized marriage vows and baptized children in the Dutch Reformed Church. By the middle of the seventeenth century, New Netherland was coalescing into a slave society. When the English assumed control of the province in 1664, people of African descent—who comprised approximately ten percent of the colony's population—were not only performing critical economic roles but also leaving an indelible imprint on provincial culture.[3]

The development of the Mid-Hudson region proceeded slowly. Seventeenth-century Dutch settlement was concentrated in two distinct regions: New Amsterdam and its environs in the lower Hudson Valley and the area surrounding Fort Orange and the patroonship of Rensselaerswyck to the north. Preoccupied with the fur trade and imperial commerce, the Dutch West India Company found little of value in the extensive region lying between its principal fur trading post in the upper Hudson Valley and its commercial entrepôt on the tip of Manhattan Island. Interest in the central valley increased moderately after the English seized the colony from their Dutch rivals. Europeans first settled the west bank, as English, Dutch, French Huguenot, and Palatine German settlers spread out slowly from Esopus (Kingston), a small outpost established in the 1650s. For the most part, however, population growth remained modest for several decades. Ethnic conflict, political factionalism, the absence of representative government, and the proximity of hostile French and Native American nations retarded settlement in New York for much of the late seventeenth and early eighteenth centuries. Restrictive patterns of land tenure rendered the Hudson Valley especially unattractive to prospective immigrants. For much of the colonial period, provincial governors regularly dispensed patronage in the form of extensive land grants to political allies. By the early eighteenth century, landlords and speculators held title to hundreds of thousands of acres in the province; fewer than one dozen landlords held title to virtually every acre in Dutchess County alone.[4] In theory, the owners of such vast tracts would entice migration to their estates and stimulate economic development. In practice, however, the awarding of such extensive patents to a privileged gentry retarded population growth for several decades. Although lease agreements in colonial New York were not necessarily onerous and tenancy provided colonists of modest means opportunities to cultivate land they would not have been able to purchase, the leasehold system discouraged the immigration of ambitious yeomen who eschewed New York in favor of opportunities to purchase freeholds in Pennsylvania and the Chesapeake region. Settlement of the river's east bank proceeded especially slowly. It is unclear whether any European resided in Dutchess County when it was organized in 1683, and its population remained so small that colonial authorities provisionally attached the county to neighboring Ulster until 1713. As late as 1731, Dutchess ranked dead last in population among the province's ten counties, numbering a mere 1,724 (non-Indian) persons.[5]

Profound economic changes beginning in the early eighteenth century brought about a dramatic reversal in the region's fortunes. For many years, the lure of the fur trade, restrictive patterns of land tenure, exorbitant transportation costs, and the absence of lucrative markets discouraged settlement and limited acreage under cultivation. However, a long-term recession in the fur trade beginning in the latter part of the seventeenth century encouraged New Yorkers to diversify their economic activities.[6] By the second quarter of the eighteenth century, an expanding trade in foodstuffs encouraged producers to look to the fertile soils of the central Hudson region. The less mountainous eastern bank proved especially attractive. Dutchess' soils proved superior to rockier soils west of the river, while gently rolling hills provided excellent irrigation and drainage. The many creeks and streams on the eastern bank provided water power for a variety of milling enterprises, while multiple sites for river landings provided ideal access to more distant markets. Dutchess' rich soils beckoned land-hungry immigrants from New York City, Long Island, and neighboring New England. After decades of halting growth, Dutchess became the fastest-growing county in the colony by the middle of the eighteenth century. During the half century between 1723 and 1771, the county's population increased an astounding twentyfold to more than twenty-two thousand residents. Within a mere twenty-five years, Dutchess jumped from the position of least to second most populous county in the province, a rank it held for the rest of the century.[7]

The region's rapid economic development exacerbated a chronic shortage of labor. In the semi-subsistent economy of the eighteenth-century Hudson Valley, most farmers produced largely for themselves and exchanged small surpluses in local markets. Most farms were small in size, and growers relied predominately on family labor.[8] However, the increasing volume of extra-local trade and expanded enterprises of larger farmers and landlords intensified labor demands. The majority of masters and employers in the Hudson Valley, however, struggled to attract and retain workers. J. Hector St. John de Crevecoeur, a French commentator of eighteenth-century American life who became a landholder and slaveowner on the west bank, lamented that when it came to hiring laborers, employers had to "pray and entreat them" and concede virtually anything they demanded.[9] Landlords offered a variety of incentives to prospective tenants, but many newcomers left not long after they arrived to purchase freeholds elsewhere. Indentured servants, moreover, were too few and costly to meet the pressing labor need. Like other prospective immigrants, servants regarded their prospects brighter in colonies other than New York.[10]

Unable to attract or retain a sufficient number of free or bound European immigrants, producers in the Hudson Valley turned to slaves as a more convenient source of labor. Although black labor proved critical to early colonial development, the importation of slaves into the province was comparatively modest during the seventeenth century. New Netherland and New York occupied the periphery of the Atlantic World, and slave importations were irregular. Slaves typically arrived in small parcels from the Caribbean and southern mainland colonies—rarely from the African continent directly. Although New York buyers often complained that merchants in the West Indies dumped unhealthy, unproductive, and intractable slaves onto northern markets, such slaves remained attractive because they had survived the "seasoning" process and had become at least partially acculturated to European and American ways. Skilled cosmopolitan "creoles" born elsewhere in the Atlantic World were especially prized. The supply of enslaved laborers, however, remained inadequate to meet the needs of a rapidly growing economy. As production and commerce expanded, authorities took steps to promote the importation of slaves directly from the African continent. As early as 1709, the Crown directed New York's Governor Hunter to give "all due encouragement and invitation" to merchants engaged in the African trade and directed the Royal African Company to provide the colony with "a constant and sufficient supply of Merchantable Negroes at moderate process."[11] New York buyers continued to face stiff competition from purchasers in the West Indies and southern colonies, but the fantastic growth in the transatlantic slave trade and a discriminatory tariff policy that promoted African importations provided New Yorkers with an expanded supply of enslaved laborers. By midcentury, slaves comprised as many as one-third of all immigrants to the colony.[12] New York's black population doubled between 1723 and 1756 and tripled during the six decades between 1731 and 1790, jumping from 7,231 to 25,983 persons, making the province the largest slave society north of the Chesapeake.

The rate of increase was particularly dramatic in the Hudson Valley, where more than half of the colony's slave population lived and worked. Dutchess County's black population almost tripled between 1756 and 1790, exceeding the rate of increase for the colony and state as a whole. By the beginning of the final decade of the eighteenth century, Dutchess was home to 2,300 people of color, 1,856 of whom were slaves.[13] The county's black population was heavily concentrated in the more populous western regions along the Hudson River, the foci of economic activity. At the time of the first federal census in 1790, three of every four slaves in the county lived and worked in the four townships of Clinton, Fishkill, Poughkeepsie, and Rhinebeck.[14] Although slaves comprised only four percent of the county population as whole, twelve percent of residents in Rhinebeck, ten percent in Fishkill, and eight percent in Poughkeepsie were held in bondage.[15] Comparatively few residents of eastern and southern Dutchess were slaveowners, but between one in five and one in four households in Fishkill, Poughkeepsie, and Rhinebeck included slaves at the end of the century.[16]

Slaveowners in the region relied not only on the specific skills of their slaves but also on their adaptability to the myriad labor demands of the regional economy. Grains like barley, maize, oats, rye, and especially wheat were the mainstay of the eighteenth-century economy, but over time, farmers increasingly diversified their activities to include flax, hay, hemp, and a wide variety of vegetables. Virtually all farmers tended orchards that produced apples, cherries, plums, and peaches. The rhythms of work varied with the changing seasons. When not engaged in plowing, planting, and harvesting, slaves busied themselves felling trees, clearing fields, tending livestock, constructing barns, repairing fences, fixing tools, and carting produce to market.[17] Hudson Valley farmers and their slaves were "jacks of all trades" who labored as their own blacksmiths, butchers, carpenters, cobblers, coopers, distillers, joiners, masons, rope makers, sawyers, tanners, tailors, and weavers. The phrase "understands all kinds of farm work" appeared regularly in newspaper advertisements for male slaves during the late eighteenth and early nineteenth centuries. Abel Noble, for example, boasted that his twenty-seven-year-old slave was "a handy fellow at many sorts of business."[18] Slaves not only performed multiple tasks but also mastered specific skills. Caesar, an accomplished farmer who labored for Thomas Dearin of Poughkeepsie, was a talented mason adept at making "a very good stone-wall."[19] The versatility of male slaves extended beyond the farm to include rural manufacture and commerce. Mill operators in Dutchess County employed slave labor, and slaves worked in local forges.[20] Merchants utilized Africans and African Americans in their warehouses, while black teamsters and boatmen transported goods along local highways and waterways. Well acquainted with farm work, one twenty-year-old offered for sale was also "used to the boating business," and another skilled farmhand came well recommended as "an excellent teamster."[21] While engaged in farming,

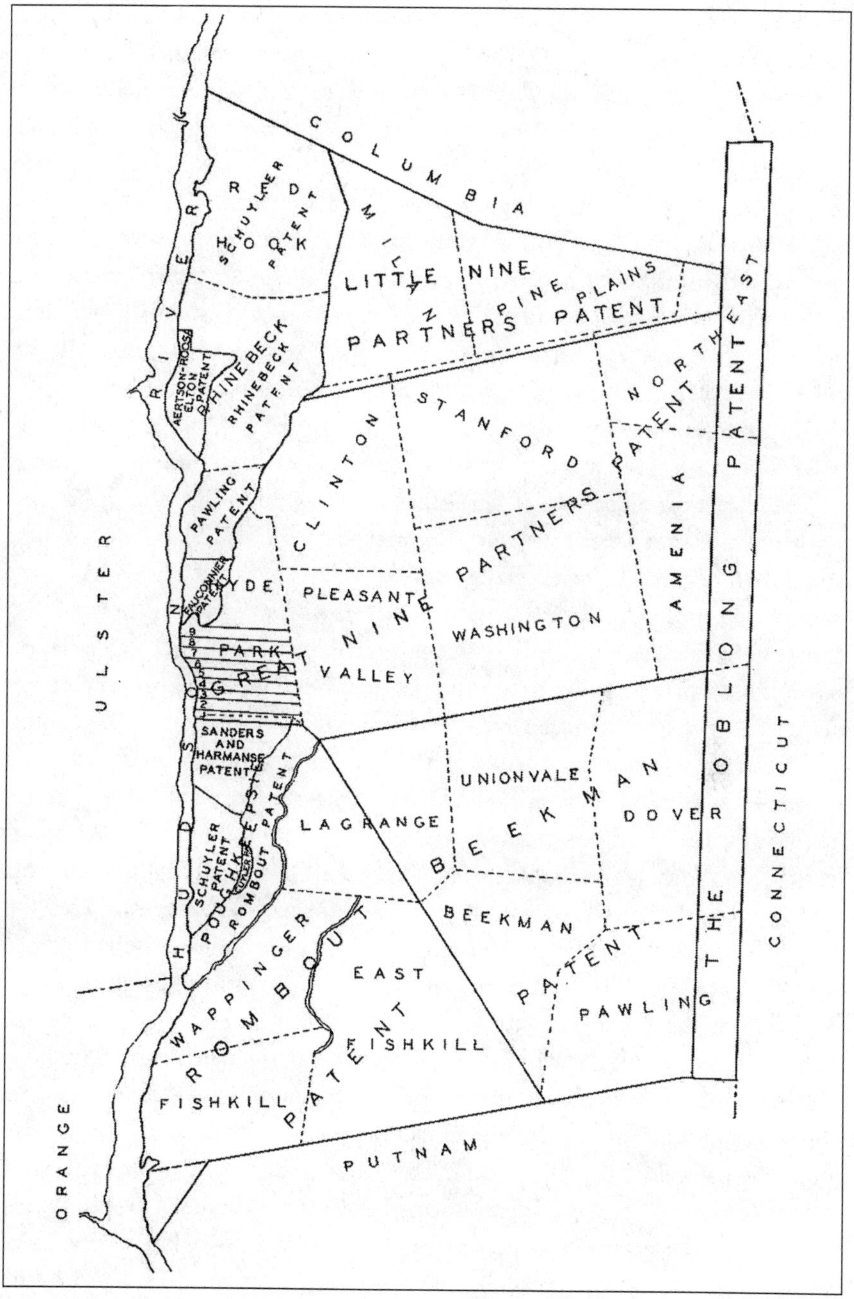


Map 1.1 Map of Dutchess County including townships and original patent boundaries. The towns comprising Putnam County were part of Dutchess until 1812. *Yearbook*, Dutchess County Historical Society 24 (1939): 52. Courtesy Dutchess County Historical Society.

rural manufacture, and commerce, male slaves also worked within their masters' households. Boys typically labored as house servants, while men in genteel families served as coachmen, porters, and waiters. Slaveowners particularly valued those capable of work on both the farm and in the home. One young man offered for sale in 1782 not only tended his master's farm but also served as a "genteel waiter" and "good teemsman."[22]

Enslaved women and girls labored predominately as domestics, whose responsibilities around the home were likewise numerous and wide-ranging. While the phrase "understands all kinds of farm work" typically appeared in ads for male slaves, advertisements for women regularly noted familiarity with "all kinds of house work." Domestics maintained individual households, assumed responsibilities of child care, and engaged in rural manufacture. Advertisements for female slaves enumerated skills in baking, cooking, ironing, knitting, needlework, scrubbing, sewing, spinning, starching, and washing. Butter and cheese were important commodities in local trade, and ads routinely identified slaves' skills in dairying, milking, and butter making. Responsibilities of slave women, however, extended beyond the domain of the household. As they valued the versatility of their male slaves, slaveowners prized the adaptability of female slaves to different tasks. Sellers described their slave women as "remarkably nimble" and "exceeding [sic] handy," capable of performing "any kind of business" and "all kinds of work."[23] One seller boasted that the woman he offered for sale—recommended for her "sobriety and honesty"—was the "most compleat [sic] house wench."[24] Women were not absent from the fields, particularly during harvest and other busy times. One twenty-four-year-old woman offered for sale by Thomas Palmer in 1783 was not only familiar with "kitchen work" but also "capable of working in hay or harvest, as a common Negro man."[25] Across the river in Ulster County, the region's most famous slave—a young woman named Isabella who assumed the name Sojourner Truth later in life—supposedly performed the work of two laborers. Slaveowner John Dumont boasted that Isabella was in fact more valuable than a man since she could "do a good family's washing in the night, and be ready in the morning to go into the field," where she performed as well as Dumont's best hands.[26]

Work in the eighteenth-century Hudson Valley was hard. Whether laborers toiled indoors or out, the workday began before daylight and ended long after the sun set in the evening. Labor on farms and in shops, mills, forges, and homes was not only long but often dangerous. Physical descriptions of fugitive slaves provide glimpses into the rugged and violent lives slaves led. Advertisements for runaways regularly noted bruises, lumps, scars, and other distinguishing marks. Caesar, a young man approximately fifteen or sixteen years of age, bore a "remarkable scar" on his forehead from the kick of a horse.[27] One of Faurt's middle fingers "stood square" due to an accident.[28] Anyone who worked around fireplaces ran the risk of burns. Thirty-year-old Sook appeared cross-eyed "on account of a burn upon the eye lid."[29] Many slaves carried the marks of injuries and illnesses throughout their lives. As a young man, Maurice still bore the scar from an accident he suffered years earlier as a child.[30] Masters frequently described their fugitives as being lame or suffering a limp; such slaves typically walked "a little stooping," "a little stiff," "considerably bent," or "rather one-sided."[31] Even less fortunate slaves suffered the loss of extremities such as fingers and toes; Christopher, a "stout" twenty-three-year-old man from Clinton, "lost a piece of one ear."[32]

Scars and disabilities attested not only to the harsh reality of life and labor in the eighteenth-century Hudson Valley but also to the violence of an institution that grew more brutal over time. As the colony's black population increased and as white fears of an increasingly alien and potentially dangerous population intensified, New York was transformed from what Ira Berlin has characterized as a "society with slaves" into a "slave society." What few opportunities and privileges Africans and African Americans had enjoyed under the Dutch disappeared as a more oppressive racially based system of bondage emerged in the province during the 1700s.[33] The creation and adaptation of slave law both reflected and shaped this transformation. The emergence of slavery in English America over the course of the seventeenth century raised troubling legal questions. First, common law presumed that only a heathen could be a slave; did conversion and Christian baptism liberate someone held in bondage? Second, patrilineal descent had awkward implications for free white men—notably slaveowners—who fathered children born of slave women. Could such children sue for freedom on the basis of paternity? New York took steps early in the eighteenth century to clarify legal confusion and close avenues of potential emancipation. Following the lead of the Caribbean and southern colonies, provincial lawmakers in 1706 decreed that Christian baptism presented no "Cause or reason" for emancipation and stipulated that the legal status of a child born of a slave followed that of the mother, that is, such a child was to be "adjudged a Slave." Passed ostensibly to assist "good subjects" in their efforts to proselytize the colony's black population, the "Act to Incourage the Baptizing of Negro, Indian and Mulatto Slaves" effectively solidified the property rights of slaveowners while guaranteeing them a potentially self-reproducing labor force.[34] The 1702 "Act for Regulateing [sic] of Slaves" and subsequent revisions confirmed the near absolute power slaveowners and civil authorities wielded over the province's enslaved population. Masters enjoyed the right to punish slaves at their full "discretion," short only of premeditated murder or willful mutilation. Municipalities were authorized to employ a "common whipper" of slaves at public expense to administer physical punishment. Legislation attempted to circumscribe slave life by curtailing movement, prohibiting unauthorized assembly, barring the ownership of guns, and criminalizing illicit trade. In an attempt to separate the colony's enslaved and free populations and reinforce the dependence of slaves on their masters, the law imposed penalties on any colonist who engaged in illegal commerce with slaves or who employed, harbored, concealed, or entertained a slave without the permission of the slave's master. Enslaved New Yorkers were subject to a legal double standard. Legislation denied slaves the right to a jury trial; criminal cases against slaves were heard by a panel of freeholders and three justices of the peace who wielded significant discretion in administering punishment. On the west bank, a special court in Kingston was demonstrative in sentencing a slave named Thom of the murder of a black woman in 1696, ordering that Thom be hung by the neck until "dead, dead, dead"—after which his throat was to be cut and his corpse "hanged in a Chaine [sic] for an Example to others."[35] Slaves could testify only against other slaves—in no case whatsoever could a slave testify against a free person. Any slave convicted of striking a free man or woman was subject to imprisonment or corporal punishment. In 1707, for example, the Court of Sessions in Ulster County sentenced a slave named Pierro to be whipped publicly in every corner of the town of Kingston for assaulting Catrina Cortregt, the wife of Hendrick Cortegt.[36] Periods of conflict and social unrest heightened fears of the province's enslaved population. Anxious colonists were particularly inclined to suspect their slaves during wartime. In an attempt to prevent slaves from escaping and carrying intelligence to their French enemy in Canada, lawmakers authorized the execution of any fugitive captured above Albany.[37] Most terrifying were incidents of slave violence and conspiracy, which prompted the adoption of yet more stringent and oppressive controls. Passed after the "Execrable and Barberous [sic]" murder of a Queens County slaveowner and his family by a slave, the 1708 "Act for preventing the Conspiracy of Slaves" authorized the execution of any slave convicted of murdering or conspiring to murder any free person.[38] In the aftermath of a deadly slave uprising in New York City in 1712, lawmakers strengthened slave controls, explicitly designating murder, conspiracy, arson, rape, and the mutilation or dismemberment of a free person as capital crimes. "An Act for preventing[,] Suppressing[,] and punishing the Conspiracy and Insurrection of Negroes and other Slaves" also denied the right of black colonists to hold property and stiffened penalties for those who illegally harbored, entertained, or traded with slaves. And, in a move of far-reaching consequence, lawmakers all but closed avenues toward emancipation by rendering the costs of freeing a slave prohibitively expensive; after 1712, a slaveowner wishing to manumit human property needed to post a hefty two-hundred-pound bond.[39]

The legal authority to sell a slave as an object of property was one of the most terrifying weapons a master wielded. Slaveholders frequently justified northern slavery as an allegedly benign institution that recognized and protected slave families. Orange County farmer J. Hector St. John de Crevecoeur claimed that adult slaves freely married partners of their choosing, spent regular time together, and enjoyed the privilege of "educating, cherishing, and chastising their children."[40] De Crevecoeur's idyllic portrayal grossly misrepresented reality. Throughout the colonial period, the slave family enjoyed no legal protection; not until 1809 did state law recognize slave families. The threat of sale was particularly salient in the Hudson Valley, where the seasonal economy meant that slaveowners frequently hired out their slaves during slack times. Selling slaves for days, weeks, months, or even years not only allowed slaveholders to adjust their labor needs to the changing seasons and shifting economic fortunes but also provided masters supplemental income and relieved them from costs of slave maintenance. The comparatively cheaper cost of hiring also put enslaved labor within reach of smaller farmers, artisans, and shopkeepers of more modest means.[41] Consequently, slaves in the Mid-Hudson region like Diana Jackson were "sold from one Person to another" and relocated from place to place during their lives in bondage.[42] Phillis Anthony spent the most productive years of her life serving no fewer than seven different masters.[43] Rachel Pride labored for at least eight, making her way to the central Hudson Valley from her native New Jersey over the course of several years.[44] The threat of sale was a source of constant anxiety; actual separation produced gut-wrenching anguish. Sojourner Truth's mother, "Mau-Mau Bett," saw most of her children sold away; Sojourner herself never knew several of her older siblings.[45]

Patterns of slaveholding had an especially devastating impact on black family life in the Mid-Hudson Valley. A discernable preference for male slaves to perform heavy labor and the hesitancy to purchase women of childbearing age who could burden masters with the maintenance of slave children meant that black males outnumbered females for most of the eighteenth century. Since settlement of the central Hudson region proceeded later than other parts of the province, the sex ratio remained more skewed in Dutchess than in other counties, stabilizing only in the 1770s and 1780s.[46] Most devastating was the small size of slaveholdings that fragmented slave families. Unlike most slaves in the southern colonies who typically worked and lived with or near other bondmen and women, slaves in the Mid-Hudson Valley were comparatively isolated. The mean slaveholding in Dutchess County at the beginning of the final decade of the eighteenth century was 2.8 slaves. Almost three-quarters of county slaveowners held fewer than four; more than two of five slaveholders owned only a single slave. Slaveholding on such a small-scale often separated spouses and parents from children. Almost half of all African Americans in white households in 1790 resided in homes with three or fewer blacks; fully one-third lived only with whites. Conceivably as many as three-quarters of slaves in the central Hudson Valley lived apart from loved ones.[47] Similar slaveholding patterns existed in seaports, but concentrated settlement in urban environments allowed city dwellers to associate with other slaves on a daily basis—on streets and docks, and in markets, shops, and alleyways. However, comparatively dispersed settlement in the countryside served to isolate African Americans in the central Hudson Valley. While many of the region's black residents might have traveled only to neighboring farms to visit friends or loved ones, others undoubtedly had to traverse greater distances. Even when family members resided nearby or within the same household, demanding work routines meant that members spent precious little time together. Dutchess County's black residents enjoyed little privacy. Slaves typically resided in their masters' homes, usually in attics, basements, cellars, garrets, or kitchens that were often dark, cramped, and uncomfortable. Even as an adult, Sojourner Truth could still vividly recall the small basement quarters she shared with several other slaves as a young child, its little light streaming through a "few panes of glass," and "annoying" and "noxious" odors emanating from the mud floor below the floor boards.[48] Such spatial intimacy could have devastating consequences. The master undermined the position of husbands, wives, and parents as providers and protectors.[49] Sojourner Truth knew far too well how capricious and devastating a slaveowner's power over slave family life could be. Incensed by an intimate romantic relationship his slave Robert had cultivated with the young Isabella, Robert's owner brutally beat the young man, forbade him from seeing Isabella again, and forced him to marry someone else.[50] Women, children, and men who lived under the same roof as their owners were constantly vulnerable to physical, emotional, and sexual abuse. Scars and injuries hint at such brutality, but explicit details of such traumatic encounters will likely remain forever hidden. When composing Sojourner Truth's narrative, Oliver Gilbert recorded only that it was during the young woman's time in the Dumont household that there "arose a long series of trials in the life of our heroine, which we must pass over in silence."[51]

However, if the familial nature of slavery in the Hudson Valley bred cruelty and engendered fear and distrust, it also fostered bonds of genuine affection. Slaves and their owners became intimately acquainted with each other. Hudson Valley slaves were integral, if clearly subordinate, members of their owners' households. As Melvin Patrick Ely has demonstrated in his study of black life in rural Virginia, there existed a wide gap between how whites perceived slaves in the abstract and how they interacted with those with whom they were intimately acquainted. However unequal, interracial relationships in smaller rural communities were personal, casual, and familiar.[52] White and black residents of Dutchess County worked, lived, ate, drank, played, sang, and danced together. Patterns of rural social life dictated such intimate exchange. Family and community celebrations regularly mixed free and slave. J. Hector St. John de Crevecoeur recalled how white and black residents shared life's "joys and pleasures" and partook of "the mirth and good cheer" of festive seasons.[53] Several slaves were accomplished fiddlers and musicians who played at country frolics and dances to the enjoyment of white and black revelers alike.[54] Strict legal controls on slave behavior and prohibitions on illicit social intercourse between slaves and free colonists proved practically unenforceable.[55] A county grand jury indicted Johannis Radcliff, a Rhinebeck cooper, for entertaining slaves and encouraging them to drink "to excess" and engage in "riotous and rude behavior."[56] Slaves could be not only companions, confidants, and friends but also lovers. "Mulatto" and "yellow" slaves were products not only of forcible rape but also of more consensual unions. Even De Crevecoeur admitted that intimacy between black and white in the valley sometimes degenerated into "licentiousness" despite laws to the contrary.[57] In 1762, Adreyan Van Voorhees was accused of having "Carnell [sic] knowledge" of a slave belonging to Captain Nicholas Emigh and having "gotten her with Child." An affidavit sworn by Adreyan's brother Stephen vehemently denying the charges maintained that the slanderous accusation had impugned Adreyan's good character—especially among "Young Ladies of Credit and Reputation"—and had damaged his business.[58] Men, however, were not the only ones to stand accused of improper sexual activity. John and Mary Van Camp sued Polly Knap for slander in 1792 after Polly alleged that Mary had miscarried a black child fathered by Van Camp's "servant" Peat. According to the Van Camps' complaint, Polly envied Mary's "happy state and condition" and maliciously attempted to discredit her "good name[,] credit[,] and esteem." Like Stephen Van Voorhees, the Van Camps claimed that neighbors and friends had "withdrawn themselves" from Mary's company.[59] In both instances, however, scandal seemed to have arisen from the accusation of an illicit sexual union—not necessarily the racial identity or legal status of the alleged sexual partner.

Slaves in Dutchess County and the wider region exploited the familial nature of slaveholding to extract concessions from their owners. A struggle for power lay at the heart of the master-slave relationship. Slavery entailed the constant and daily negotiation between slave and master that required accommodation and resistance on the part of each party. Slaves occupied a clearly inferior position in such dealings, but the master's authority was never absolute, and slaves were never completely powerless. The physical and emotional intimacy of slavery in the Mid-Hudson Valley enhanced the bargaining position of bondmen and bondwomen in the incessant "give-and-take" between master and slave. Slaves exerted some say in the tasks to be performed and lobbied their masters for improved conditions, extra provisions, time off, and opportunities to visit loved ones.[60] Some exercised voice in determining where and for whom they labored. According to his master's 1771 last will and testament, William Doughty's slave Sampson could not be sold against his will.[61] Benjamin Roe's slave Nann enjoyed full "liberty to chuse [sic] herself a master to live with," as did Abraham Kip's slaves, who were free to be hired by "honest persons" whom "they shall think best."[62] Genuine compassion and a sense of paternalism obviously informed a slaveholder's willingness to make such concessions, but slaves undoubtedly influenced such decisions, and some agreements were likely the consequence of lobbying by slaves themselves. Of course, the leverage slaves wielded vis-à-vis their owners was limited. Ignoring the entreaties of their bondmen and women, the vast majority of colonial slaveholders bequeathed or sold slaves without a second thought. Even when making concessions, masters typically circumscribed slaves' freedom of action by limiting the choice of a new master to heirs, requiring the approval of a prospective sale by executors, and insisting on adequate compensation for their estates. John Montross' slave, for example, enjoyed the right to select a new owner only if he earned a "reasonable sum."[63] An opportunity to negotiate or reject a sale usually required some concession on the part of the slave. A recalcitrant bondman or woman did not earn a master's goodwill. Abraham Kip, Peter Jay, and Catherine Reade indicated that it was only in recognition of loyal and obedient service that they permitted their slaves some discretion in choosing new masters.[64] Nonetheless, although slaveholders restricted slaves' choice of new masters, demanded fair compensation, and insisted on the involvement of their executors, the fact that such masters and mistresses made such allowances at all is suggestive of the intimacy of slaveholding in the region.

Concessions to slaves served a master's interest by providing incentive and positive reinforcement for dutiful service, but they simultaneously eroded a slaveholder's authority in other ways. Independent economic activity such as hunting, fishing, and gardening allowed slaves opportunities to supplement their diets and reduce their material dependence on their owners. Moreover, the sale of goods in local markets provided discretionary income to purchase articles of clothing, household items, and small gifts for family members. For a period of time, Sojourner Truth's parents cultivated tobacco, corn, and flax on a small plot along a mountain slope on the west bank.[65] Although liberty to engage in such activities was clearly circumscribed, the small informal slave economy allowed enslaved women and men to assume roles as actors and decision-makers who exercised a small degree of control over their lives.[66] Theft of a slaveowner's goods and engagement in illegal economic activity was even more subversive of a master's authority. Illicit trade and social intercourse between slaves and nonslaveholding whites persisted throughout the colonial period—to the consternation of provincial authorities. Writing to the justices of the peace in Dutchess County amid the hysteria precipitated by the discovery of an alleged slave conspiracy in New York City in 1741, Lieutenant Governor George Clarke pleaded with the judges—in the name of "Peace, the Safety of the Province, and your own Preservation"—to enforce legal controls vigorously and aggressively prosecute those colonists who illegally consorted with slaves.[67] At times authorities were indeed vigilant. In late 1741, justices in Ulster County fined several local slaveowners for allowing their slaves to meet illegally at the home of Abraham Stoubergh.[68] Finding William Lester of the Rombout Precinct guilty of harboring slaves at different times between May and September of 1746, the Court of General Sessions in Dutchess County concluded that the shoemaker must not have had "God before his Eyes" but had been "seduced by the Instigation of the Devil."[69] For the most part, however, legislation prohibiting illicit economic intercourse between slaves and free colonists was largely ineffective in the rural Mid-Hudson Valley, where blacks and whites consorted with each other on a regular basis. As late as 1791, the black market in stolen goods had grown so alarming to a group of slaveowning farmers in Ulster County that they petitioned the legislature for redress. Decrying the frequent theft committed by slaves and the "scandalous custom" of many citizens in trading with black residents, the petitioners exhorted their representatives to adopt measures to quell such "destructive" commerce.[70]

African Americans in bondage not only exercised a modicum of economic independence but also carved out a unique social and cultural space in the Mid-Hudson Valley. Born and raised in their masters' homes, often separated from kin, and working and living with their owners on a daily basis, African Americans rapidly acculturated to the particularly rich and diverse cultural world of the eighteenth-century Hudson Valley. The vast majority of native-born slaves typically spoke different European languages heard in the region, notably Dutch or English.[71] New Yorkers of Dutch descent clung fiercely to traditional ways, and some slaves raised in such households knew no language other than Dutch. Having been brought up "among Low Dutch," for example, Tom, a seventeen-year-old mulatto in the Fishkill home of Adrian Brinckerhoff, spoke but "bad English."[72] However, black residents of the central Hudson Valley were just as frequently conversant in both languages; Hendrick Benner's slave Abraham was even multilingual, fluent in English, Low Dutch, and German.[73] Levels of language proficiency varied greatly. Some black residents spoke poorly—at least to the ears of their owners. Slaves like James, Daniel, and Tom stuttered or stammered.[74] While someone like Rachael spoke "quick and hoarse," others like James and Jack were "slow in speech" or spoke "thick and slow."[75] Alleged deficiencies in speech stemmed from different causes. A physical disability afflicted nineteen-year-old Harry, who spoke "awkwardly" due to a drooping lower lip.[76] Speech difficulties could also indicate ignorance or insecurity when conversing with whites. Some, however, demonstrated an excellent command of language; Caesar and William, for example, each spoke "very good" Dutch and English.[77] However, if African Americans in the central Hudson Valley spoke the languages of their owners and imbued many different European values, they retained a unique cultural identity and exercised a degree of social autonomy. Surrounded by whites, people of color consciously sought out and nurtured relationships with other black men and women on neighboring farms and in nearby shops and homes. Different historians of the rural African American experience have demonstrated the existence of informal black social networks in the countryside, and fragmentary evidence suggests that such networks existed in the Mid-Hudson Valley. De Crevecoeur, for example, observed that slaves in the region occasionally managed to escape white supervision to conduct "their own meetings."[78] Black New Yorkers occupied a clearly distinctive religious and spiritual world. Slaves appeared periodically in the baptismal and marriage records of eighteenth-century churches—typically recorded without surnames and identified by their owners—and occasionally accompanied their masters to religious services. Christianity, however, made only limited inroads among the region's black population during the colonial era. The principal denominations evinced limited interest in proselytizing among New York's black population, while slaveowners for their part remained decidedly hesitant to catechize their slaves. Despite legal assurance that Christian baptism did not alter a slave's status, masters feared the potentially subversive consequences of the Gospel; white New Yorkers blamed both the 1712 slave uprising and alleged 1741 conspiracy in part on efforts to proselytize and instruct slaves. White opposition alone, however, was not the only reason for the limited conversion of slaves. Many in bondage remained indifferent and even hostile to the creed of their enslavers. Resistance intensified as the number of African-born slaves in the colony increased over the course of the eighteenth century.[79] The cultural divide between white colonists and their black slaves widened as the infusion of foreign-born slaves served to "Africanize" black life and culture—religious beliefs, rituals, burial practices, language, naming patterns, work ways, healing practices, material culture, food ways, music, dance, and folklore.[80] Typically identified by their Hudson Valley owners simply as "Guinea born" regardless of nativity, some native Africans struggled to adjust to their new environment. Although Pomp managed to become proficient in English, Ananias Cooper's slave Tom spoke "broken English," and the "Guinea Negro" Adam could only "read English broken."[81] Retention of native languages and traditional ways could provide a powerful weapon of individual resistance. A woman with an "ungovernable temper" who spoke only broken English, John L. Holthuysen's slave supposedly laughed when spoken to and only pretended "to understand the person who speaks to her."[82]

Although the importation of African-born slaves served to "Africanize" eighteenth-century black life, black culture in the Hudson Valley in fact represented the fusion of multiple European, African, and American cultural forms. Since its inception, the colony of New York was the most culturally heterogeneous in North America. White colonists traced their origins to the British Isles, France, the Netherlands, Iberia, and different Germanic kingdoms in Central Europe. The colony's black population, however, was yet more diverse. Enslaved New Yorkers came from many different regions in West Africa, Central Africa, East Africa, Madagascar, the Caribbean, and other parts of the Atlantic World.[83] Although the rural Hudson Valley was less ethnically diverse than the "melting pot" of New York City, slaves borrowed from different ethnicities in the region and fused them to fashion new cultural forms. Language is one example. Black speakers of European languages created their own structures, idioms, and dialects; what slaveowners like Ananias Cooper and John Holthuysen heard as poor speech was just as likely "Africanized" variants of Dutch and English.[84] The syncretization of European and African cultural forms in the Hudson Valley is perhaps best demonstrated by the Afro-Dutch celebration of Pinkster. Black New Yorkers appropriated and transformed the Dutch and German religious holiday over the course of the eighteenth century. Lasting for several days after Pentecost Sunday, the festival was an especially powerful sensation of sights, smells, tastes, and sounds. Days were filled with sporting events, games, feasting, and drinking. Dressed in elaborate, colorful, and even gaudy costumes, revelers paraded and marched about festival grounds in grand style. By the turn of the nineteenth century, evidence of African cultural influences was unmistakable. Musicians played on drums, rattles, and stringed instruments that closely resembled African counterparts. One observer of Pinkster festivities in Albany in 1803 recorded that during the evenings prior to the festival blacks roamed the streets beating a "Guinea drum" to announce the upcoming holiday and awaken "the latent spark of love for his native country and native dance in the bosom of the African."

The frenzied, expressive, improvisational, and sexually provocative style of dance shocked white observers. In a ritual of role reversal, an African "king" ruled the festivities, lording over white and black alike. The white witness to the 1803 festival considered the whole spectacle "a chaos of sin and folly, of misery and fun" where "every vice" was "practiced without reproof and without reserve."[85] Like other festivals of misrule, Pinkster had contradictory implications. On the one hand, an inversion of the social hierarchy and seemingly unrestrained revelry served to reinforce the existing social order by providing a "safety valve" of sorts that released anger and discontent among the oppressed. On the other hand, by the turn of the nineteenth century, black New Yorkers had transformed the festival into a celebration of a unique creole culture, creating and expressing a distinctive identity and racial consciousness that nurtured individual and communal pride. African Americans in the Hudson Valley ultimately engaged in what William Piersen has called a "resistant accommodation," never directly challenging the existing order, but adapting different cultural forms to meet their own emotional, cultural, and spiritual needs.[86]

By the latter part of the eighteenth century, Africans and African Americans occupied an important economic and unique social space in the Mid-Hudson Valley. Although a distinct minority, slaves played vital roles, performing varied tasks and plying multiple skills in the region's mixed economy. The institution of slavery as it evolved in the region, however, could be extraordinarily brutal and violent. Slave law gave masters near absolute control over their slaves, and the small scale of slaveholding in the rural Hudson Valley severely circumscribed black life. Paradoxically, however, intimate familiarity with their owners empowered slaves in their dealings with their masters and enabled some to extract concessions from them. Neither fully African nor fully European, African Americans drew upon and fused different cultural traditions to construct a unique social and cultural identity. Often isolated from family and friends and living in their masters' households, African Americans rapidly acquired European languages and values. Given their comparatively smaller numbers and relative isolation, slaves in Dutchess County could never recreate the rich, complex, and dynamic cultural world of New York City. However, the shared experience of bondage and common ancestry united all people of color in the central Hudson Valley and set them apart from their white owners. That sense of cultural distinctiveness and the intimacy of slaveholding in the region empowered African Americans in the freedom struggle during the eighteenth and early nineteenth centuries.

# 2
# Resistance and Revolution

THE FREEDOM STRUGGLE WAGED by Ebenezer Hulsted's slave Rachel was as heroic and as dramatic as that waged by any other American during the War for Independence. The thirty-five-year-old fled her owner in Great Nine Partners, Dutchess County, during the early summer of 1781 despite the threat of capture and the significant danger she assumed as a lone black woman on the run. In doing so, she joined thousands of slaves across North America who fled to British lines seeking freedom during the war. Rachel, however, was not content simply to flee from bondage. One week after her initial escape, she allegedly returned to her master's home with an accomplice and burned Hulsted's house to the ground. In the newspaper advertisement her traumatized owner posted after the incident, Hulsted described Rachel as a "tall and lusty woman"—physically imposing and sexually intimidating—who was devious and calculating, "as cunning and subtle a creature as any of the kind." An outraged—and homeless—Hulsted exhorted "all well-wishers to their country to apprehend and secure her, so that she may be brought to justice."[1]

Rachel was only one of a countless number of ordinary but largely unknown Americans whose decisions and actions helped to determine the course of the Revolution in the Mid-Hudson Valley and beyond. Historians have long debated the extent, depth, and duration of social upheaval during the Revolutionary era, but it is clear that the convulsive experience of war had dramatic social consequences. What began ostensibly as a political conflict between the mainland British colonies and the Mother Country over taxation and the right to self-government had profound and unanticipated social consequences. The experience of the Revolution irrevocably eroded traditional patterns of deference and undermined a hierarchical social order where a privileged elite—many of whom owned slaves—wielded disproportionate political, social, and economic power. Slavery provided a powerful metaphor for colonists who struggled against British tyranny, and many Americans came to recognize the hypocrisy of slaveholding in an enlightened republic founded on liberty and the defense of inalienable natural rights. Slaves were not casual observers but active participants in the freedom struggle. Emotional appeals to "life," "liberty," and "freedom" had profound, immediate, and personal meanings to those held in bondage. Drawing upon a long history of resistance, slaves in the central Hudson Valley seized opportunities available to them during the War for Independence. Their actions—and, just as significantly, what leaders on both sides of the conflict feared African Americans would or could do—directly informed political decisions and military strategy. Determining allegiance, however, could be a complicated and agonizing experience. The conflict precipitated a "crisis of conscience" for blacks as well as whites, and the loyalties of many African Americans in Dutchess County and the surrounding region were torn. The vast majority of slaves did not act as boldly as Rachel did but instead chose to tread cautiously and act more prudently. The wartime experience, however, politicized African Americans, who grew more assertive, self-confident, and even defiant. In so doing, slaves mounted a serious challenge to slavery in the Mid-Hudson Valley.[2]

African Americans in Dutchess County found allies among local members of the Society of Friends, or Quakers. For Christians opposed to slavery, the institution of human bondage was an abomination in the sight of God; its abolition was the only means of purifying American society and averting the divine judgment to come. For Friends, the holding of a fellow human being in bondage violated the Quaker tenet of the equality of all humankind before the Creator. Slavery bred worldliness and nurtured vice, and the violence associated with the brutal institution affronted Quaker pacifist principles. Overcoming initial resistance, outspoken antislavery evangelists such as Benjamin Lay, Anthony Benezet, and John Woolman forced Quakers in the Middle Colonies to confront slavery and adopt a more definitive antislavery stance during the third quarter of the eighteenth century. John Woolman's itinerant ministry carried him to Quaker Hill, Nine Partners, and the Oblong in eastern Dutchess, where he found receptive audiences.[3] As early as July 1759, the Preparative Meeting at Nine

Partners brought complaints to the Oblong Monthly Meeting against two members, Jonathan Lapham and Daniel Tobias, for each buying a slave. The Monthly Meeting appointed members to convince the pair of the sinfulness of their actions and warn them of the possibility of disownment if they failed to offer "satisfaction" for their offenses. Tobias complied, promising to free his slave within "some reasonable time." Although the fate of Lapham's slave is unclear, the Oblong Monthly Meeting disowned Lapham in May 1760 for participating in militia musters.[4] However, if the meeting had hoped to set examples, it was soon disappointed. The Nine Partners Preparative Meeting accused John Keese and Benjamin Lapham in 1763 and Stephen Haight in 1764 of buying slaves. The charge against Benjamin Lapham was particularly grievous since the accused was also charged with being "familiar" with his female slave "in a Carnal Manner." Although Keese and Haight expressed remorse and promised to make restitution for their offenses, both men were slow to act, and their cases dragged on for several months. Its patience exhausted, the Monthly Meeting disowned Keese in May 1765 for "Neglecting to make Suitable Satisfaction & Still Continuing in the Offence." Haight's behavior was even more disconcerting. In February 1766, the meeting determined that Haight (who had been found guilty of fighting and using profane language) had not only violated his promise to manumit his slave but had actually sold him. Seeing no "Likelihoods of Reformation," the meeting disowned Haight in March, condemning his most "unjust and immoral conduct."[5]

The Oblong Monthly Meeting not only policed its own membership and disciplined those who purchased or sold slaves but also played a role in initiating debate over slavery within the wider New York Yearly Meeting. In April 1767, Dutchess County Friends raised the issue of the "Inconsistency of Slave Keeping with our Religious Principles" and forwarded its query to the Quarterly Meeting in Purchase. The Quarterly Meeting in turn referred the question to the Yearly Meeting, inquiring "If it is not consistant [*sic*] with Christianity to buy and sell our fellow-men for slaves during their lives, and their posterity after them" and "whether it is consistant [*sic*] with a Christian Spirit to keep these in Slavery that we already have in possession." The Yearly Meeting at Flushing in May 1767 deferred consideration of the matter until the following year, when it again demurred to take up the issue. The 1768 Yearly Meeting warned that "an Answer to this Querie, at least at this time" was likely to cause divisions and "Introduce heart burnings and Strife amongst us, which ought to be Avoided." Although acknowledging African Americans to be rational creatures who were born free and who ought not be enslaved, the assembly noted that to "turn them out at large Indiscriminately" would result in a great "Inconveniency." Three more years elapsed before the New York Yearly Meeting formally prohibited the sale and purchase of slaves and urged slaveholding members to liberate their human property. In 1777, the meeting authorized the disowning of members who refused to relinquish their property. Nevertheless, it was not until a full decade later that the Yearly Meeting was able to report that no member owned slaves.[6]

Although Friends in Dutchess County provided a driving force behind the New York Yearly Meeting's endorsement of antislavery, local Quakers were hardly of one mind on the question. In September 1768, almost a year and a half after the Oblong Monthly Meeting forwarded its query on slaveholding to the Quarterly Meeting, the clerk of the Oblong meeting recorded the purchase of a slave by one of its members.[7] Joseph Hustead of Nine Partners did so in early 1769, fully aware that the purchase was "contrary to Friends' principles"; he further antagonized the meeting when he hired out his slave—an accomplished fiddler—to entertain young people in the area. Hustead, who had stopped attending meetings, rebuffed visits from representatives of the newly organized Nine Partners Monthly Meeting, which disowned him in July 1769.[8] That same summer, the Oblong Meeting heard disturbing allegations against Nathan Birdsell and his son for having been "active or accessory in making a Slave of a free Subject." The investigation into "So Sorrowful a Case" lasted for several months, as the Birdsells refused to give satisfactory account either of their actions or of the whereabouts of the free black child allegedly sold into bondage. In August 1770, after learning of the child's tragic drowning, the Monthly Meeting promptly disowned both father and son.[9]

Although the Nine Partners and Oblong Meetings disciplined members who engaged in slave trafficking and organized committees to lobby slaveholders, local Friends were slow to emancipate those whom they already held in bondage. To be sure, Quakers who liberated their slaves acted out of genuine moral conviction. When registering his intent to manumit a thirteen-year-old girl in May 1774, Ebenezer Cook admitted that he had become convinced of the "iniquity" of slaveholding since purchasing the girl ten years earlier. Jacob and Dorothy Thorn and William and Jemima

Thorn acted out of "tenderness of conscience," while Jonathan and Martha Hoag acted "Especially for the sake of justice and Equity to fulfill the Royal Laws of God to do to all men as we would be done unto." However, records of manumission also reveal how slaveowning Friends attempted to balance moral conviction with self-interest. Owners of multiple slaves frequently registered the manumission of certain individuals but retained others for months or even years. Zebulon Hoxsie, for example, emancipated a woman named Ziphro in January 1773 but did not liberate six other slaves until almost three years later. A number of slaveholders in the record postponed the effective date of emancipation for months and even years. Aaron Haight, for example, provided for the manumission of his slave Thomas only after a full decade of additional service. Masters commonly retained younger slaves by postponing the manumission of girls until the age of eighteen and of boys until twenty-one.[10] It was not until 1778 or 1779 that both the Nine Partners and Oblong Monthly Meetings were free of slavery.[11]

Despite their conservatism, the Society of Friends remained an almost solitary antislavery voice in Dutchess County. In 1778, a small Baptist congregation in the town of Northeast declared slavery contrary to the Gospel and resolved to do nothing to uphold it.[12] However, no other records of organized antislavery activity during the period exist. Moreover, the position Quakers occupied mitigated the force of their message. Friends in Dutchess comprised a distinct minority that was partially isolated both socially and geographically. Concentrated in the eastern portions of the county separated by the Taconic Mountains, Quakers exerted little influence over slaveowners in the westernmost river towns along the Hudson, where the vast majority of the county's slaves lived and worked.[13] Moreover, many local residents interpreted the pacifist stance many Friends assumed during the War for Independence as sympathy for the Loyalist cause. Local Quakers could ill afford to be outspoken in their antislavery views during the Revolutionary period, particularly in a region where slavery was as well entrenched as in the Hudson Valley.[14]

The manumission of slaves was uncommon in Dutchess County during the colonial and Revolutionary eras. Prior to 1783, merely two of fifty-three Dutchess County wills mentioning slaves contained articles of manumission.[15] The sizable bond required obviously served to dissuade many masters from liberating their human property. Additionally, for individuals like Valentine Wheeler, who stipulated that his slave Tom was to serve Wheeler's wife "as long as he or she lived," concern for the economic security of widows and heirs superseded any consideration of emancipation.[16] During the War for Independence, the increased demand for labor, the economic and social dislocations wrought by the conflict, and the fear of insurrection presented additional impediments to manumission. Indeed, the exigencies of war forestalled any legislative efforts to free New York's slaves. When the subject of abolition arose at the state's first constitutional convention in 1777, delegates deferred the entire question on the grounds that "it would be highly inexpedient to proceed to the liberating of slaves within this State, in the present situation."[17] With the outbreak of war and the refusal of New York to take any steps to legislate the end of slavery, the onus fell on African Americans themselves to secure their own freedom.

The black freedom struggle in the Revolutionary Hudson Valley was only one episode in a broader saga of slave resistance and rebellion in early New York, British North America, and the wider Atlantic World. Resistance to bondage was most often indirect. Slaves resorted to a variety of tactics in the struggle for power that slave and master waged on a daily basis. Slaves defied their masters by slowing the pace of work, feigning illness, sabotaging tools, vandalizing property, talking insolently to their owners, stealing from the master's storehouse, assembling with others in defiance of law, and engaging in other illicit activities. Certain forms of resistance could be self-destructive. Some slaves, for example, succumbed to the temptation to escape the brutality of bondage through alcohol. Sellers of slaves not infrequently vouched for their slaves' sobriety, suggesting that whites typically associated slaves with the abuse of strong drink. As if his runaway Jerry was exceptional, Stephen Mitchell of Poughkeepsie explicitly noted that the twenty-year-old was *not* "addicted to the use of spirits."[18] Slaves who abused alcohol could be unproductive and unmanageable. Hannibal, a young man "very fond of liquor" who labored in the Livingston and Beekman mills in Poughkeepsie, allegedly had a "sulky temper."[19] Henry G. Livingston evidently found one twenty-four-year-old woman ungovernable. When advertising her, Livingston admitted that he sold her "for no fault but her love of liquour [*sic*]."[20]

Resistance could also be direct and violent. Slave rebelliousness in New York only intensified during the eighteenth century as the black population increased and the slave institution grew increasingly brutal and oppressive. As early as 1702, the "Act for Regulateing [*sic*] of Slaves" noted apprehensively that the number of slaves in the province "doth daily increase, and that they have been found oftentimes guilty of Confederating together in running away, or other ill practices."[21] Tensions exploded in New York City during the spring of 1712, when a couple dozen insurgents set fire to a building and murdered several whites who rushed to the blaze. Hysterical recriminations followed. Panicked authorities brutally executed twenty-one alleged conspirators, and lawmakers rushed to strengthen the colony's slave code.[22] More stringent controls, however, only exacerbated tensions. In 1715, Governor Hunter warned the Lords of Trade in London that the prohibitive costs imposed on manumissions three years earlier only frustrated slaves; with their hopes of liberation all but dashed, those in bondage were prone to "insurrections more bloody than any they have yet attempted."[23] The influx of African-born slaves during the middle decades of the century inflamed the racial fears of New Yorkers. Rumors of slave conspiracies prompted the assembly to update its slave statutes yet again in 1730.[24] The hysterical response to another supposed plot in New York City eleven years later resulted in the arrest of 175 alleged conspirators, the execution of more than 30 slaves, and banishment of another 70 from the colony.[25] The alleged conspiracy reverberated throughout the province. Lieutenant Governor George Clarke castigated slaveowners and public authorities for their lack of vigilance. In his letter to the justices of the peace of Dutchess County, Clarke questioned how New Yorkers could be so complacent "After the Providential Discovery of the late most Execrable Conspiracy and the Hellish and barbarous designs for the Ruin and Destruction of this whole Province."[26] However, for all the fear of slave rebellion, organized conspiracies in colonial New York were few. Violent resistance more commonly took the form of individual acts. Arson, assault, murder, and rape committed by slaves struck terror in the hearts of Hudson Valley residents. During the winter of 1714–1715, Tom attempted to murder his master Johannes Dykeman, a tenant on Livingston Manor.[27] Such acts resulted in swift and brutal punishment. Authorities executed a Kingston slave named Tom for the attempted rape and murder of a white woman. Jack, convicted of torching a barn full of wheat in Kingston in 1732, and a Red Hook slave found guilty of the same offense were each burned alive for their crimes.[28] Although isolated acts of violence did not themselves threaten the slave system, they generated fears and anxieties that profoundly shaped how free colonists perceived the province's growing black population.

Slave resistance and white fears of rebellion in the central Hudson Valley intensified as the imperial crisis unfolded during the third quarter of the eighteenth century. Slaves such as Minsor, who was accused of assaulting Fenner Palmer of Pawling in early 1774, grew increasingly bold and insolent as war approached.[29] Entertaining near hysterical fears of insurrection, authorities responded decisively and even ruthlessly to individual acts of defiance. One young man terrified the residents of Poughkeepsie shortly before the Revolution when he allegedly torched his master's barn and outbuildings. Detected by smoke that emanated from combustible materials in the man's pocket, the twenty-year-old confessed to the crime, and local justices sentenced him to death by burning. His horrific execution was a public spectacle that must have been indelibly imprinted upon the collective memories of those who witnessed it. The crowd surrounding the pyre was allegedly so dense that it "excluded the air, so that the flames kindled but slowly, and the dreadful screams" of the victim could be heard as far as three miles distant.[30]

Individual acts of defiance intensified fears of broader conspiracies. According to some accounts, insurrectionists came extremely close to executing one carefully orchestrated plot in Ulster County in February 1775. Johannes Schoonmaker, a Kingston-area farmer, allegedly overheard a conversation between two leaders of the conspiracy only hours before the event. Schoonmaker rushed to spread the alarm; authorities quickly arrested twenty alleged conspirators and confiscated a sizeable cache of powder and shot. The subsequent investigation uncovered a chilling conspiracy. According to the insurgents' plan, rebels from the four towns surrounding Kingston were to organize themselves into three groups. While one group set fire to several Kingston buildings, a second contingent was to assume the grisly task of murdering the occupants who fled their burning homes. The third group, meanwhile, was to beat drums to muffle the cries and screams of the victims. After the initial assault, the insurgents allegedly planned to join forces with as many as five to six hundred Indians.[31] Whether the conspiracy was a genuine and well-planned operation or the product of white imagination (or a little bit of both), accounts of the Ulster plot appeared in newspapers throughout the colonies. The episode had a chilling effect in the Mid-Hudson Valley. It almost certainly weighed heavily on the minds of the freeholders in the Rombout Precinct who assembled in Fishkill in the spring of 1775 to organize a committee of defense charged with monitoring "affairs of the Negroes."[32] Immediately across the river in Newburgh, the town council imposed a sundown curfew on all slaves and ordered up to thirty-five lashes for any individual found in violation of the ordinance.[33]

Provincial lawmakers also responded to the perceived threat, authorizing any individual in time of invasion to shoot any slave found more than one mile from his master's abode.[34]

The course of events and the military campaigns that unfolded in New York intensified fears of subversion and insurrection. The Hudson Valley occupied a precarious but pivotal strategic position during the War for Independence. The Hudson River served as a major avenue of transportation and commerce that linked the port of New York with the interior and Canada. British control of the waterway would have severed New England from the other states, conceivably strangling the rebellion itself. Defense of the valley became critical after New York City fell to British forces during the late summer and early autumn of 1776. The central Hudson Valley also provided a wealth of resources vital to the American war effort. Dutchess and Ulster counties not only boasted a large number of potential recruits for American armies, but local farms, mills, shops, shipyards, and forges also provided large quantities of foodstuffs and other materials essential to the military campaign. Communities on both banks of the river became armed encampments crowded with soldiers, laborers, camp followers, and refugees. Fishkill served as a major supply depot, hospital, prison, and burial ground, while New York's provisional government and revolutionary committees sat in Fishkill, Kingston, and Poughkeepsie at different times during the war.[35]

Residents of the Mid-Hudson Valley, however, were sharply divided as the Revolution unfolded. The crisis exacerbated internal tensions and conflicts that had been simmering for years prior to the outbreak of war, particularly on the east bank. More so than in Ulster County, where smaller yeoman farmers predominated and where social, economic, and political inequalities were less pronounced, life in Dutchess during much of the eighteenth century remained decidedly hierarchical and undemocratic. A landed aristocracy wielded inordinate wealth and power, and traditional patterns of deference dictated political and social relationships. By midcentury, however, tenants, freeholders, rural manufacturers, shopkeepers, merchants, and other ambitious men from the middling ranks increasingly challenged the political and economic hegemony of the county's landed gentry.[36] The struggle for power tore individual loyalties. Conflicting allegiances and ambivalence on the part of many inhabitants were evident before the outbreak of war. At an August 1774 public meeting, residents in the Poughkeepsie Precinct expressed alarm at the "dangerous consequences flowing from several late acts of the British Parliament" but also swore loyalty to the King and emphatically rejected any attempt to break from the mother country.[37] Radicals who expressed more incendiary sentiments risked recrimination. Loyal Poughkeepsie residents reacted quickly when local Whigs erected a Liberty Pole a couple of miles outside of the village in March 1775. A large posse that included the Loyalist sheriff, local constable, several justices, and "other friends to constitutional liberty and good order" acted swiftly to cut the pole down as a "publick nuisance" before an angry crowd.[38]

The outbreak of war brought the question of loyalty to a head. As many as one-third of almost 2,800 Dutchess County residents refused to sign the Continental Association and swear allegiance to the Continental and Provincial Congresses during the summer of 1775.[39] Although it is likely that a majority of those refusing to sign were desperately attempting to maintain their neutrality, some actively joined the Loyalist cause. Local Tories organized small partisan bands and recruited residents for His Majesty's service. In Dutchess' Charlotte Precinct, a trio of heavily armed Tories allegedly terrorized local residents and threatened to abduct and turn Whig leaders over to British authorities. The chairman of the Dutchess County Committee, Egbert Benson, repeatedly warned New York's Provincial Congress that the number of "disaffected" residents in the county was so great that only "spirited measures" would eliminate the Loyalist threat. Dubious of the loyalty of the local militia, Benson appealed for military assistance from outside of the county. The state complied in early summer 1776 and authorized the organization of two new companies in Dutchess (and one company in Westchester) to pacify the "sundry disaffected and dangerous persons" who disturbed the peace and threatened to take up arms against the American cause.[40] Violence and partisan activity intensified in the wake of the decision for independence and the subsequent capture of New York City by British forces. The proximity of His Majesty's forces and rumors of British advances up the river emboldened Loyalists in the central valley. As violence escalated on the western frontier and popular discontent over wartime shortages erupted into mob violence, Loyalists in Ulster and Orange Counties began to enlist recruits for His Majesty's cause.[41] The more serious threats to the rebellion, however, continued to come from the east side of the river. Only weeks after the state ordered the organization of troops to quell "disaffection" in Dutchess, a group of between 150 and 200 Tories launched an uprising in Nine Partners in early July, which was put down only by local units and a sizable contingent of Connecticut troops.[42] In early autumn, Whigs in the Southeast Precinct, the southernmost part of Dutchess County perilously close to British forces, appealed for military assistance to suppress Loyalism and restore law and order. Conflict erupted on the county's northern border as well. Reporting the violence and destruction in Claverack and on Livingston Manor to the Committee of Safety, Colonel Livingston concluded that the northern regions of the county were "infested with disaffected persons." Full-scale rebellion broke out on Livingston Manor in May 1777, followed by an uprising of as many as four hundred Tories at Washington Hollow a couple of months later.[43] To meet the threat, the committee and subsequent Commission for Detecting and Defeating Conspiracies engaged in a zealous campaign to root out disaffection in the region. Meeting alternately in Fishkill, Poughkeepsie, Rhinebeck, and Kingston between September 1776 and 1778, authorities arrested hundreds of suspected traitors for assault, conspiracy, desertion, espionage, murder, sedition, theft, and other criminal activities. The Loyalist threat in the region gradually receded after General Burgoyne's defeat at Saratoga in October 1777 and British strategists redirected their attention southward, but angry popular demonstrations against rising prices and wartime shortages and other expressions of "disaffection" in the central valley continued until the end of the war, at times degenerating into banditry and indiscriminate violence.[44]

African Americans in the Mid-Hudson Valley seized opportunities created by the wartime crisis. Many exploited the breakdown of law and order to flee from their owners. Short of violence, flight represented the most direct challenge to a master's authority. The sixty fugitive slaves from the region appearing in local newspapers between 1777 and 1783 likely represent only a fraction of those who absconded during the conflict.[45] A fugitive's motivations could be complicated, and the intentions of runaways are not easily decipherable. While flight could be a spontaneous response to a specific incident or a tactic employed by slaves in negotiating with their masters, permanent escape from bondage was likely the goal of most fugitives during the war.[46] Absconding with different items suggests a degree of forethought and provides circumstantial evidence that runaways did not intend to return. As many as twenty-five of sixty advertised fugitives carried various items with them. Additional articles of clothing not only afforded protection from inclement weather but also provided a means of disguise to reduce the risk of detection. In June 1780, Joseph Reynolds' slave Joe fled with a brown bearskin shortcoat, a yellow flannel waistcoat, a pair of leather breeches, a felt hat, and striped linen trousers. The wardrobe Rufus Herrick's slave Pompey took with him was yet more extensive. When fleeing his owner in Nine Partners during the winter of 1782, Pompey took a full suit of homespun, one suit of brown linen, one pair of white linen breeches, two pairs of white linen stockings, another two or three pairs of woolen stockings, one white Holland shirt, one checked woolen shirt, a good pair of shoes, and a pair of silver buckles. The black horse Pompey took—complete with a nearly new bridle and fine saddle "with a crimson colour'd plush housing, scallop'd all round"—undoubtedly allowed him to transport such a large bundle.[47] Horses were not only a means for speedy escape but also valuable commodities that could be sold for cash. When two slaves named Frank and Pete stole horses, their owner, Frederick Jay of Fishkill, offered a full $1,000 reward for their apprehension.[48] Proximity to military encampments and supply depots provided fugitives access to uniforms and various military supplies. Jack purportedly fled Poughkeepsie with a large bundle of several items taken "at Mr. Anthony's from the regulars."[49] Stephen Hogeboom's slave Adam took with him a very fine green soldier's coat faced with red, while the blue and red wool coat worn by the fugitive York had buttons inscribed with the letters "U.S.A."[50]

Fugitives attempting to escape bondage most frequently fled southward, seeking haven behind British lines. Although cautious not to endorse full emancipation for all slaves, British strategists appealed to Africans and African Americans both to deprive American rebels of their slaves' labor and to meet their own pressing manpower needs. As early as November 1775, Virginia's Royal Governor Lord Dunmore took the highly provocative step of promising freedom to slaves of rebel masters who fled their owners and rallied to the king's standard. The governor's incendiary appeal had an electrifying and far-reaching impact. Thousands of slaves from across the colonies fled to the British, who put them to work in a variety of military and nonmilitary capacities. General William Howe offered refuge to slaves of rebel masters after British forces seized New York City in 1776. Three years later, British Commander-in-Chief Sir Henry Clinton officially endorsed what had become a well-established practice when he formally offered sanctuary and employment to any slave belonging to a rebel master reaching British lines.[51]

Between the late summer of 1776 and the conclusion of the war, British-occupied New York City served as a magnet for fugitives from the Mid-Hudson region. Several local slaveowners, including Ananias Cooper, Cornelius Haight, Zaccheus Newcomb, Comfort Sands, Stephen Hogeboom,

Herman Pest, Ebenezer Hulsted, and Lewis Barton, all suspected that their fugitives were heading toward the enemy.[52] Marmeet, a slave belonging to the Verplanck family, joined other slaves in the vicinity of southern Dutchess and northern Westchester in a plot to flee to freedom during the summer of 1780. Whether one of the conspirators became an informant or Whig authorities learned of the plot through other means, the local constabulary upset the group's plans and apprehended Marmeet. Marmeet, however, refused to see the plan thwarted and his hopes dashed. While being escorted to the county jail, he set upon his captors and wrestled from them forty shillings of "hard money" and "a very handsome carbine." Marmeet then fled and, under cover of darkness, made his way to the Verplanck household, where he waited silently. Once the dwelling's occupants were asleep, he crept into his quarters, gathered his belongings, and then hastened to the river and southward to New York City. Perhaps despairing of actually apprehending the fugitive, the advertiser who took out the notice in the *New York Journal and General Advertiser* expressed only a desire to recover the gun.[53] Proximity to British forces and porous military lines facilitated escape for slaves in the lower Hudson Valley, but the prospect of freedom in New York City beckoned slaves from more distant locations. Tom, who fled from his master in Rhinebeck in northern Dutchess in May 1780, was spotted ten days after his escape several miles to the south.[54]

Not all fugitives who rallied to the British cause fled as far distant as New York City. Some remained in the region and found refuge among local Loyalists. Pomp, a "Guinea born" slave belonging to the Whig Comfort Sands, was allegedly harbored by "disaffected people" on the west bank who assisted him in his escape.[55] Some runaways enlisted in Tory paramilitary organizations. Black Loyalists served with partisan bands such as "Rodger's Rangers" and otherwise served His Majesty's cause by engaging in sundry seditious activities in the region. Jonathan, a mulatto slave in the hire of James Doughty, allegedly enticed a group of young men to flee conscription by escaping to Long Island. Another African American operating in the vicinity of southern Dutchess and northern Westchester assisted Loyalists attempting to flee to New York City by hiding them in the woods and piloting them on the Croton River.[56] The British, for their part, encouraged seditious activity by actively employing black agents and operatives in the region. During the summer campaigns of 1777, as General Burgoyne's army in northern New York marched southward, a mulatto woman allegedly brought intelligence from British authorities in New York City to local

Tory organizations. After passing on the critical information, the woman purportedly continued northward in hopes of reaching Burgoyne's army.[57]

If many African Americans in the central Hudson Valley were sympathetic to the Loyalist cause, their willingness to act on those sympathies was another matter. Fugitives assumed tremendous risks. Although British-occupied New York served as a powerful beacon for slaves in the greater region, the geographic distance remained daunting. Moreover, while the dislocation of war presented opportunities to escape, disorder and violence in war-torn New York also made flight that much more dangerous. Apprehension could mean brutal punishment and reenslavement. Whigs considered captured slaves of Tory masters spoils of war liable to be impressed into service. Seized when heading to the enemy in early 1777, James Weeks and Pompey were put to labor at "the works" in New Windsor.[58] Another black Loyalist who served with a partisan organization in the Pawling vicinity was even less fortunate. After the band ransacked the home of an elderly man in Quaker Hill, a posse pursued and eventually caught up with the raiders. Finding the black partisan wearing the shoes and carrying a handkerchief belonging to the victim, the captors proceeded to hang the man "as a sort of scapegoat for the rest of the party."[59]

Not only did African Americans have to consider the formidable risks of flight, but they also had to evaluate their prospects in occupied New York City. Many of those finding refuge behind British lines discovered economic and social opportunities unavailable to them in the countryside. African Americans readily found wartime employment, some earning wages for the first time in their lives. Black Loyalists served His Majesty as artisans, couriers, guides, interpreters, laborers, musicians, partisans, pilots, pioneers, privateers, servants, soldiers, spies, and teamsters. Men and women from the countryside must have found the social opportunities available in the city particularly exciting. Mixing with other fugitives, refugees, residents, and soldiers, African Americans engaged in a vibrant cultural life on the city's streets and in taverns, gambling halls, theaters, and dance halls.[60] However, fugitives also joined thousands of refugees and soldiers in an overcrowded city that suffered from serious wartime shortages of food, fuel, and housing. The poorest residents clustered in the filthiest and least healthy neighborhoods. Labor for the British Army, moreover, could be grueling, and military authorities regularly impressed laborers. And although British leaders promised freedom to slaves of rebel masters, African Americans had reason to question the British commitment to black freedom. The institution of slavery persisted in occupied New York City, and buyers and sellers participated in a brisk wartime slave trade. No black Loyalist was completely secure from kidnapping and reenslavement.[61]

If African Americans had reason to doubt British designs, British authorities in turn entertained suspicions about the loyalty of their black allies. Tories in the central Hudson Valley knew that they could not take the allegiance of African Americans for granted. Conspiring with fellow Loyalists in April 1777, "Captain Jacocks" warned that "Blacks in the Kitchen" could betray them and admonished his comrades to keep slaves ignorant of the group's plans.[62] Norma, a slave of the Van Voorhis family in Fishkill, and Dinah, a slave in the Anthony household in Poughkeepsie, were just two such women. Each stood faithfully at her owner's side when a British expedition sailed up the Hudson River in October 1777; according to local lore, Dinah even spared her master's home from the ravages of an enemy raiding party by softening British hearts with her freshly baked bread.[63]

Defense of homes and families, loyalty to their owners, hope in the egalitarian rhetoric and republican principles of the Whig Revolution, or simple circumstance compelled African Americans like Norma and Dinah to side not with the Crown but with the cause of Independence. Although opportunities to enlist in rebel forces were fewer in New York than in neighboring New England, a handful of African American men from the Mid-Hudson Valley took up arms in defense of the American cause. Fierce resistance on the part of slaveholders to black military service originally led Congress and individual states to prohibit the enlistment of black troops, but pressing manpower needs ultimately forced New England and the Mid-Atlantic states to accept African American soldiers. In 1776, New York authorized the substitution of slaves for slaveholders drafted into state militia organizations; five years later, the state authorized the emancipation of slaves who enlisted and served for three years or until honorably discharged—while providing a land bounty to a slave's owner.[64] A handful of African Americans served in different Dutchess and Ulster county militia companies, and a group of slaves in the vicinity of Marlboro in Ulster County even organized their own company, drilling under the command of a slave named Harry.[65] Philip Field, a Dutchess County native who served in Captain Pelton's Second New York Regiment, made the ultimate sacrifice for the cause of Independence, dying at Valley Forge in 1778.[66]

Although a sizeable proportion of fugitives from the central Hudson Valley ran away to occupied New York City or sought refuge among local

Loyalists, others rejected British appeals and fled instead to American forces. Young men such as John Johnson, who fled his owner and assumed a new name and identity as a free man, did so in order to enlist in military service.[67] The prospect of wartime employment also attracted some fugitives. As did the British, American armies employed African American laborers in a variety of military and nonmilitary capacities.[68] Other runaways, however, sought simply to disappear among the large numbers of soldiers, laborers, camp followers, and refugees who flooded local communities. Charles Clinton, for example, surmised that his slave Bob would "put on regimental clothing" to disguise himself as a soldier, having been "frequently in camp when the army were dispersing."[69] Yet others, such as one poorly clad African American boy who wandered into the Fishkill encampment of the Second Maryland Regiment, might have had no other place to go.[70] Military encampments were destinations for women as well as men. Joshua Shearwood's thirty-year-old female slave was supposedly "lurking about Col. Butler's Regiment" in Fishkill during the summer of 1782.[71] As long as soldiers were willing to provide refuge for fugitives or at least tolerate their presence, women like Shearwood's slave managed to support themselves as servants, cooks, nurses, and washerwomen for the army.

The matter of choosing sides ultimately proved to be an agonizing experience for most slaves in the Mid-Hudson Valley. Practical considerations weighed heavily. The proximity of British forces in New York City, the sizeable presence of American troops throughout the region, social unrest, political instability, and partisan violence in the countryside rendered the position of African Americans especially tenuous. Running away, moreover, was a particularly dangerous undertaking; prudence, attachment to family or home, and fear of the unknown prevented the vast majority of slaves from absconding. Given the formidable risks associated with flight, younger men clearly predominated among fugitives during the war years. Only four of the sixty runaways appearing in the wartime newspapers were females. Almost nine of ten fugitives during the war whose ages were specified were between sixteen and thirty-five years of age; three-fifths of all runaways were under twenty-six. Ambivalent and uncertain of the war's outcome in embattled New York, most African Americans, like many of their free white neighbors, adopted a "wait and see attitude," hoping to maintain a cautious neutrality as long as possible.[72] When circumstance or conscience dictated a commitment to one side in the conflict, African Americans not atypically arrived at different conclusions. For example, two men in the

Rhinebeck Precinct of Dutchess County, each named Jack, found themselves on opposite sides of the struggle. One, presumably a fugitive slave, joined Teunis Peer and other Loyalists in a guerilla campaign against local Whigs in northern Dutchess. During the summer of 1777, Jack and Peer made repeated attempts to coax the second Jack, a slave in the Freligh family, to escape from his "Damn'd Rebel" master and join their band. Freligh's slave, however, treaded cautiously. He originally resisted their entreaties, but he also kept his silence—at least for a while. When Peer attempted to recruit Freligh's slave to torch a local barn—immediately after his own master's barn burned under suspicious circumstances—Jack concluded that it was "his duty" to inform Freligh and local authorities. Freligh's slave, however, went beyond serving as a mere informant. He proceeded to join Peer's partisan band "while in concealment" to gather incriminating evidence that the Commission for Detecting Conspiracies ultimately used to convict Peer and his accomplices of seditious activity.[73]

African Americans in the central Hudson Valley ultimately made decisions and pursued courses of action that best served their personal interests or improved their own positions. Some runaways acted out of motivations that had little to do with either Toryism or Whiggery. Some fugitives took advantage of the circumstances simply to take some time off or to visit loved ones. John Elsworth, for example, suspected that his twenty-three-year-old slave Jack was likely in the neighborhood of his former master in "Wiccoppy" in eastern Dutchess. Henry G. Livingston's fugitive mulatto boy Caesar was likely to be found during the winter of 1782 in either Nine Partners or Rhinebeck, having lived previously in both places.[74] The quest to be reunited with loved ones actually made the Mid-Hudson Valley a destination for fugitives from outside of the region. Sam, a slave from Stono Ferry six miles north of Albany, allegedly headed to Fishkill to see his wife and nine-year-old daughter. In another especially powerful testament to the strength of family bonds, one thirty-four-year-old woman from Maryland named Sarah (who also used the alias Rachel) was "big with child" when she fled Baltimore with her six-year-old son to join her husband in Fishkill, who served in the First Maryland Regiment.[75]

Personal freedom was the most powerful inducement to flee one's owner, but freedom could be found not only with the British or in American military service. For Job Mulford's slave Levi, it lay northward and westward; in the fall of 1779 Levi allegedly crossed the Hudson River from Staatsburg in a bold attempt "to get beyond our frontiers."[76] Loyalty to one side in the struggle was ultimately a means to an end for most black participants. Allegiance could be fickle; those who actively supported one side at one point in the conflict did not hesitate to shift allegiance when necessary. Stephen Haight placed an advertisement in the *New York Packet* in June 1779 seeking information on the whereabouts of a twenty-eight-year-old slave named Caesar, who had "hired into" Captain Wright's Company the preceding summer. According to Haight, Caesar had been discharged at Valley Forge on account of ill health but had failed to return to his master in Albany County.[77]

Whichever course of action they chose, and whatever their allegiances, African Americans in the Mid-Hudson Valley grew increasingly self-confident and assertive. Often literate, multilingual, and skilled, fugitives could be intimidating. Owners of runaway slaves typically characterized their fugitives as calculating and devious. Hezekiah Collins, for example, regarded twenty-five-year-old Nero a "smooth-tongued fellow."[78] Cornelius Haight was obviously unsettled by the flight of his slave Prim in 1780. The twenty-three-year-old woman had evidently planned her escape well in advance, secreting all of her clothing to an unknown location prior to her flight. In the advertisements he took out in both the *New York Journal and General Advertiser* and *New York Packet*, Haight warned readers to be "particularly careful to secure her, so that she does not give them the slip, as she is very sly and artful . . . and if they trust her [she] will certainly deceive them."[79] Fugitives who absconded repeatedly—such as Margaret Poyer's slave Caesar in Fishkill and Tight on Livingston Manor—must have seemed particularly incorrigible.[80] Even those who did not flee grew increasingly self-confident and even insolent in dealing with their owners. Petitioning the Provisional Congress in February 1777 for their release from detention for refusing to swear allegiance to the American cause, Dirck Gardenier and Matthew Goes complained that, "having no person at Home to Superintend their Domestic Affairs but Females," their slaves "Absolutely Refuse all Obedience, Taking Advantage from your Petitioners' absence."[81]

Despite the bold actions of runaways and the growing defiance of slaves toward their owners, ultimately only a handful of African Americans in the central Hudson Valley procured their freedom by war's end. Among them were at least some of those who successfully found refuge behind British lines. Francis Griffin, a slave who once belonged to Jacob Duryea of Dutchess County, was one who narrowly escaped reenslavement. Early in the war, Duryea had entrusted to Griffin the care of the family's New

York City home when Duryea and his family fled northward in 1776. As the months and years passed, Griffin evidently found life in British-occupied New York to his liking; acting largely as a free man, Griffen even married a free woman of color. As the war approached its close, Duryea reestablished contact with his slave to negotiate the terms of their postwar relationship. Duryea proposed what he must have considered generous terms; he not only offered to hire Griffin's wife as a free laborer but also extended to the couple the option of remaining in New York City. Having tasted freedom in British-occupied New York, however, Griffin balked at the offer. Incensed at the rebuff, Duryea hired two men and proceeded to New York City to retrieve his defiant slave. After locating Griffin, Duryea and his accomplices seized him and attempted to return up the river on a sloop. However, a bystander who witnessed the abduction quickly spread the alarm, and the city inspector pursued and overtook the kidnappers with the assistance of several Hessian soldiers. At Duryea's subsequent trial, a British magistrate affirmed Francis' freedom and ordered Duryea to pay a fine to contribute to the relief of the city's indigent black population.[82]

Francis was only one of more than three thousand African Americans from throughout the colonies in New York City at war's end. Resisting the insistent demands of American authorities to return slave property, Sir Guy Carleton, commander-in-chief of His Majesty's forces in North America in 1783, refused to turn over black Loyalists who had managed to reach British lines before November 1782, when American and British delegates agreed to preliminary terms of peace. Among them were several refugees from the central Hudson Valley. Lists of black Loyalists boarding British vessels compiled by inspectors and commissioners in 1783 identify at least a dozen men from the region, ranging in age from twenty to forty-eight. From Fishkill came twenty-two-year-old Casar Nicholls, formerly the slave of "Dr. Van Wyck," and forty-year-old Bristol Storm, who had fled from his master Garnet Storm in 1780. York, a "stout fellow" of twenty-three, had escaped from Leonard Van Klock in Poughkeepsie five years earlier; thirty-one-year-old Joseph Bartlet had fled another Poughkeepsie slaveowner, Gilbert Livingston, in 1779. Forty-three-year old John Simonsbury and twenty-year-old Abraham Thomas had escaped their respective owners in Fredericksburg in southern Dutchess; Thomas, a "stout lad" identified by inspectors as the former slave of Lemuel Willet, claimed to have been born free in Westchester County. Twenty-seven-year-old John Cooper had successfully made his way from as far distant as Livingston Manor.

From Esopus in Ulster County came thirty-nine-year-old Robert James and forty-eight-year-old John Been. Other black refugees from the west bank included William Sampson, who had escaped from his master in New Windsor in 1777, and forty-year-old Nero Denton, who had fled his owner in Goshen in 1776. A twenty-seven-year-old mulatto, Robert Freeman, who had served time with a powder maker near Goshen, claimed to have been born free. Among the women who crowded New York City in 1783 were thirty-year-old Massey Antin, who had formerly served Joseph Tomkins in Dutchess County, and fifty-year-old Catharine Livingston, who had fled eight years earlier from none other than Robert Livingston of Livingston Manor.[83] Having successfully escaped bondage, however, black Loyalists boarding English vessels at war's end faced very uncertain futures in other parts of the British empire. While some exiles struggled against poverty and discrimination in attempts to build lives as free people in Canada, Britain, or West Africa, others ultimately became servants or even slaves in the British Caribbean.[84]

The institution of slavery in New York survived the war, but African American resistance to bondage before and during the War for Independence laid decisive groundwork for the long antislavery struggle that followed. The Revolutionary experience proved to be a transformative one for black New Yorkers. Evangelical Christianity and republican ideology undermined the ideological justifications for slavery, but African Americans in the Mid-Hudson region acted largely alone. The Society of Friends assumed a moral stance against slavery prior to Lexington and Concord, but they comprised a distinct minority in Dutchess County. Manumission of slaves was exceptionally rare during the eighteenth century; emancipation even proved to be a drawn-out process among Friends themselves. Drawing upon a long tradition of resistance to bondage, slaves in the central Hudson Valley seized opportunities created by war. Capitalizing on the Hudson Valley's pivotal geographic position and exploiting the breakdown of law and order in the region, African Americans waged their own freedom struggle against an oppressive system of small-scale slavery that was both part of and separate from either the American struggle for Independence or the British effort to crush the rebellion. A sizeable number of African Americans in the region answered British appeals and defied their rebel masters to become Loyalists, either by fleeing to New York City or by joining partisan organizations in the countryside. The matter of allegiance, however, proved a difficult one for slaves in the valley. Some fugitives fled to join American forces. Others exploited the breakdown of authority to take time off from work routines and to visit loved ones. In the end, comparatively few slaves in the region resorted to violence or ran away. And while some became Patriots and perhaps a larger number became Loyalists, many more went to great lengths to remain neutral. Whatever their loyalties and whatever courses of action they pursued, African Americans were central actors in the Revolutionary drama that played out in the Mid-Hudson Valley. By the cessation of hostilities, however, the war against slavery had yet to be won.

# 3

# The Ordeal of Emancipation

Zaccheus Newcomb's slave Pomp was one of many slaves in the Mid-Hudson Valley who were thwarted in their attempts to procure freedom during the War for Independence. Between thirty and thirty-five years of age in 1780, Pomp was older than most other fugitives, but he otherwise typified runaways during the war—intelligent, courageous, confident, and resourceful. Although "troubled with a rupture," the five-foot-ten-inch Pomp was a "spry" and "well made" man. Fluent in English and Dutch, he was a "talkative" individual with a "likely" engaging personality. Although he labored predominately on the farm, he was an intelligent man who was "handy and ingenious about anything else"—including cobbling and fiddling. Pomp could read and write, and he might very well have forged a pass when he attempted to flee to the enemy in the summer of 1780. It is uncertain whether he ever reached British-occupied New York City. Pomp remained Newcomb's slave at war's end, and he continued to serve his master until Newcomb's death in 1791. When composing his last will and testament several months before his death, Newcomb made provisions for Pomp's manumission—not immediately but "nine months after next January." Pomp presumably became a free man in the late summer or early autumn of October 1791—eleven years after he had fled Newcomb for British lines during the War for Independence.[1] Runaway advertisements and Newcomb's will are revealing, but the fragmentary historical record raises as many questions as it answers. Was Pomp apprehended when he originally fled during the war? Newcomb took out advertisements in both the *New York Journal and General Advertiser* and *New York Packet* offering a sizeable reward for the fugitive's capture. Did Pomp entertain doubts after taking flight and decide to return on his own? Or could it be that he never intended to escape to the British at all but instead decided to absent himself for a period of time? What was the relationship between the two men like after the war? Did a chastened Pomp resolve himself to his lot—or did he remain assertive and restive? Did master and slave reach some sort of accommodation? What was the significance of the date of manumission recorded in Newcomb's will? Did "nine months after next January" indicate some prior arrangement between the two men? At the end of his life, did Newcomb entertain doubts about the moral legitimacy of slaveholding? If so, how could he have postponed emancipating his slave until well over a year later? Could it be that the dispensation of Newcomb's slave property was simply part of the settlement of his estate and had nothing to do with moral scruples?

The story of Pomp and Zaccheus Newcomb highlights the complicated and contested relationship between masters and slaves in the central Hudson Valley in the aftermath of the War for Independence. The revolutionary crisis undermined slavery in the region, but the institution proved remarkably resilient. While neighboring states adopted measures to end slavery during and immediately after the war, proslavery lawmakers thwarted similar antislavery efforts in New York. Even after the state's adoption of a conservative scheme of abolition at the close of the century, slaveowners in Dutchess County pursued a variety of strategies to retain their human property as long as possible. At the same time, however, if the Revolution failed to destroy slavery and even reinforced the property rights of slaveholders, it also emboldened African Americans in their own freedom struggle. Bondmen and women in Dutchess County accelerated the pace of emancipation by adopting different strategies and tactics to exercise greater autonomy and even negotiate their own manumissions. Slavery in New York largely ended by the third decade of the nineteenth century, but the protracted battle over emancipation in the central Hudson Valley during the post-revolutionary period proved particularly arduous.

Ultimately the War for Independence had contradictory implications for slavery and race in New York and the nation. On the one hand, African American resistance and the emergence of an organized antislavery movement during the era brought the question of slavery and the place of black Americans in the infant republic to a head. The natural rights philosophy of the Revolution provided a formidable ideological weapon for slavery's opponents. While antislavery evangelists preached the immorality of slavery, republican theorists attacked the hypocrisy of slaveholding in a free republic. Vermont expressly prohibited slavery in its constitution of 1777. A series of judicial decisions during the early 1780s effectively abolished slavery in Massachusetts and New Hampshire. Pennsylvania was the first state to legislate emancipation when in 1780 it adopted a scheme that eliminated slavery over several years. Connecticut and Rhode Island passed similar statutes in 1784. Southern states never adopted similar measures, but individual slaveowners across the Upper South liberated thousands of men and women at the end of the eighteenth century. Paradoxically, however, the Revolution simultaneously reinforced the slave system in other ways. If the natural rights philosophy of the Revolution undermined ideological justifications for slavery, Enlightenment thought simultaneously enshrined the fundamental right to property. Freedom and slavery had been inextricably linked in the American colonial experience. The existence of a permanently degraded underclass identifiable by race served to elevate the status of all free people; Euro-Americans were free and equal precisely because they were neither enslaved nor black. Moreover, the disruption and dislocation of war that allowed black Americans to flee their owners also intensified racial fears and fueled opposition to emancipation. The radical tide of the 1770s and early 1780s ebbed as different political, economic, and social crises precipitated a conservative "counterrevolution" during the final years of the century. Compromises made at the 1787 Constitutional Convention—including the "three-fifths clause" that prescribed the counting of each state's slave population for the purposes of apportionment and taxation, the restriction on the authority of Congress to interfere with the transatlantic slave trade for twenty years, and a "fugitive slave clause" that guaranteed the right of citizens to retrieve persons "bound to service" who fled to other states—legitimized slavery in the new nation. Meanwhile, events abroad—specifically the French Revolution and war in Europe—heightened conservative fears of the contagion of revolution; the bloody war of liberation in Saint-Domingue (Haiti) and Gabriel's Rebellion in Virginia in 1800 raised the specter of race war throughout the Americas. Powerful economic interests meanwhile staunchly defended the slave system. In the North, resistance to abolition was nowhere more pronounced than in New Jersey and New York, where African Americans comprised a comparatively larger proportion of the total population and played more vital economic roles than in neighboring New England. New Yorkers confronted a shortage of labor during the immediate postwar period, and many ambitious shopkeepers, artisans, and farmers embraced slave ownership as a means of achieving economic success, displaying newfound status, and exercising political influence in the new republic. Racial slavery lay at the very foundation of the economic, political, and social order, and the prospect of full and immediate emancipation threatened catastrophe.[2]

Even if slavery emerged from the war as firmly entrenched in New York society and economy as before, the institution did not go unchallenged. Hundreds of black New Yorkers had procured their freedom during the conflict, and the ordeal had empowered and politicized those who remained in bondage. Events in neighboring states meanwhile bolstered the antislavery cause; Connecticut and Rhode Island's adoption of gradual abolition in 1784 left New York and New Jersey as the only northern states not to have taken some action against slavery. Lawmakers in New York engaged in substantive debate the following year when they considered a draft proposal modeled after gradual abolition laws in neighboring states. Such measures that postponed the liberation of slaves until adulthood ensured slaveowners access to black labor while ostensibly preparing African Americans for freedom.[3] The proposed bill initially enjoyed support in both houses, but the prospect of emancipation mobilized defenders of slavery in the Hudson Valley and elsewhere in the state. Residents of the Ulster County towns of Hurley, Marbletown, and Rochester—whose nine hundred slaves comprised almost one of every five people in those communities—petitioned Governor Clinton and the state legislature to demand "most strenuously" the defeat of the bill. Citing scriptural passages and legal principles to defend the moral and constitutional legitimacy of slaveholding, the petitioners defended slavery in New York as more merciful and civilized than human bondage under the "barbarous Moors" and other non-western peoples. The Ulster residents also made practical economic arguments; the prohibitive costs of the proposed plan fell exclusively and unfairly on the shoulders of the state's slaveholders. In the event that theoretical and economic arguments failed to convince lawmakers, the petitioners also stoked racial fears. Among the "unavoidable consequences" of abolition was intermarriage between the races—a prospect "next to death to many virtuous citizens of this state." Emancipation of such a depraved and ignorant population prone to "plundering, stealing, ravishing, uncleanness, murder, &c." would impose overwhelming burdens upon society. In the end, the petitioners argued that the abolition of slavery in the state would have precisely its opposite effect, "that is, to free slaves, in order to enslave freemen!"[4]

Lawmakers were sensitive to such remonstrances, especially in the popularly elected assembly. Debate in the lower house grew especially acrimonious when New York City assemblyman Aaron Burr introduced a radical proposal for the immediate emancipation of all slaves in the state. After representatives from the Hudson Valley joined a decisive majority in rejecting Burr's motion, proslavery legislators successfully added a series of amendments to the proposed bill that prohibited interracial marriage and barred African Americans from voting, holding office, serving on juries, and testifying against whites in court.[5] The senate balked at the restrictions the assembly imposed on the civil liberties of black New Yorkers; after intense negotiation, a joint committee ultimately agreed to eliminate all restrictions except the denial of suffrage. The Council of Revision, however, rejected the compromise bill on the grounds that the voting restriction was "repugnant" to republican principles. Undaunted, the bill's supporters in the senate overcame opposition from Dutchess County's Jacobus Swartwout and other proslavery senators from the Middle and Southern Districts to override the council's veto. However, opponents managed to kill the measure in the assembly, where the effort to override fell one vote short of the required two-thirds majority. Proslavery lawmakers from the Hudson Valley coordinated with colleagues from Albany, Kings, and Richmond Counties to stave off New York's first attempt to legislate the end of slavery. Antislavery was a credible force in post-revolutionary New York, but under no circumstances were the majority of New Yorkers willing to endorse a proposal that abridged the property rights of slaveholders or recognized freed persons as social or political equals.[6]

The antislavery cause made incremental progress in New York during the 1780s despite the defeat of the abolition bill. The political battles in Albany sensitized New Yorkers to emancipation and intensified public debate over slavery. Established in 1785, the New York Manumission Society, which counted among its members James Duane, Alexander Hamilton, John Jay, Philip Schuyler, Melancton Smith, and other prominent New Yorkers, emerged as the most significant antislavery organization in post-revolutionary New York. Although conservative in its goals and committed to gradualism, the organization pursued a multifaceted strategy. The society waged an aggressive propaganda campaign and promoted black improvement in the hope that intellectual achievement and moral uplift would dispel racial prejudice. Defeat of the gradual abolition bill derailed any hope of adopting similar legislation in the immediate future, but the society lobbied for more modest measures intended to chip away at the legal edifice of slavery. Antislavery advocates achieved two modest but important legislative victories in 1785, when the state banned the importation of slaves into New York and removed the two-hundred-pound security that had significantly curtailed manumission for several decades.[7] A small number of enslaved New Yorkers received their freedom the following year when the state emancipated slaves of Loyalists who had become public property by virtue of the state's confiscation acts.[8] The 1788 "Act Concerning Slaves" not only confirmed the suspension of the bond requirement for manumission and the ban on slave importations but also outlawed the sale of slaves out of state. The statute also suspended the special slave courts of the colonial era, provided jury trials for slaves accused of capital crimes, and brought punishments for enslaved criminals in line with those for white convicts. Such incremental victories, however, were overshadowed by other provisions of the 1788 law. The very first section of the statute declared unequivocally that every "negro, mulatto, or mustee" within the state at the time of the law's passage was to serve for life unless manumitted by law. Additionally, the act reaffirmed two fundamental tenets of slave law, notably that the legal condition of any child born of a "negro, mulatto, or mustee woman" followed that of the mother and that Christian baptism did not alter a slave's legal status. Although opponents of slavery achieved notable legislative victories in the years after the war, the 1788 slave code largely reaffirmed the property rights and legal authority of slaveholders.[9]

More than a decade passed before New York finally legislated the end of slavery in the state. Despite the persistent efforts of the New York Manumission Society and its allies, fears of black dependency and the complicated questions surrounding compensation and the political status of freed slaves effectively subverted attempts to renew any meaningful legislative discussion of emancipation for several years. As David Gellman has demonstrated, only the confluence of several different factors during the late 1790s—a burgeoning print culture that allowed antislavery propagandists to press their case, rapid population growth, an expanded supply of free labor, and party politics—provided the preconditions necessary for adoption of abolition in New York.[10] Proslavery lawmakers successfully parried antislavery efforts during the decade after the defeat of the 1785 bill, but the legislative deadlock was finally broken in early 1799 when antislavery legislators successfully introduced a gradual emancipation bill—the fourth attempt to do so in as many years. As they had in 1785, opponents mobilized to defend the state's slaveholding interests. Unsuccessful in their initial attempt to kill the bill out of committee, proslavery assemblymen, including Abraham Adriance and John Van Benthuysen of Dutchess County and their Ulster colleagues, made a series of motions to delay emancipation as long as possible. In the other house, Dutchess' Peter Cantine Jr. and Thomas Tillotson—both slaveholders—joined the majority of their senate colleagues in demanding compensation for slaveowners and insisting that the state assume the costs of emancipation. The Council of Revision endorsed the bill two days after senate approval.[11]

Although it had been unable to forestall passage of the 1799 act, the state's slaveholding interest exacted a high price. Emancipation under "An Act for the Gradual Abolition of Slavery" was gradual in the truest sense of the word. The law liberated no one. The statute decreed all children born of slaves in the state after July 4, 1799, to be free, but it stipulated that females were to serve their mothers' masters until the age of twenty-five and males until age twenty-eight. By binding the children of slaves until adulthood, lawmakers guaranteed their mothers' owners access to their labor during their most productive years.[12] Slaveowners managed to protect their economic interests in other ways. Under the provisions of the statute, slaveholders could abandon legal claim to the labor of children born of their slaves within one year of birth, thereby shifting liability for their maintenance to the state. The state in turn remunerated local overseers of the poor for their care. Since overseers routinely bound out abandoned children to the very persons who originally surrendered them and subsidized masters for their maintenance, slaveowners effectively received double compensation. In 1803, for example, the justices of the peace for the Town of Beekman bound out to Peter G. Palen the very child whom he had abandoned, awarding Palen two months' compensation.[13] Although black New Yorkers heralded the adoption of gradual abolition as a profound historic moment, the 1799 statute had little practical meaning for most of New York's slaves. Those born before July 4, 1799, faced the prospect of spending the rest of their lives in bondage. Those born after that date bound to serve until adulthood—whose indentures could be bought and sold—led lives agonizingly similar to those of their parents. As James Gigantino has argued, the indenture of children born of slaves effectively created another form of unfree labor, and gradual abolition might be understood more accurately as the perpetuation of slavery under a different name.[14]

The demography of slavery reveals the painfully slow pace of emancipation in the central Hudson Valley. At the time of the first federal census in 1790, the almost 1,900 slaves who lived and worked in Dutchess comprised more than four-fifths of the county's black population. The county's slave population declined by a mere 247 individuals during the 1790s. Dutchess included as many as 1,200 slaves a full decade after the adoption of the abolition law, and the number of free African Americans in the county did not surpass the enslaved population until the 1810s. Even as late as 1820, almost one-third of black county residents had yet to taste freedom.[15] Emancipation proceeded particularly slowly in those western townships that boasted the largest black populations. During the final decade of the eighteenth century and the first decade of the nineteenth, the slave populations of Clinton, Fishkill, Poughkeepsie, and Rhinebeck declined at slower rates than those elsewhere in the county. The number of slaves in Clinton and Poughkeepsie dropped notably during the 1810s, but the institution proved resilient in the two other towns. While the slave population of the rest of the county dropped by more than seventy percent during the thirty years between 1790 and 1820, the number of slaves in Fishkill and Rhinebeck (and Red Hook)—collectively comprising more than half of the county's enslaved population—declined by less than half (see table 3.1).[16]

Figures on slaveholding are equally suggestive. After a negligible decline in the number of slaveholding households in the county during the final decade of the eighteenth century, such households dropped only fifteen percent during the first decade of the nineteenth century and twenty percent during the 1810s.[17] Again, the decline was slowest in those towns of western Dutchess that boasted the largest slave populations. The number of slaveholding households in Poughkeepsie and Rhinebeck actually *increased* slightly during the 1790s, and Rhinebeck (and Red Hook) witnessed yet another marginal increase in the 1810s. Poughkeepsie saw an appreciable decline in the number of slaveholding households only during the second decade of the century. Over the course of thirty years, Fishkill witnessed a modest decline of twenty-eight percent, while the number of Rhinebeck and Red Hook families who held slaves remained relatively constant. As late as 1820, more than four hundred Dutchess County families—including one of ten Rhinebeck households, eleven percent of Fishkill households, and almost two-fifths of Red Hook households—continued to hold slaves. The number of slaveholding households throughout the entire county declined by less than two-fifths during the three decades between 1790 and

Table 3.1
Slave Population and Proportion of African Americans in Slavery, Dutchess County, New York, 1790–1820

| Town | 1790 | | 1800 | | 1810 | | 1820 | |
|---|---|---|---|---|---|---|---|---|
| | N | (%) | N | (%) | N | (%) | N | (%) |
| Amenia | 52 | (64.2) | 40 | (37.0) | 57 | (69.5) | 32 | (32.7) |
| Beekman | 106 | (90.6) | 78 | (58.2) | 39 | (27.3) | 25 | (15.6) |
| Carmel | — | — | 16 | (80.0) | 6 | (22.2) | — | — |
| Clinton | 176 | (85.0) | 182 | (74.3) | 152 | (62.6) | 59 | (20.9) |
| Dover | — | — | — | — | 18 | (28.6) | 1 | (1.5) |
| Fishkill | 601 | (93.6) | 524 | (81.5) | 400 | (65.7) | 266 | (38.5) |
| Franklin | — | — | 19 | (36.5) | — | — | — | — |
| Frederickstown | 63 | (60.6) | 2 | (66.7) | 1 | (100.0) | — | — |
| Milan | — | — | — | — | — | — | 18 | (26.9) |
| Northeast | 80 | (78.4) | 72 | (51.4) | 57 | (45.6) | 25 | (39.1) |
| Patterson | — | — | — | — | 8 | (18.2) | — | — |
| Pawling | 42 | (31.6) | 34 | (30.0) | 6 | (18.2) | 4 | (5.2) |
| Philipstown | 25 | (92.6) | 10 | (27.8) | 8 | (20.5) | — | — |
| Poughkeepsie | 199 | (80.6) | 177 | (55.8) | 131 | (39.8) | 52 | (14.7) |
| Red Hook | — | — | — | — | — | — | 182 | (61.7) |
| Rhinebeck | 421 | (86.4) | 361 | (73.5) | 313 | (74.9) | 74 | (52.1) |
| Southeast | 13 | (81.3) | 17 | (45.9) | 15 | (40.5) | — | — |
| Stanford | — | — | 44 | (45.8) | 27 | (21.8) | 24 | (24.0) |
| Washington | 78 | (58.6) | 33 | (31.1) | 6 | (8.2) | 10 | (13.7) |
| **Total:** | **1,856** | **(80.8)** | **1609** | **(63.3)** | **1244** | **(52.1)** | **772** | **(31.3)** |

*Notes:* Carmel was organized from Frederickstown in 1795; Dover was organized from Pawling in 1807; Franklin was organized from Frederickstown and Southeast in 1795; Milan was organized from Northeast in 1818; Franklin was renamed Patterson in 1808; Red Hook was organized from Rhinebeck in 1812; Stanford was organized from Washington in 1793; Carmel, Frederickstown, Patterson, Philipstown, and Southeast were set off to form Putnam County in 1812.

*Sources:* Heads of Families at the First Census of the United States Taken in the Year 1790: New York (Baltimore: Genealogical Publishing Co., 1976); Population Schedules of the First Census of the United States, 1790, microcopy 637, roll 6, New York, vol. 2 (Washington, DC: 1965); Population Schedules of the Second Census of the United States, 1800, microcopy 32, roll 21, New York (Washington, DC: 1959); Population Schedules of the Third Census of the United States, 1810, roll 30, New York (Washington, DC: 1968); and Population Schedules of the Fourth Census of the United States, 1820, roll 71, New York, vol. 10 (Washington, DC: 1959).

1820—hardly evidence that slaveowning families were eager to relinquish their slave property (see table 3.2).

Manumission records not only illuminate the gradualism of emancipation in Dutchess County but also reveal the different mechanisms slaveholders employed to protect their interests. Facilitated by the state's suspension of the bond requirement, individual manumissions did become more frequent after the Revolution. While merely two of fifty-three Dutchess County slaveholders before 1783 included provisions in their wills for the emancipation of

**Table 3.2**
**Households with Slaves in Dutchess County, 1790–1820**

| | 1790 | | 1800 | | 1810 | | 1820 | |
|---|---|---|---|---|---|---|---|---|
| Town | N | (%) | N | (%) | N | (%) | N | (%) |
| Amenia | 22 | (5.0) | 16 | (3.8) | 26 | (5.8) | 21 | (4.2) |
| Beekman | 46 | (9.0) | 34 | (6.1) | 24 | (3.9) | 21 | (3.3) |
| Carmel | — | — | 10 | (3.2) | 4 | (1.2) | — | — |
| Clinton | 67 | (9.6) | 58 | (7.7) | 53 | (6.3) | 38 | (3.5) |
| Dover | — | — | 12 | (3.4) | 1 | (0.3) | | |
| Fishkill | 195 | (22.0) | 179 | (19.8) | 151 | (14.2) | 140 | (11.3) |
| Franklin | — | — | 13 | (5.2) | — | — | — | — |
| Frederickstown | 36 | (3.9) | 2 | (0.7) | 1 | (0.3) | — | — |
| Milan | — | — | — | 14 | (4.6) | — | — | — |
| Northeast | 33 | (6.6) | 28 | (5.9) | 32 | (6.3) | 17 | (5.4) |
| Patterson | — | — | — | — | 6 | (2.4) | — | — |
| Pawling | 19 | (2.8) | 19 | (2.8) | 3 | (1.0) | 4 | (1.3) |
| Philipstown | 12 | (3.6) | 7 | (1.6) | 4 | (0.8) | — | |
| Poughkeepsie | 81 | (21.8) | 85 | (17.4) | 73 | (10.7) | 30 | (3.2) |
| Red Hook | — | — | — | — | — | — | 73 | (18.1) |
| Rhinebeck | 121 | (23.5) | 133 | (23.8) | 112 | (16.9) | 45 | (10.1) |
| Southeast | 6 | (4.3) | 7 | (2.4) | 12 | (3.8) | — | — |
| Stanford | — | — | 20 | (5.8) | 15 | (4.4) | 14 | (3.4) |
| Washington | 33 | (4.5) | 12 | (3.1) | 4 | (1.0) | 7 | (1.6) |
| **Total:** | **671** | **(10.0)** | **623** | **(8.7)** | **532** | **(6.7)** | **425** | **(5.7)** |

*Sources:* See table 3.1.

slave property, thirty percent of testators freed slaves during the decade and a half after the war. The rate of manumission accelerated after the adoption of gradual abolition in 1799; during the first two decades of the nineteenth century, more than two-thirds of testators who held slaves included provisions in their wills authorizing the manumission of slave property.[18] A gradual increase in the frequency of manumission alone, however, obscures the conservatism of the majority of slaveholders in Dutchess County. A closer examination of manumissions recorded by the Town of Poughkeepsie clerk between 1790 and 1826 suggests that slaveholders hardly rushed to free their slaves after the passage of the abolition statute. After recording only eight manumissions during the final decade of the eighteenth century, the town clerk registered twenty-seven manumissions between 1800 and 1810, thirty-two during the subsequent decade, and another fifteen after 1820. In other words, more than half of manumissions appearing in the town record book were dated after 1810.[19]

Slaveowners not only sought to retain their human property as long as possible, but they also attempted to maintain control over when and under what terms their slaves received their freedom. The state's gradual abolition law largely codified practices of slaveowners themselves. Three-quarters of testators who manumitted slaves after 1783 postponed the effective date of emancipation or otherwise made it conditional. Concern for the economic security of heirs remained the principal reason for delaying emancipation, as it was for refusing to manumit slaves at all. Husbands commonly directed the manumission of slaves only after the deaths of both themselves *and* their spouses, thereby ensuring that their widows would continue to have access to their slaves' labor throughout their lifetimes. John Ostrom of Clinton made such intentions explicit when he stipulated in 1814 that the young woman Dinah was "to faithfully wait on and attend" Ostrom's wife until her death.[20] In almost half of wills freeing slaves after the Revolution, slaveowners authorized manumission only at a specified future date, usually when bondmen and women reached a specific age. Manumitted slaves typically received their freedom when they reached their late twenties, but slaveowners did not hesitate to delay manumission even later. According to the terms of Isaac Mitchell's will, Rose, Jerry, Vinar, and Rachel were not to be liberated until each reached thirty years of age. John Ackerman of Fishkill bequeathed his slaves Adam and Isaac to his two sons and authorized their manumissions only on their thirty-sixth birthdays.[21] Age, legal restrictions, and potential labor value discouraged the emancipation of younger slaves.[22]

Joseph Lancaster of Beekman claimed to act out of only the most altruistic motives when he purchased a three-year-old girl named Aner in May 1796. Believing it to be "wrong and wicked to hold any people . . . in a State of Slavery," Lancaster swore his intent to manumit the girl—when she reached eighteen years of age.[23]

Financial considerations restrained the antislavery impulses of many Dutchess County slaveowners. Jacob Smith and William Williams permitted the manumission of their slaves only if their liberation did not place undue financial burdens on their estates; Myer Hermance of the town of Northeast went so far as to require his slave Phillip to indemnify his heirs upon his manumission.[24] Egbert Bogardus of Fishkill was yet more direct. If his executors proved unable to manumit his slave Pegg without legally discharging his estate from financial liability for her maintenance, they were simply to "dispose" of her.[25] Even after the Revolution, testators such as Hendrick Palen of Beekman, Isaac Balding of Poughkeepsie, and John Germond of the Washington Precinct did not hesitate to liquidate their slave property either to satisfy financial obligations or bequeath the proceeds from such sales to their heirs.[26]

Given the economic costs of emancipation, slaveowners regarded manumission as a beneficent gift bestowed only to the most deserving of slaves. Masters who liberated their bondmen and women often indicated that they acted "in consideration of faithful services." Abraham Schenck of Fishkill, for example, provided for the manumission and maintenance of his aged female slave Hannah, "who from her youth has deserved well of me and the family."[27] Zacharias Van Voorhis of the Rombout Precinct went so far as to orchestrate a ritual demonstration of his magnanimity, instructing his executors "to order my . . . negroes into that apartment in my house where I died, and there in the most solemn manner proclaim to them their freedom."[28] Conceiving of manumission as a reward for loyal service, slaveowners attempted to wield the prospect of freedom as a means of control. Some slaveholders stipulated explicitly that manumission was contingent upon appropriate behavior. Richard Davis of Poughkeepsie authorized his executors to liberate Charles and Sarah when they reached thirty years of age, "provided they behave with coming decency so as not to become chargeable by Running Away."[29] Adonijah was approximately nineteen years of age when his master, Daniel Lewis of Stanford, drafted his last will and testament in 1795. According to that document, Adonijah was to receive his freedom at age thirty and only if "not guilty of any crime such as Stealing running away or some other criminal misdemeanor." If disobedient, Adonijah was to remain a slave for life.[30] Johannes De Wit of the Rombout Precinct was yet more proscriptive. Although set at liberty to provide for themselves, De Wit's slaves remained under "the care and inspection" of his executors until they reached twenty-five years of age. Until that time, De Wit's executors exercised authority to bind out his slaves if they failed to support themselves or proved "disobedient" and unable "to behave themselves well and keep sober." De Wit made it very clear that his executors were to liberate his slaves only if they abided by his injunctions.[31]

The selectivity with which slaveowners manumitted their slaves meant that emancipation in Dutchess County proceeded piecemeal. Owners of multiple slaves frequently liberated one or more while leaving others in bondage. William Radcliff of Rhinebeck manumitted Sally and Margaret in 1806 but still owned five slaves in 1810; his estate included twenty-five-year-old Isaac at the time of his death four years later.[32] Almost half of slaveholders who can be positively identified in town manumission records continued to hold slave property at the time of the subsequent federal census. Several slaveholders appear more than once in town manumission records. James Dearin of Poughkeepsie, for example, freed his slave Nanny in August 1804 but postponed the manumission of Benjamin James until 1807. He appeared in the record a third time a decade later when he liberated Sarah Blakesly.[33] Wills provide additional insights into the selectivity of manumission. Only approximately a quarter of slaveowners who freed slaves after 1783 provided for the immediate manumission of their entire slave property upon their deaths. Several who liberated one or more slaves also bequeathed others to heirs or even ordered their sale. Benjamin Knickerbocker of Northeast, who not only liberated Peter and his wife but also provided the couple with a horse and twenty-five dollars, willed four other slaves to various family members.[34] Perhaps the most illustrative example of all is that of Fishkill farmer Adolph Myers, who manumitted two slaves named Harry and Jane, willed one slave to each of his three children, and directed the sale of yet another, the money from the transaction to be "put at interest" for his grandchildren.[35]

Even the espousal of antislavery sentiments did not preclude slaveholding itself. Articles of manumission typically included language indicating that a slaveowner acted out of enlightened republican principles or "divers good causes and considerations." In 1795, Zephaniah Platt—delegate to the state constitutional convention of 1777, member of the Committee of Public Safety, Second Provincial Congress, and Continental Congress, military officer, justice, and delegate to the 1788 ratifying convention—manumitted his slave Tone "Agreeably to the Republican Spirit of the Constitution of our Country."[36] However, some masters who expressed such convictions when liberating individual slaves saw no contradiction in retaining ownership of other bondmen and women. George Emigh, for example, provided for the manumission of Isabel upon his death out of the conviction that he could not "in justice leave a fellow creature behind me in a state of slavery"—but he did not hesitate to postpone the emancipation of his slave boy Saul until age twenty-one.[37] The experiences of two statesmen who represented Dutchess County in the state legislature in 1799 are particularly illustrative. Former assemblyman Henry Dodge of Poughkeepsie professed to act out of "good and valuable considerations" when he decreed that Ishmael Frasher was to enjoy forever all "liberties, rights, privileges and Immunities of a free Man." Dodge did so, however, fully seven years after the passage of the 1799 act. Moreover, he delayed freeing thirty-five-year-old Floro for two more years. Dodge still owned three slaves in 1810, and it was not until 1819 that he emancipated twenty-three-year-old Bet Stephens.[38] Like Dodge, Thomas Tillotson, who endorsed the gradual abolition act as a state senator, continued to hold slaves long after the passage of the law. The Rhinebeck slaveholder owned five slaves in 1800 and actually increased his holding to six by 1810. It was not until 1815 that he emancipated his slave Catherine, and as late as 1820—two decades after the passage of the abolition act—the former senator still held two individuals in bondage.[39] Even if manumission in Dutchess County became more frequent in the decades after the Revolution, it hardly represented a categorical rejection of slavery as a moral or political evil.

Given the entrenched resistance of slaveholders to emancipation, it was incumbent upon African Americans themselves to wield the decisive blow against slavery in the central Hudson Valley. Ironically, slaves exploited the very system of small-scale slavery that was so oppressive. The leverage slaves wielded vis-à-vis their owners only increased in the aftermath of the Revolution, and bondmen and women grew more assertive in demanding concessions from their owners. In some cases, slaves instigated their own sales to improve their positions. A 1795 advertisement in the *Poughkeepsie Journal* for the sale or exchange of a young man, his wife, and the couple's child noted that the prospective sale was made at the family's request.[40] In another instance, one skilled and versatile young man adept at farming, the care of horses, and domestic service compelled Henry Livingston to sell him to a local buyer when the twenty-year-old objected to relocating to New York City.[41] The fervent resolve to protect families often lay behind attempts to prevent or instigate sales. One of Thomas Tillotson's own slaves forced her master's hand when she simply refused to accompany him to Albany and be separated from her free husband. The senator not only complied with her request to be sold but also recommended the woman's husband for a position in her buyer's family.[42] While some slaves sought new owners to be close to loved ones, other bondmen and women such as Israel Smith's slave Dick, John Hageman's slave Harry, and Nathaniel Pendleton's slave girl Sarah enjoyed protection from sale and potential separation from family and friends.[43] Even when sold, some slave families remained together as a single unit. One slaveholder in August 1799 offered to sell a young couple with their four-month-old child; yet another seller a year later indicated that he would consider selling a husband, his wife, and their one-year-old boy separately only if they remained in the same neighborhood.[44] Of course, the influence slaves wielded vis-à-vis their owners should not be overstated. Although many bondmen and women successfully negotiated concessions from their owners, others continued to be sold or bequeathed to heirs without a second thought. When advertising an eighteen-year-old woman in 1798, Abraham Teller stated plainly that she came "with or without a male child of about one year old, as may best suit the purchaser."[45] Nevertheless, the more frequent sale of women with their children attests to the increasing ability of many mothers to entreat and cajole their owners. John Pottenburgh expressly stated that the twenty-five-year-old woman he advertised in 1803 was to be sold with her eighteen-month-old child.[46]

The prevalence of slave hiring in the central Hudson Valley enhanced the bargaining position of slaves. Facing the potential depreciation in the value of their human property and the growing restlessness of their bondmen and women, slaveholders found slave hiring increasingly attractive after 1799. The practice of slave hiring, however, had contradictory implications. If the sale of slaves for specific terms proved lucrative for buyers and sellers, it also provided slaves with economic and psychological weapons of resistance. While frequent sale could be disruptive and emotionally painful, movement from place to place also brought slaves into contact with new people—black as well as white—and expanded their knowledge of the wider world and awareness of their place in it. A native of Fairfield, Connecticut, Hagar Davis lived in different parts of Dutchess County during her life in bondage, serving multiple masters in Fishkill, Poughkeepsie, and Nine Partners.[47] Some versatile and skilled slaves hired out by their owners exercised extraordinary discretion in determining the terms of their own employment. One "excellent house servant" and farmer adept in the care of horses enjoyed the right to stipulate the terms of his own sale.[48] The impact of such autonomy was far-reaching. Refining existing skills and acquiring new ones, hired slaves learned the value of their labor and grew increasingly self-confident. Its effect, moreover, was cyclical. Working for others and for themselves in different settings, increasingly confident slaves grew more assertive in their dealings with their masters and demanded yet greater concessions.[49] Several slaves in the region exercised a remarkable degree of autonomy in the early nineteenth century. Peter Livingston's slave John Francis received permission to work for himself; Rachel Pride likely moved and acted as a free woman of color during the full year she received leave from her master to attend to her ill daughter across the river.[50] Samantha Lewis was a slave in name only during the final months of her bondage. Although her master's will stipulated that she was to be manumitted at the age of twenty-two, Lewis effectively earned her freedom before that date; she left Fishkill and relocated to Poughkeepsie in October 1814 when her new master agreed that he no longer required her services.[51]

Slaves who worked for themselves endeavored to make virtual freedom real by purchasing their freedom outright. Hired out by his master's widow, Thomas Atkins ultimately earned the fifty pounds required for his manumission.[52] A woman named Betty similarly "undertook to pay her freedom" from James Emott of Poughkeepsie in 1807.[53] Self-purchase agreements were made largely at the instigation of slaves themselves. The case of Rachel Pride, who approached Moses Downing to negotiate her own sale for two years of service and fifty dollars, was not necessarily atypical.[54] In some instances, the costs of self-purchase could be modest. Twenty-five-year-old Deyone paid five shillings to Roelf and Garret Kip of Rhinebeck for his freedom in 1804.[55] James Kypher paid Amos Thorn of Poughkeepsie a nominal fee of one dollar.[56] Nevertheless, self-purchase could also be an arduous and expensive process. Since many slaveowners insisted on full compensation for their loss, costs could be prohibitive. Moreover, opportunities for employment were fewer in the countryside than in the city.[57] Slaves like Thomas Atkins and James Vandeburgh's slave Ompador managed to pay for their freedom in installments.[58] A series of smaller payments, however, only delayed emancipation, and those with very limited means found even modest installments difficult to meet. According to the agreement she concluded with Robert Livingston, Caty Stevenson was to receive her freedom after a period of six years for the sum of thirty dollars. However, after hiring herself out for four years, Stevenson had managed to earn a mere five dollars toward her purchase price.[59] Those who could not earn wages paid for their freedom with their own labor. In 1804, Robert Newkirk negotiated with Abraham Flagler of Clinton to obtain his freedom after a specified term of service.[60] As William Wright and Prince discovered, however, laboring for their freedom could be onerous. Under the contract he concluded with his master, Wright was to be liberated only after five and a half years of "honest" and "faithful" service. Moreover, Wright's failure to conduct himself appropriately would postpone his emancipation for an additional year.[61] Prince labored for an even longer term, earning his freedom only after seven years of service to Doctor John Masten of Rhinebeck.[62] Given the sizeable costs of self-purchase, slaves turned to others for assistance. Under the terms of an agreement reached in February 1807 among Joseph Scott of Kinderhook, Scott's slave James, and James Sleght of Poughkeepsie, James was to receive his freedom after he served Sleght for ten and a half months and Sleght paid forty dollars.[63] Liberated slaves went to great lengths to redeem relatives and friends still in bondage. Husbands and fathers in particular endeavored to purchase their wives and children; both Robert Churchill and Permete Bloom purchased their wives' freedom shortly after procuring their own manumissions.[64] At times family members could overcome seemingly insurmountable odds. A young woman named Jane was only seventeen in 1801 when her master allowed her to work for herself in consideration of a promise made by Moses Hallem, a black man, to pay one hundred dollars at a future date. Amazingly, the couple met that price and married shortly after Jane's manumission.[65]

Even with the assistance of kin and opportunities to work for themselves, self-purchase remained a very uncertain proposition. Any agreement required the willingness and ability of a slaveowner to enter into it. In the eyes of the law slaves could not contract, and self-purchase agreements enjoyed no legal standing. As Anthony Murphy discovered, slaveowners could arbitrarily alter and even abrogate such agreements. Although Murphy had originally contracted to buy his wife's freedom for ten dollars, for unknown reasons he ended up having to pay twice that figure.[66] Slaves had no legal recourse if and when masters violated the terms of their agreements or reneged on their promises. Even an agreement made in good faith by both parties was threatened with dissolution. A slaveowner could die before manumitting a slave, or desperate financial circumstances could force the liquidation of slave property before a slave had purchased his or her freedom.[67]

Nevertheless, if slaveowners could abrogate self-purchase agreements negotiated with their bondmen and women, it was not in their long-term interest to do so. Entering into contracts whereby slaves purchased their own freedom guaranteed masters a reliable source of labor, encouraged good behavior, and provided compensation for the loss of slave property. Conversely, an obdurate slaveowner who refused to accede to the entreaties and demands of his or her slaves risked retaliation. In the aftermath of the Revolution, African Americans in the Mid-Hudson Valley were hardly content to wait passively as they witnessed the disintegration of slavery in neighboring states and the excruciatingly slow pace of abolition in New York. Slaves intensified their resistance during the post-revolutionary era, resorting to traditional tactics such as slowing the pace of labor, feigning illness, performing shoddy work, stealing property, and sabotaging tools. Running away remained an effective weapon of resistance. Slaveowners in the central Hudson Valley grew increasingly vulnerable to flight during the post-revolutionary period. While twenty-two fugitives appeared in local newspaper advertisements during the ten years between 1785 and 1794, ads for two dozen slaves were published in the five years immediately preceding the passage of the 1799 abolition act. The growing restiveness must have been palpable. On the river's west bank, residents organized the "Slave Apprehending Society of Shawangunk" in response to the "uneasiness and disquietude" among local slaves who mistakenly believed that the legislature had liberated them.[68] The frequency of slave flight increased notably after the adoption of the gradual abolition statute in 1799, as the average number of runaways appearing in newspaper advertisements doubled. While printers published notices for 46 runaways between 1785 and 1799, as many as 108 fugitives appeared on the pages of the local press between 1800 and 1817. By 1810, the increasing frequency of flight in the region prompted several slaveholders in the vicinity of New Paltz in Ulster County to organize the "Society of Negroes Unsettled," an association contracted for the express purpose of retrieving runaways.[69] In total, advertisements for as many as two hundred fugitives appeared in Dutchess County newspapers between 1785 and 1827, when slavery legally ended in the state.[70]

Runaways who fled the region headed in different directions. Offering social and economic opportunities and the relative safety afforded by the anonymity of an urban environment, New York City served as a powerful magnet for fugitives from across the Mid-Hudson region. In 1809 William Davis of Poughkeepsie warned ship captains and ferrymen to look out for his slave Caroline, whom he suspected of heading to Manhattan.[71] While a majority of fugitives likely sought refuge among the throngs of New York City, other runaways sought haven in neighboring states and on the northern and western frontiers; even after 1787 it remained difficult and costly to retrieve fugitives who left New York.[72] In 1802, two slaves named Will fled their masters in Fishkill for Vermont, following the general path taken by Tone in 1798 and Tom in 1800.[73] Neither the frontier nor New England, however, sufficed for Henry Livingston's slave Solomon, whom Livingston suspected would "apply for a passage to some foreign country."[74] Solomon was not alone; African Americans were well represented among seamen and laborers in the maritime trades. One young man of seventeen had already completed several sea voyages when he fled his owner in 1808 wearing a "blue Sailor coat."[75]

As they had during the war years, runaways during the post-revolutionary period frequently absconded with items to facilitate their escape. Lists of pilfered articles published in advertisements for fugitives could be extensive. In addition to providing an exceptionally detailed description of what his slave Ned wore when he took flight in 1799, Abel Smith indicated that Ned absconded with two pairs of shoes, an old blue shortcoat, a striped under-jacket, two pairs of bearskin trousers, a white cotton shirt, and a white jacket with pewter buttons.[76] Other advertisers noted simply that their runaways carried bundles or fled with "other clothes too tedious to mention."[77] Well aware that clothing afforded disguises, slaveholders like William Rider did not even bother to describe their fugitives. Placing an advertisement for the capture of his slave Sukey in the *Poughkeepsie Journal*, Rider commented wryly in August 1799 that it was "needless to give a description" of what the woman took with her since "she took away a considerable bundle of clothing, and will probably change it."[78] Fugitives most commonly absconded with articles of clothing, but runaways took whatever might assist them in their escape. James and Abraham rode off on horses; Lew fled with a seven-year-old mare and a young colt.[79] Money—and articles that could be sold—were obviously valuable. When fleeing Henry Livingston in 1805, Jack not only stole a sizeable amount of cash but also took with him property valued at 140 pounds.[80] Artisans fled carrying the tools of their craft, and musicians typically absconded with their fiddles and other instruments.[81]

Peter Waldron's slave Tom was particularly bold; the eighteen-year-old fled from his Fishkill master in the summer of 1810 carrying a gun.[82]

Permanent escape from slavery, however, need not have been the principal objective of most fugitives during the post-revolutionary era. The desire to reunite families remained a powerful motivation for many runaways. Approximately half of fugitives whose intentions or destinations were surmised by their owners allegedly absconded to visit loved ones or return to previous places of residence.[83] The obstacles to reuniting with family members could be more formidable in the countryside than in a compact urban environment; while fugitives in a seaport might have escaped to a nearby neighborhood, dispersed settlement and distance separated rural slaves. However, familial bonds were powerful enough to draw runaways across many miles. Sukey fled William Rider allegedly to reunite with her husband in Boston.[84] A surprising number of fugitives, however, remained in the region. Both Tom, who escaped from his master in Rhinebeck Landing, and Stephen Huston, who fled from Abiah Palmer in Amenia, were suspected to have returned to their birthplaces on the west bank.[85] Larger communities like Fishkill and Poughkeepsie attracted truant slaves. Mary Hasbrouck of New Paltz suspected that her bondmen Harry and Caesar were "loitering" in the Poughkeepsie vicinity, and Jacob Bockee's seventeen-year-old servant Si supposedly made her way from the town of Northeast to the county seat and was "lurking about" the village.[86]

Remaining in the region entailed risk, and fugitives who "loitered" about local neighborhoods successfully avoided detection only by constant vigilance. Runaways could not remain at large for extended periods without assistance. Family members and friends aided runaways in their flight, and small black neighborhoods in the countryside and in larger villages provided fugitives a modicum of protection. Peter, a free man who worked in Poughkeepsie, helped his wife Susanna and their nine-year-old son escape from Robert Gill in 1803.[87] Henry Livingston of Rhinebeck suspected that his twenty-seven-year-old slave Jack had joined his mulatto wife and taken up residence with a free black man whom Jack had visited the previous winter along Wappinger's Creek.[88] Fellow slaves and free blacks, however, were not the only individuals willing to assist fugitives. Fraternization between slaves and their free white neighbors was a regular part of life in the rural Hudson Valley, and periodic warnings inserted in runaway advertisements against aiding and abetting runaways suggest that the practice was not necessarily uncommon. In 1798, Stephen Legget of Stanford accused physician

Leonard Barten of "persuading away" his slave Tom.[89] John Oppie's slave Harry allegedly had been harbored "at Mr. Reuben Fowler's in Fishkill for some time past" before being spotted "lurking about" in Beekman.[90] Accomplices who provided haven for fugitives did so out of genuine moral conviction, self-interest, or a combination of both. John Coonley of the town of Washington might have feared that an unscrupulous employer would hire his fugitive blacksmith Harry when he warned that all individuals who harbored the fugitive did so "upon their peril."[91] Sheltered by family and friends, runaways who remained in the region attempted to assume new identities. Medad Raymond of Peekskill in northern Westchester County was confident that his seventeen-year-old servant Sam was with his parents in Fishkill using an alias.[92] Jonathan Lockwood of Beekman similarly suspected that his twenty-three-year-old fugitive Vas would change his name.[93] The frequency by which slaves and servants "loitered" about different neighborhoods might help to explain the tendency of several slaveowners to delay placing notices in local newspapers in hopes that their fugitives would eventually return voluntarily.[94] Occasionally, notices appeared long after the event. The fugitive Nicholas had been at large for more than two years before an advertisement for his capture appeared in the *Poughkeepsie Journal* in September 1808.[95] Ann Long took out an advertisement for her servant girl Mary only after the young woman had been spotted in Nine Partners—fully three years after she had originally absconded.[96]

Flight could be the spontaneous response to a specific event. It was his master's death and the impending threat of his own sale, for example, that likely prompted Peter to flee in early 1798.[97] The determination to protect family members could also provide a powerful motivation for escape. It might have been the prospective breakup of his family that convinced Ishmael to flee with his two sons and infant daughter in the summer of 1789.[98] However, slave flight during the final years of the eighteenth century and the first part of the nineteenth must be understood within the broader context of the contested negotiated relationships between slaves and owners in the post-revolutionary Hudson Valley. Running away—and the threat of flight—provided slaves a potentially formidable weapon in their dealings with their masters. Gilbert Livingston was particularly incensed when Sam "ungratefully" absconded in 1804. As Livingston explained in an unusually detailed advertisement, the nineteen-year-old's "dereliction of service" was particularly "base" because the young man had solicited Livingston to purchase him "on an express contract to work out his freedom."[99] The protracted power struggle between James and his master Israel Vail lasted for years. Like the contract concluded between Livingston and Sam, James' original purchase agreement stipulated that the slave was to receive his freedom after serving Vail for a specified period. Like Sam, James ran away before the end of that term, fleeing on the night of July 30, 1803. Whether authorities apprehended the fugitive or James had a change of heart, the runaway returned. Although both men agreed to adhere to the terms of their original agreement, James fled again in September 1805. If James had no qualms about violating the informal contract he had concluded with Vail, his owner was indignant at James' breach of faith for a second time. In a postscript to the advertisement for James' apprehension, Vail fumed, "As the aforesaid Negro man was purchased at his own request, this dereliction of service must be considered by every person as notoriously base." The infuriated slaveowner entreated "printers throughout the United States" to place the advertisement in their newspapers.[100] In the eyes of Israel Vail and Gilbert Livingston, contracts for freedom were beneficent gifts awarded for loyal service, and the terms of such agreements were binding. For slaves like Sam and James, however, such agreements were only means to an end—their ultimate liberation—to be discarded whenever a better opportunity for freedom arose.

In the eyes of their masters, slaves like Sam and James were sinister and devious. Runaways were typically intelligent, shrewd, and calculating. Slaves who worked as teamsters and boatmen exploited their intimate knowledge of geography. A coachman, the fugitive Charles was very "well known" along the roads to Albany and New York City.[101] Fugitives also tended to be articulate; two-thirds of forty-two runaways whose language proficiency was recorded by their owners were literate or identified as "talkative" "well spoken," "good speakers," or "great talkers."[102] Such articulate and intelligent individuals displayed great confidence in dealing with whites. Jacob Cholwell of Red Hook described his fifteen-year-old fugitive as "a very cunning fellow," having been taught how to read and write.[103] Masters considered self-assured and smooth-talking slaves threatening and devious. Bernard Matthewson of Stanford believed that his bilingual sixteen-year-old fugitive Gin "had rather tell a lie when the truth will answer well."[104] In the eyes of her master, Matsey, a well-spoken sixteen-year-old from Red Hook, was "artful enough to deceive Satan himself."[105] Advertisers for runaways occasionally noted the intractability of their fugitives, describing them as having a "down" or "sour" look, a "surly countenance," or a "sulky" or "ungovernable" temper.[106] Dealing with such cantankerous and uncooperative slaves undoubtedly exacted a heavy psychological toll. James Bramble of Poughkeepsie evidently had his hands full dealing with his slave Tom. Although the nearly forty-year-old man had a fondness for "strong liquor" and was in fact too "slow in his motion" to run, Tom was "addicted to walking off" and frequently loitered about the Poughkeepsie race grounds.[107]

If flight and other forms of direct and indirect resistance rendered slaveholding more onerous and costly to slaveowners, such defiance also entailed significant risk. Rather than acceding to their slaves' demands and negotiating self-purchase agreements, slaveholders could respond to such threats by imposing harsh punishments or even by selling their troublesome property altogether. In advertising for the capture of the fugitive Simon in 1818, for example, John Drake indicated his intent to sell the remaining time of his incorrigible servant after Simon had fled "for the fifth time within a few months."[108] Drake certainly had interested buyers; even after the adoption of gradual abolition, slave ownership remained an important form of conspicuous consumption, and advertisements for the sale and hiring of slaves after 1799 reflect a vibrant local market. The most lucrative markets lay in the Southern states. In defiance of state law, slaveowners and traders resorted to a variety of stratagems—from ostensibly voluntary "indentures" to outright kidnapping—to sell slaves out of state. The precise number of slaves illegally exported from New York during the Early National period is unknown, but the figure was likely significant. Although hardly conclusive, the decline of Dutchess County's African American population from 2,541 to 2,390 during the decade following the passage of the act of 1799 after decades of continuous growth is suggestive.[109]

For the most part, however, the pace of emancipation slowly but steadily accelerated during the decades after 1799. The depreciating value of slaves in New York and penalties associated with illegal slave sales more often encouraged slaveowners to reach some accommodation with their bondmen and women. Guaranteeing labor for a set period of time, encouraging good behavior, and securing some form of compensation for the eventual loss of the slave was preferable to risking flight and losing the slave altogether.[110] However, the bargaining position of masters vis-à-vis their slaves weakened over time. The success of some slaves in procuring freedom through negotiated contracts or flight and a growing population of freed slaves only emboldened those yet in bondage and increased the likelihood of their own success. The sheer momentum of events in the Mid-Hudson Valley and elsewhere in the state forced state lawmakers to take more decisive antislavery measures by the 1810s. Adopted in 1817 after a number of years of discussion and debate, "An Act Relative to Slaves and Servants" hastened abolition in New York by providing for the emancipation of slaves unaffected by the original gradual abolition statute. In a nod to property rights and the state's slaveholding interest, however, the 1817 law postponed the date of those born before July 4, 1799, another ten years until 1827. In addition, the act confirmed the indenture of children born of slaves after July 4, 1799, but reduced the age of servitude to twenty-one.[111]

The changing profile of fugitives during the opening decades of the nineteenth century hints at the growing assertiveness of African Americans during the waning years of slavery. Running away was a bold act. As elsewhere in the Americas, fugitives in the central Hudson region were predominantly young, healthy, single males who acted alone.[112] Flight was not a viable option for the very young, the very old, or women, who shouldered familial responsibilities and who had fewer opportunities to support themselves. However, both the increasing frequency of female runaways and the declining age of fugitives over the course of the post-revolutionary era are striking. Men comprised almost nine of every ten runaways between the end of the Revolution and 1799 and more than eight of ten fugitives between the adoption of gradual abolition and 1817. Females, however, comprised fully one-third of all fugitives appearing in the local press after the passage of the 1817 abolition law. The average age of runaways dropped during the same period. Fugitives under twenty-six years of age accounted for three of every four runaways between 1785 and 1799, almost eighty percent of fugitives between 1800 and 1817, and as many as nine of ten runaways after 1817.[113] With the demise of slavery in New York assured, bound service must have become even more objectionable to younger African Americans, female and male alike. Advertisements in the local press capture the intractability of such younger fugitives in slavery's waning years. Bound to serve for another ten to twelve years, John Drake's "lazy and sloven" sixteen-year-old servant Simon chewed tobacco and used "harsh speech."[114]

The increasing restiveness of African Americans during the opening decades of the nineteenth century hastened the demise of slavery in Dutchess County and beyond. The institution was all but dead in New York by 1827, but the battle for emancipation in the Mid-Hudson Valley had been exceptionally grueling and painful. Resisting the more radical impulses of the Revolution, slaveowners during the post-revolutionary period maneuvered to reassert their authority and legitimize slavery in the new republic. After delaying abolition as long as possible, slaveholders acquiesced only to a conservative scheme of emancipation that phased out slavery over time and protected their financial interests. Emancipation in Dutchess County proceeded only slowly during the decades after the War for Independence, especially in those western townships along the river with the densest enslaved populations. Individual slaveowners postponed manumission and granted freedom selectively, often demanding obedient behavior and even compensation from those whom they chose to liberate. The intransigence of their owners ultimately compelled slaves in Dutchess County to resort to their own devices. Exploiting their own value in the regional economy and the intimacy of slaveholding in the central Hudson Valley, bondmen and women exacted concessions from their owners. Some requested or rejected sales and lobbied successfully to keep slave families intact. As their leverage vis-à-vis their owners increased over time, many pressured their masters into negotiating self-purchase agreements, and an increasing number absconded when their owners refused to do so. The ability of slaves to exact concessions from their masters was clearly limited, but increasing restiveness and flight rendered slaveholding more onerous for their owners. African Americans were clearly protagonists in the battle for emancipation, and their actions are fundamental to understanding the demise of slavery in the Mid-Hudson Valley. Emancipation, however, was only the beginning of the struggle. Freedom brought challenges of its own.

# 4

# An Arduous Struggle

## *From Slavery to Freedom*

MANY YOUNG WOMEN OF COLOR at the dawn of the nineteenth century might have identified with Sarah Tabor. Sarah was born to Abby Lattimore and John Ogden in Poughkeepsie during the Revolution. Her mulatto parents were unique; Abby and John were not only free at a time when the overwhelming majority of the region's black residents were held in bondage, but they also managed to support themselves on a small plot of land they leased across the river in Marlboro. Tragically, John's premature death left his family in difficult circumstances. After the expiration of the family's lease, Abby—a widow and single mother—returned with her children to the east bank, where she found employment as a servant in the Murray home in Poughkeepsie. Once old enough to work herself, Sarah left her family to assume a position as a domestic in the Mesier home in Fishkill. Domestic service was not only taxing but also impermanent. Sarah spent two years with the Mesiers but then moved from household to household, eventually making her way to Dover in the eastern part of Dutchess County. There, she met and fell in love with Jacob Tabor, a twenty-four-year-old slave from neighboring Pawling. Sarah's brother, a man named Absalom Titus, purchased Jacob's freedom, and the couple married. Sarah and Jacob migrated from eastern Dutchess to Poughkeepsie in 1805 in search of new opportunities. Life in the village, however, proved difficult. Although they rented several different tenements in Poughkeepsie, the Tabors failed to establish a permanent residence in the village. Perhaps it was because of his inability to find steady employment that Jacob turned to illegitimate means to support his family. In August 1809, a prostitute by the name of Maria Herrick testified to authorities that she had been "induced" to the Tabor home and forced to flee after an "altercation" with several men. The town justices convicted another woman at the residence of being a "disorderly person" and fined Jacob for keeping a "disorderly house." Shortly afterward, Jacob was imprisoned for an unspecified offense, leaving Sarah and the couple's children dependent on public relief. Jacob served his sentence, but Sarah and the Tabor children found themselves alone yet again when Jacob died less than two years after his release from prison. Their patience exhausted, the justices of the peace ordered the indenture of the Tabor children and the breakup of the family.[1]

The Tabors' ordeal poignantly illustrates the formidable challenges African Americans in the Mid-Hudson Valley confronted during the transitional period between slavery and freedom. Historians have traditionally identified the late eighteenth and early nineteenth centuries as the formative period of free African American life in the urban North. In the aftermath of the Revolution, thousands of liberated slaves asserted their independence by migrating to seaport cities such as Boston, New York, and Philadelphia in search of social and economic opportunities not available in the countryside. African Americans occupied the lowest rungs of the socioeconomic ladder, but a notable number of black city residents enjoyed modest success as artisans, peddlers, and small proprietors. Free African Americans established independent households and founded black congregations, fraternal orders, benevolent societies, and other organizations to meet the material, social, and spiritual needs of the community.[2] The experience of African Americans in the central Hudson Valley, however, differed from that of their urban counterparts in important respects. Gradual abolition proved especially devastating in a rural environment. The inclination of slaveholders to retain their slave property as long as practicable, their insistence on remuneration in the form of monetary compensation or additional labor, and the selective manner by which slaveowners granted manumission posed formidable obstacles to African Americans in the central Hudson Valley. Dispersed settlement, the comparative isolation of the countryside, and economic dependency further constrained the ability of the region's black residents to build free lives during the early decades of the nineteenth century. Emancipated slaves in Dutchess County were more likely than their urban counterparts to remain as dependents in white households, while those unwilling or unable to labor for their former masters found economic opportunities severely circumscribed. A largely propertyless population of wage laborers struggled to maintain a bare subsistence during the transitional period between slavery and freedom. Perhaps it was out of desperation that Jacob turned to crime, but his incarceration ultimately deprived his family of a husband and father, and his death meant the dissolution of his family. However, if the Tabors' story attests to the painful transition from slavery to freedom in Dutchess County, it also testifies to the resourcefulness and fortitude of the county's black residents in an unforgiving and hostile environment. Jacob and Sarah's marriage, Absalom Titus' purchase of his brother-in-law's freedom, and the Tabors' migration from the countryside to Poughkeepsie all attest to the determination to forge autonomous lives as free people. Despite the persistence of bondage and the constraints of rural poverty during the opening decades of the nineteenth century, freed men and women in Dutchess County turned to each other, laying the foundations for an independent community life after slavery.

In the absence of organized community institutions found in urban centers, the family assumed inordinate importance in the rural Mid-Hudson Valley. The abandonment of the master's household to establish identities as free husbands, wives, fathers, and mothers represented a powerful assertion of autonomy. An institution that formed individual and collective identity, the family was the fundamental building block of community life. New York State provided a modicum of protection to black families in 1809 when it legally recognized slave families and the right of slaves to hold property.[3] However, the 1809 statute had little practical meaning for those separated from family members. Compared to their counterparts in urban settings, African Americans in rural Dutchess County were slower to establish independent households during the transitional period between slavery and freedom. In 1790, when free people comprised almost one-third of New York City's African American population, merely one of five black residents in Dutchess County was free. Three decades later, when slavery had all but died in Manhattan, almost one of three black residents in Dutchess remained in bondage (see table 4.1).

The disparity between Dutchess County and New York City was attributable not only to the migration of African Americans from the countryside to the seaport but also to the slower pace by which slavery ended in the central Hudson Valley. Emancipation did not necessarily free African Americans from the supervision of former masters or white employers. Although the slave population of Dutchess gradually declined after 1790, both the number and proportion of white households with black members remained virtually unchanged.[4] Free African Americans in the rural Hudson Valley were more likely than liberated slaves in New York City to reside in white households; between 1790 and 1810, more than two-fifths of free blacks in Dutchess County continued to live with and work for white families.[5] As many as one-third of free black residents continued to live with white families two decades after the passage of New York's gradual abolition law; those five hundred individuals and the almost eight hundred men, women, and children still in bondage collectively accounted for just over half of Dutchess County's black population in 1820 (see table 4.2).

Different factors explain the persistence of emancipated slaves in white households. Manumission proceeded largely piecemeal in the Mid-Hudson Valley. While masters remained reluctant to relinquish their human property, liberated slaves hesitated to leave spouses and children still in bondage. Emancipation, moreover, brought not only joy but also anxiety. While many freed people seized opportunities to escape oppressive circumstances, others hesitated to abandon whatever security they had enjoyed or separate themselves from masters and mistresses with whom they had forged intimate emotional bonds.[6] Emancipated slaves faced an uncertain economic

**Table 4.1**
**African American Populations of Dutchess County and New York City, 1790–1820**

| | Dutchess County | | New York City | |
|---|---|---|---|---|
| **Year** | **Slaves (N/%)** | **Free (N/%)** | **Slaves (N/%)** | **Free (N/%)** |
| **1790** | 1,856 (80.8) | 440 (19.2) | 2,369 (68.3) | 1,101 (31.7) |
| **1800** | 1,609 (63.3) | 932 (36.7) | 2,868 (45.0) | 3,499 (55.0) |
| **1810** | 1,244 (52.1) | 1,146 (47.9) | 1,686 (17.2) | 8,137 (82.8) |
| **1820** | 772 (31.3) | 1,696 (68.7) | 518 (4.8) | 10,368 (95.2) |

*Sources:* Heads of Families at the First Census of the United States Taken in the Year 1790: New York (Baltimore: Genealogical Publishing Co., 1976); Population Schedules of the First Census of the United States, 1790, microcopy 637, roll 6, New York, vol. 2 (Washington, DC: 1965); Population Schedules of the Second Census of the United States, 1800, microcopy 32, roll 21, New York (Washington, DC: 1959); Population Schedules of the Third Census of the United States, 1810, roll 30, New York (Washington, DC: 1968); Population Schedules of the Fourth Census of the United States, 1820, roll 71, New York, vol. 10 (Washington, DC: 1959). New York City figures come from Gary B. Nash, "Forging Freedom: The Emancipation Experience in Northern Seaport Cities," in *Slavery and Freedom in the Age of the American Revolution*, ed. Ira Berlin and Ronald Hoffman (Charlottesville: University Press of Virginia, 1983), 5.

future. The regional economy was beginning to undergo profound and sometimes unsettling change during the opening decades of the nineteenth century. Although Hudson Valley foodstuffs had been important commodities in imperial commerce during the colonial period, practically few local farmers during the eighteenth century engaged in long-distance trade. As late as 1800, the overwhelming majority of Hudson Valley residents engaged predominately in a small-scale semi-subsistent economy where families produced principally for themselves and bartered goods and services with their neighbors.[7] Traditional preindustrial modes of production and exchange persisted into the nineteenth century, but the capitalist Market Revolution was beginning to transform the regional economy as black residents emerged from bondage. Newly constructed roads such as the Dutchess Turnpike, which extended the width of the county from Poughkeepsie to the Connecticut border, connected the rural hinterland with villages along the river and drastically reduced the costs of transporting goods to market. Farmers continued to produce predominately for local buyers, but an increasing volume of goods found its way to river landings in the long-distance trade. More than a dozen landings in Fishkill, Poughkeepsie, Hyde Park, Rhinebeck, and Red Hook—studded with wharves, storehouses, workshops, offices, and stores—were sites of bustling activity as an increasing number of sloops, schooners, packets, and eventually steamboats sailed weekly up and down the river. The expanding

**Table 4.2**
**Free African Americans in Dutchess County, 1790–1820**

| Year | Total Free African American Population | Free African Americans in White Households (N/%) | Free African Americans in Black Households (N/%) |
|---|---|---|---|
| **1790** | 440 | 178 (40.5) | 262 (59.5) |
| **1800** | 932 | 448 (48.1) | 484 (51.9) |
| **1810** | 1,146 | 471 (41.1) | 675 (58.9) |
| **1820** | 1,696 | 505 (29.8) | 1,191 (70.2) |

*Sources:* See table 4.1.

marketplace encouraged more intensive cultivation. Horatio Spafford's 1813 *Gazetteer of the State of New York* ranked Dutchess among the most productive and "opulent" farming counties in the state and observed that no other county exceeded Dutchess in "style of improvement."[8] While clearing land and expanding tillage of most fertile soils, farmers converted less-productive plots to meadow and pasturage. The populations of sheep, horses, cattle, and dairy cows soared to meet the rising demand for woolens, draft animals, meat, and dairy products. Farm women devoted more time to the marketing of produce and the production of butter and cheese. Property owners also extracted wealth from land ill-suited for cultivation. Densely wooded lots provided timber, barrel staves, and other wood products. Small deposits of iron ore could be found in eastern and southern Dutchess, while limestone was dispersed across the county. Amenia was known for high-quality marble; slate quarries in Clinton employed as many as three hundred workers.[9] Perhaps the most striking development was the transformation of manufacturing. Most manufacture in rural Dutchess remained centered on the farm and in the home, but manufacturing establishments proliferated across the county during the opening decades of the nineteenth century. The introduction of new technologies and significant national events—notably the War of 1812 and the embargo that preceded it—spurred manufacture in the central valley. The topography of the east bank provided ideal natural environments for manufacturing enterprises. Larger creeks such as the Crum Elbow, Fall, Fishkill, Saw, Sprout, and Wappinger's and smaller streams and tributaries provided sites for a wide variety of manufactories: carding machine works, cotton factories, distilleries, furnaces, forges, fulling mills, gristmills, hatteries, oil mills, sawmills, scythe works, tanneries, trip hammers, and woolen mills. The vast majority of mills and rural workshops were small, but entrepreneurs erected larger factories in Rhinebeck, Pleasant Valley, Poughkeepsie, and Fishkill. The overwhelming majority of Dutchess County residents remained engaged in the traditional rural economy, but by the 1820s the revolution in markets and manufacturing was beginning to leave an indelible mark on the way people lived and worked. In 1824, more than three hundred county merchants conducted an increasing volume of business and trade, while almost 2,900 workers—over one-quarter of the county workforce—labored in more than three hundred mills, workshops, and factories across the county.[10]

Free African Americans aspired to become freeholders in the region's rapidly expanding economy. Landownership was emblematic of both economic autonomy and equal citizenship in the new American republic. After procuring his freedom, Robert Newkirk migrated from Clinton to Poughkeepsie around 1804, purchased an acre of land, and erected a small house on the lot.[11] In 1818, Charles Freeman purchased three acres in the town of Beekman for the sum of $312.[12] However, Newkirk and Freeman were exceptional; very few were as fortunate as the handful of black families in Hyde Park who leased, purchased, or received small plots from the prominent Bard family.[13] By 1825, only twenty-eight black residents—a mere one percent of the county's black population—owned property assessed at $250 or higher; less than four percent of all African Americans in Dutchess paid any tax whatsoever.[14] Opportunities for landownership dwindled during the opening decades of the nineteenth century as farming and manufacture became more capital intensive and property values soared. Restrictive patterns of land tenure further limited prospects for land acquisition. Although the Revolution weakened the grip of the region's landed aristocracy, the leasehold system persisted in areas of northern Dutchess and other parts of the county.[15] In some instances, tenancy could provide an avenue toward independent property ownership. As in other parts of the rural North, some former slaves without the means to purchase land outright negotiated agreements with landowners whereby they worked small plots and earned income as cottagers or sharecroppers. Released from slavery, Permete Bloom and his wife originally worked for Gilbert Titus in Beekman but eventually became tenants, first leasing a house and eight acres from Israel Titus and then renting property from the Livingston family. Tenancy allowed the Blooms to accumulate modest savings; Permete, his wife, and their children eventually moved to Poughkeepsie, where they purchased a plot for $150 and erected a small house for $110.[16] Most liberated slaves, however, had few if any financial means with which to purchase real estate. The least fortunate, including eighteen-year-old domestic Bet Taylor and fifty-seven-year-old Deverix Milbur, owned little more than their personal belongings.[17] Slaveowners rarely provided their slaves with material or financial assistance upon their manumission. When they did so, they typically bequeathed to slaves only their personal belongings; only occasionally did masters provide small cash payments, tools, or a cow or horse. In no instance did masters provide real estate upon their deaths. Few men or women were as fortunate as Michael Vincent's slaves Sambo, Pompey, Jane, and Sarah, who, in addition to sharing 135 pounds in cash, each received a bed, bedding, and a chest filled with clothing upon their manumission.[18]

Largely propertyless and effectively barred from landownership, the majority of freed men and women in Dutchess County struggled to support themselves as laborers, domestics, and hired hands. The revolution in markets and production had contradictory implications for black workers. On the one hand, farmers and producers who increasingly relied on wage labor provided opportunities for men and women in the countryside to supplement their income by performing labor and piecework for local manufacturers. Skilled black labor remained no less valuable than it had been during the colonial period, and talented workers were capable of earning decent wages and commanding the respect of white employers.[19] For the most part, however, work on farms and in local workshops in the early nineteenth century was largely unpredictable and insecure. Wage laborers in the countryside were particularly vulnerable to the vagaries of the emerging market-oriented economy.[20] As wealth became increasingly maldistributed and traditional relationships between masters and their workmen deteriorated, laborers found fewer opportunities for upward mobility. A series of editorials in the *Dutchess Observer* in 1817 lamented the alarming number of working people who had been reduced to living "hand to mouth" and warned of the enslavement of the "poor, honest, and industrious citizen" by "money interests."[21] In an increasingly competitive and unforgiving labor market, the least skilled black laborers lived on the verge of destitution. Anthony Murphy, for example, barely managed to support himself and his family on what he earned as a day laborer.[22] Employment for the laboring poor was often temporary. Wandering from place to place in search of work, migrant laborers failed to establish residency in any community. After securing their freedom, Harry and Jenny Van Brunt rented a variety of different places in Clinton, Pleasant Valley, and Poughkeepsie, moving with their children every one to three years.[23] Benjamin Furman was even more traveled. After serving as a printer's apprentice in New York City, Furman resided in Horseneck, Greenfield, and Newtown before moving with his family to Dutchess. Once in the county, the Furmans moved from Amenia to Poughkeepsie to Beekman and back to Poughkeepsie again within the span of approximately two years.[24] Such migration did not escape the notice of local authorities, who viewed the growing transient population with alarm. At its June 7, 1810, meeting, the Poughkeepsie Overseers of the Poor resolved to conduct a census of the town's black population, instructing the census taker to identify those "not having a family" and those likely to become chargeable to the town.[25]

Contrary to what municipal authorities perceived, migration throughout the county was neither random nor aimless. Whether seeking to reconstitute families, find work, or purchase property, migrants operated from distinct motives and pursued definite destinations. Having procured their freedom, Dutchess County's black residents relied on those informal networks forged in bondage. Small black enclaves in the countryside attracted some migrants. Baxtertown, a cluster of African American households located in a low swampy area two miles west of the village of Fishkill, might have originated as a maroon settlement of Native Americans and fugitive slaves during the colonial period.[26] East of the village of Hyde Park, black residents who occupied small plots along a small rural roadway called "Fredonia Lane" constituted a small neighborhood popularly known as "Guinea" or "New Guinea."[27] Charles Freeman's holdings in the town of Beekman provided a nucleus for the small community of "Freemanville," or "Guinea Town."[28] It might have been that neighborhood that attracted Moses and Jane Hallem, who migrated to Beekman from Orange County.[29] The number of black residents in Beekman increased by more than one-third between 1790 and 1820, while the African American populations of the neighboring towns of Dover, Fishkill, and Pawling grew at a more modest rate of eight percent.[30] North of Beekman, the black population of the towns of Washington and Stanford increased by almost one-third; several former slaves belonging to the Johnston family and other slaveholders in central Dutchess clustered in the vicinity of Lithgow and Millbrook near the Nine Partners Meeting House and Boarding School.[31]

While small rural neighborhoods provided havens in the Dutchess countryside, many freed people who abandoned their masters' households tended to migrate to the village of Poughkeepsie and surrounding communities. Eighteen-year-old Freelove Marsh, for example, migrated to the county seat after completing her indenture to the Matthison family of Amenia. Robert and Sarah Churchill followed Jacob and Sarah Tabor, making their way to Poughkeepsie from their homes in the Oblong.[32] Census returns hint at this migration. While the slave population of Poughkeepsie declined by 147 individuals during the thirty years after 1790, the town's free black population jumped by 253 persons. Indeed, the growth of Poughkeepsie's black population between 1790 and 1820 surpassed that for all other towns in the county. While the number of African Americans residing elsewhere rose by a modest eleven percent, Poughkeepsie's black population grew forty-three percent, from 247 to 353 people. The number of black residents in the neighboring town of Clinton (including Hyde Park and Pleasant Valley) increased by more than one-third. The small but growing free African American population of the greater Poughkeepsie area promoted further immigration. The number of free black residents in Poughkeepsie surpassed the town's slave population in the 1810s; by 1820, when almost one-third of African Americans across the county remained in bondage, fully eighty-five percent of the town's black population was free. In neighboring Clinton, the ratio was almost four of five residents. Conversely, the African American population remained static in those towns where slavery persisted the longest. Fishkill's black population increased by less than eight percent between 1790 and 1820; in northwestern Dutchess, where the majority of African Americans remained in bondage as late as 1820, the black population of Red Hook and Rhinebeck actually declined by ten percent (see table 4.3).

While many freed people migrated to make a fresh start, economic security remained elusive for many emancipated slaves in Dutchess County. Flora Francis' mother was sincere when she "thanked God" that she was in good health and able to support herself.[33] Illness or injury daily threatened to reduce the laboring poor from bare subsistence to destitution. Charles Lee and his lame and rheumatic sister were left in desperate circumstances when an unspecified physical complaint incapacitated Charles.[34] Misfortune could even devastate those who had managed to carve out a modicum of success. After relocating from Beekman and purchasing their Poughkeepsie property, Permete Bloom and his wife struggled to make their mortgage payments; the couple eventually defaulted when Permete's wife fell gravely ill and rheumatism prevented Permete from working.[35] The position of single women could be precarious. Although the labor performed by women was less seasonal, opportunities were limited in other ways. Samantha Lewis, a cook in the employ of the Jewett family in Poughkeepsie, worked occasionally on the farm, but women typically found few options outside of domestic service, where they earned low pay and remained vulnerable to harassment and abuse. The loss of a position could be devastating. Women comprised almost three of every five African Americans in the poor record for the town of Poughkeepsie between 1807 and 1815, the majority of whom were either single, separated from their spouses, or widowed. Propertyless widows had few resources on which to rely. Hagar Davis, whose consumptive husband had received support from the town prior to his death, became dependent on public relief when an unspecified "female complaint" so debilitated her that she was unable to labor.[36] Few were as fortunate as Hannah or Molly,

Table 4.3.
African American Population of Dutchess County by Town, 1790–1820

| Town | Total Population (Slaves/Free) | | | |
|---|---|---|---|---|
| | 1790 | 1800 | 1810 | 1820 |
| Amenia | 81 (52/29) | 108 (40/68) | 82 (57/25) | 97 (32/65) |
| Beekman | 117 (106/11) | 134 (78/56) | 143 (39/104) | 160 (25/135) |
| Carmel | — | 20 (16/4) | 27 (6/21) | — |
| Clinton | 207 (176/31) | 245 (182/63) | 243 (152/91) | 282 (59/223) |
| Dover | — | — | 63 (18/45) | 67 (1/66) |
| Fishkill | 642 (601/41) | 643 (524/119) | 609 (400/209) | 691 (266/425) |
| Franklin | — | 52 (19/33) | — | — |
| Frederick-stown | 104 (63/41) | 3 (2/1) | 1 (1/0) | — |
| Milan | — | — | — | 67 (18/49) |
| Northeast | 102 (80/22) | 140 (72/68) | 125 (57/68) | 64 (25/39) |
| Patterson | — | — | 44 (8/36) | — |
| Pawling | 133 (42/91) | 113 (34/79) | 33 (6/27) | 77 (4/73) |
| Philipstown | 27 (25/2) | 36 (10/26) | 39 (8/31) | — |
| Poughkeepsie | 247 (199/48) | 317 (177/140) | 329 (131/198) | 353 (52/301) |
| Red Hook | — | — | — | 295 (182/113) |
| Rhinebeck | 487 (421/66) | 491 (361/130) | 418 (313/105) | 142 (74/68) |
| Southeast | 16 (13/3) | 37 (17/20) | 37 (15/22) | — |
| Stanford | — | 96 (44/52) | 124 (27/97) | 100 (24/76) |
| Washington | 133 (78/55) | 106 (33/73) | 73 (6/67) | 73 (10/63) |
| Totals: | **2,296 (1856/440)** | **2,541 (1609/932)** | **2,390 (1244/1146)** | **2,468 (772/1696)** |

*Notes:* Carmel was organized from Frederickstown in 1795; Dover was organized from Pawling in 1807; Franklin was organized from Frederickstown and Southeast in 1795; Milan was organized from Northeast in 1818; Franklin was renamed Patterson in 1808; Red Hook was organized from Rhinebeck in 1812; Stanford was organized from Washington in 1793; Carmel, Frederickstown, Patterson, Philipstown, and Southeast were set off to form Putnam County in 1812.

*Sources:* See table 4.1.

whose former masters provided for their maintenance during old age in consideration of "long and faithful service."[37] Younger women confronted their own challenges. Responsible for the care of children, single mothers were particularly vulnerable. The mother of a two-year-old boy, Diana Jackson appeared before the overseers of the poor, sick, and destitute only six days after giving birth to her second child.[38] Caty Stevenson, an unwed mother of six children, was expecting her seventh when the overseers of the poor ordered her removal from the town in 1809.[39]

Women and men incapacitated by sickness, injury, or age had few options. Mutual aid societies, benevolent organizations, fraternal orders, and black churches that attempted to meet the needs of the urban poor did not exist in the central Hudson Valley. Although African Americans comprised only seven percent of Poughkeepsie's population at the beginning of the nineteenth century, the forty-nine cases of African Americans in the town poor record accounted for almost one of every five examinations conducted by the overseers of the poor between 1807 and 1815.[40] The significant proportion of black residents residing in white households renders that figure even more sobering. Individuals of any race seeking public assistance found the state's poor laws unforgiving. Residency, not race, was the principal criterion in dispensing relief. New York adopted stringent poor laws during the Early National period to meet the challenge of rising poverty rates and address public fears of a growing transient population. Distinguishing between deserving and unworthy poor and attempting to minimize costs, state law empowered overseers of the poor to deny relief to nonresidents and remove them from the community.[41] Only one-third of African Americans in the Poughkeepsie poor record whose residency status was specified met residency requirements and received relief. Authorities ordered Lucy Anderson's removal even though the pregnant woman insisted that she had a place to stay and could support herself as a spinner.[42] The overseers of the poor were not totally unmoved by Diana Jackson's desperate plight, granting the ill mother of a two-year-old and a newborn temporary assistance—but they still ordered her removal from Poughkeepsie.[43] When adjudicating cases, the costs of relief and the concern for public order superseded any compunction to keep families together. Sarah Tabor received public assistance during her husband's absence, but authorities did not hesitate to bind out her children after their father's death.[44] The overseers similarly indentured Phebe Lewis' daughters, aged four and six, when Lewis appealed for relief in October 1814.[45]

Facing the prospect of removal and the potential breakup of their families, Dutchess County's black residents turned to public assistance only as a last resort. Recently liberated from bondage, African Americans did whatever they could to avoid the stigma of dependency.[46] Although disproportionately represented in the poor record, black residents were less likely than either native-born whites or immigrants to *seek* public relief. African Americans more frequently appeared before the overseers of the poor when they were physically incapable of supporting themselves; ill and debilitated women and men comprised three of every five African Americans appearing before the authorities, a rate double that of native-born whites seeking assistance.[47] Amy Lewis, for example, supported herself for seven years after her manumission before the "King's Evil" rendered her unable to work.[48] Phebe Lewis managed to provide for herself and her two young daughters for two years after being abandoned by her husband and applied for relief only when illness incapacitated her in 1814.[49] As many as eight cases in the Poughkeepsie record were brought to the authorities by others. Two physicians, Doctor Carrel and Jonathan Ward, appeared before the overseers seeking remuneration for the treatment of black patients. Carrel cared for Robert Rutgers, a poor black man debilitated by typhus fever, and Ward attended a woman named Sylvia, who broke her leg.[50] The case of Jin ended tragically. The forty-three-year-old woman returned to her native Dutchess County from New York City during the summer of 1807, arriving at the Poughkeepsie home of Gurdon Miller. There she fell dangerously ill, "not in a situation to be moved." The overseers approved Miller's request for assistance in caring for Jin, but the woman died a month later.[51]

African Americans in need first turned to others before seeking public assistance. After a lifetime of service, some freed persons expected former owners to provide for them in their later years. Robert Rutgers' old master assumed liability for the maintenance of his former slave, but other former slaveholders were either unwilling or unable to provide such support.[52] After selling his Poughkeepsie property in 1811, an ill and widowed Robert Newkirk returned to his former master in Clinton only to be remanded to the overseers in Poughkeepsie.[53] Aaron Low and his wife Rachel Pride each found themselves in similar circumstances. Low was turned out by Peter Van Kleeck, who simply refused to support the seventy-five-year-old man after Van Kleeck married Low's mistress. Rachel felt entitled to her former owner's support and even stated her case before the overseers. Pride testified that Moses Downing granted her permission to work for herself and promised to assist Rachel whenever she found herself in need. Downing took a different view of their agreement, insisting that he had fully discharged the woman and was therefore not liable for her support. The overseers evidently agreed with Downing but awarded Rachel temporary relief.[54]

Although a few needy men and women looked to those who had provided for their material needs under slavery, many more turned to real or fictive kin networks. Mary Cary's mother and stepfather expressed willingness to take in their pregnant eighteen-year-old single daughter until she gave birth and was able to provide for herself.[55] Jane Thorn was also confident of her family's support. Although poor and afflicted with rheumatism, she testified before the overseers that she could support herself at her sister's place in Pleasant Valley.[56] Individuals like Mary Cary and Jane Thorn were fortunate to have kin to whom they could turn. The gradualism of abolition and the persistence of blacks in white households meant that many in need did not have family or friends on whom they could rely. Seasonal employment and transiency separated family members for weeks or months at a time. Lucy Anderson's husband went to sea when the twenty-three-year-old woman was four months pregnant with the couple's first child.[57] Separation and poverty took their toll on family relationships. The widower Robert Newkirk returned to his former master in Clinton perhaps because he was estranged from his daughter Betty and her family—Newkirk could not name his daughter's children.[58] Poverty constrained even the ability of families bound by powerful emotional ties to provide for their own members. Parents were commonly forced to indenture their children. Sarah Tabor and Jenny Van Brunt, daughters of free parents who spent their older childhood years as servants in white homes, were hardly atypical.[59] Mary Cary herself labored in the Newcomb household in Poughkeepsie after her father bound her for a term of seven years.[60] Ill or dependent kin could overburden families who were already struggling to eke out a bare subsistence. Lucinda Garner petitioned the overseers of the poor to take charge of Jin, another black woman who had come to Lucinda's home and refused to leave.[61] Dick Francis of Poughkeepsie managed to care for his seriously ill brother John for four months but appealed to the overseers in April 1811 when he found himself unable to support him any longer. Two years later, Dick's wife Flora claimed that she could provide for herself and her family during her husband's absence as long as her mother and lame father moved elsewhere.[62]

An increasing number of black residents managed to forge personal networks as the pace of emancipation accelerated. Although the proportion of free African Americans residing with white families remained constant between 1790 and 1810, the number of independent black households in Dutchess County slowly but steadily increased from 59 in 1790, to 100 in 1800, to 142 in 1810. The number of black households almost doubled during the subsequent decade, increasing to 272 families. By 1820, as many as seventy percent of Dutchess County's 1,700 free black inhabitants lived in African American households—a rate surpassing that in New York City. Moreover, an even greater proportion of black households in Dutchess were two-parent families; while approximately four of five black New York City households with children under fourteen years of age included at least one adult male and one adult female, the proportion in Dutchess was as high as ninety-two percent. Female-headed households with children accounted for almost one of every five black families in the city, but thirteen such families in Dutchess accounted for a mere six percent of black households in 1820.[63] Not all African American households were nuclear families. To cope with the gradual and piecemeal nature of emancipation in the Mid-Hudson Valley and the challenges of rural poverty, individuals and families clustered together in fictive kin networks to provide mutual support. As many as one-third of black county households in 1820 were augmented households that included non-kin as well as kin.[64] Ompedo Freeman evidently welcomed friends and boarders into his Poughkeepsie home, where Lucy Anderson stayed while her husband was at sea.[65] The Freeman household seems to have been a destination for newcomers to the village as well. Both the Churchill and Tabor families stayed with Freeman after their arrival from the eastern part of the county.[66]

Independent African American households provided not only material assistance but also emotional and psychological support. Interrelated networks of kin and non-kin, however small, served as the nucleus for psychological liberation and cultural self-expression. Although impressionistic and fragmentary, local records contain circumstantial evidence of a dynamic life within local black homes. Whatever was happening in the Freeman household in Poughkeepsie during the late summer and early fall of 1807 attracted the attention of public authorities. In October, the overseers of the poor admonished Freeman for "keeping a disorderly house"—the same offense Jacob Tabor committed two years later. Such historical references can obscure as much as they reveal. Public authorities routinely referred to "disorderly" houses, persons, and behaviors to denote immoral or criminal activity. During the early 1800s, Poughkeepsie residents increasingly associated poorer neighborhoods with public disorder and vice. In 1816, the *Dutchess Observer* lamented that the modest village included no fewer than twenty-three "topers shops," nine "rum grottoes," and several brothels and billiard halls that exhibited "whoredom, drunkenness, and profaneness."[67] Many of Poughkeepsie's black residents lived and worked in such neighborhoods, and some did engage in illicit activities. Investigations into the happenings at the Tabor home uncovered prostitution and violence. Jane Hallem appeared before the overseers of the poor after her husband Moses was convicted of an unspecified crime and sentenced to seven years in prison.[68] However, if obscure references to "disorderly" behavior provide evidence of vice and crime, historians have also suggested that such references also betray white apprehension of black autonomy and growing discomfort with black assertiveness in the wake of emancipation. Aaron Black, for example, must have been particularly intimidating. Having escaped arrest for an unspecified felony in 1824, the "remarkably strong" and "well formed" man had "a habit of boasting and threatening in an extravagant manner, and of giving himself ludicrous airs of quality and importance."[69] Released from the constraints of bondage, men and women daily expressed their freedom in countless ways—in the decisions they made, in the company they kept, and in how they acted and carried themselves.[70]

By the third decade of the nineteenth century, African Americans in Dutchess County were beginning to lay the foundation for an independent communal life. The struggle to reach that point, however, had been an exceptionally arduous one. While black residents in New York City forged separate households, built churches, and established other community institutions during the post-revolutionary period, freed persons in Dutchess County struggled simply to survive. Emancipation could mean poverty, insecurity, and even tragedy for African Americans in the Mid-Hudson Valley. The gradualism of abolition, the persistence of free blacks in white households, and restricted economic opportunity in the countryside seriously constrained the ability of Dutchess County's black residents to establish independent families prior to the 1810s. Free black laborers struggled to make a living with limited resources and daily faced the risk of incapacitating disease or injury. However, the African American experience in Dutchess County also points to the importance of kin networks in a rural environment. Reluctant to seek material assistance from public sources but unable to turn to relief organizations available in urban centers, freed men and women gradually left their masters' homes to create and solidify real and fictive kin networks. Individuals forged augmented households of kin and non-kin to meet the challenges presented by the slow and piecemeal process of abolition, while a comparatively balanced sex ratio allowed African Americans to forge independent two-parent nuclear families during the waning years of slavery. Although one of three black residents in Dutchess County remained in bondage as late as 1820, a majority of free African Americans lived in separate black households where they exercised their freedom in independent family life. Their resilience during the painful transitional period between slavery and freedom provided the foundation for community building and activism during the antebellum era.

# 5

# Race and the Construction of a Free Community

In September 1839, a black Poughkeepsie resident wrote to Charles B. Ray, editor of the *Colored American* in New York City, to provide an account of the free African American population of the village. Identifying himself as "A Colored American," the writer acknowledged the presence of "divisions that have taken place from time to time" among members of the community and expressed regret for "the poor and slow advancement we have made in improvements." Rather than dwelling on conflict and failure, however, "A Colored American" focused on progress and emphasized the dynamism of the village's small black population. During the mid-1830s, Poughkeepsie's African American community boasted an independent black church, a Sabbath school, a day school, a literary society, and several benevolent organizations. Unfortunately, an unidentified "ism" concerning the "why and wherefore to every thing that was or should be done among us" polarized the community in late 1838, and "every thing which tended to our improvement fell to the ground." That crisis, however, proved temporary; prospects were again bright by the spring of the following year. As divisions healed, "every thing took a change for the better" and "once blasted hopes" were "revived anew." "Instead of isms, and proscription being the order of the day," "A Colored American" wrote, "the doctrine of general good to the whole people, is held forth . . . without regard to sect or denomination." Under the direction of the newly arrived Samuel Ringgold Ward, the African school was thriving. The Sabbath school, under the control of a black superintendent, had witnessed an almost threefold increase in attendance. The community boasted a Phoenix society and debating organization, and "two or three" female benevolent associations were doing "tolerably well."

Having accomplished so much in only a few months, Poughkeepsie's black residents expected to achieve even more in the year ahead. With great hope for the future, "A Colored American" predicted that when the next celebration of West Indian emancipation came on the first of August, "we expect to have something to say as well as our friends in other parts of the country."[1]

"A Colored American's" assessment of Poughkeepsie's black community reveals both the opportunities and challenges African Americans in the Mid-Hudson Valley encountered in building lives as free people during the antebellum period. As Shane White has explained, the meaning of freedom and racial boundaries in the North were negotiated and contested in the wake of emancipation.[2] For generations, slavery had informed conceptions of freedom and had dictated relations between white and black. The institution's demise confronted New Yorkers with fundamentally new questions about the nature of freedom, equality, citizenship, and identity. During the second quarter of the nineteenth century, both white and black residents increasingly defined themselves in racial terms. As white New Yorkers constructed a racially exclusive definition of citizenship that marginalized people of African descent, black residents forged a unique collective consciousness as free people of color. Released from the debilitating constraints of gradual abolition during the long transitional period from slavery to freedom, African Americans in Dutchess County forged autonomous family lives, and residents in larger communities established separate religious, charitable, and educational institutions dedicated to racial uplift. The correspondence from "A Colored American" also reveals the extent to which Poughkeepsie's black inhabitants had come to develop a racial consciousness that united them with people of color far beyond the central Hudson Valley. In writing to the editor of the most important black newspaper of the time, "A Colored American" was eager to showcase the achievements of Poughkeepsie's black residents to readers across the North. Moreover, the writer's explicit reference to the first of August—Emancipation Day, the commemoration of the end of slavery in the British Caribbean—reveals the extent to which African Americans in the central Hudson Valley had come to identify with people of color across the Americas. Nevertheless, the struggle to construct an identity as free people was not easy in post-emancipation Dutchess County. At times, black residents themselves disagreed about how to respond to an increasingly hostile racial climate. The legacy of slavery was not easily shaken.

Slavery and race were fundamental to the construction of regional and national identity during the Early Republic. In North as well as South, race assumed inordinate importance amid convulsive economic change and social, cultural, and political ferment. The capitalist Market Revolution marginalized black Americans in several ways. In the South, the rapid territorial expansion of the slave plantation system and the ascendancy of the "Cotton Kingdom" buttressed economic, legal, and ideological justifications for bondage. In the North, anxious businessmen engaged in a competitive and unstable market, and laborers alienated from an increasingly impersonal workplace scapegoated free African Americans who supposedly competed for jobs and depressed wages. Democracy itself was racialized as whiteness emerged as a principal criterion of citizenship. Throughout the North and Midwest, restrictions on the civil liberties and political rights of African Americans accompanied the popularization of politics and the adoption of universal white male suffrage. White men who championed participatory government and exalted virtuous and independent "self-made" men perceived black ignorance, dependency, and servility as the very antithesis of democratic values. With the demise of slavery, white Northerners constructed new means of marginalizing their black neighbors, barring them from certain types of employment, denying them equal educational opportunities, relegating them to specific neighborhoods, and segregating them in public spaces. Culturally, environmentalist racial philosophies of the Revolutionary Era, which acknowledged the intrinsic humanity of nonwhites and attributed their degraded positions to bondage and racial oppression, receded in the face of racist ideologies predicated on the alleged innate and immutable biological inferiority of nonwhite peoples. Racism permeated popular culture. Blackface minstrelsy reinforced stereotypes of black buffoonery. Riddled with malapropisms that demeaned black speech and containing outrageous visual images that grossly distorted black anatomical features, the new mass print culture lampooned African Americans, ridiculed black efforts at self-improvement, and reinforced racial prejudices. During the decades preceding the Civil War, as black Southerners confronted an expansive slave system, African Americans in the North found themselves an increasingly marginalized caste.[3]

The "racialization" of Northern life was the consequence not only of disruptive change during the Early Republic but also of the North's own experience with slavery. Over the course of the colonial era, racial slavery had become interwoven into the fabric of daily life and had deeply ingrained itself in northern thought and culture. The lives of slaves, servants, and free African Americans in the Mid-Hudson Valley differed little during the long transitional period between slavery and freedom, and whites rarely made meaningful distinctions between free people of color and enslaved. The regular sale and purchase of indenture contracts, the careless misidentification of children born after 1799 as slaves in the 1820 federal manuscript census, and the inclusion of such children in manumission records suggest the extent to which white residents in Dutchess County continued to perceive their black neighbors as members of a servile caste regardless of their legal status.[4] Those who had come to associate blackness with dependence and inferiority struggled to envision a biracial republic wherein African Americans were full and equal participants. Indeed, white Northerners increasingly conceived of themselves and their communities in racially exclusive terms, expunging from historical memory their own slave past. In the wake of Northern emancipation, slavery and its evils became an exclusively Southern problem. Having abolished the institution themselves, Northerners could assume a self-righteous and vigilant stance against the Slave South—while ignoring slavery's devastating legacy in the Free States.[5] Representative James Tallmadge of Dutchess County, for example, played a pivotal role in congressional debates surrounding the admission of Missouri to the Union in 1819–1820; his famous proposal for the gradual abolition of slavery in Missouri precipitated the nation's first real sectional crisis and provoked impassioned debates on the floor of Congress. Tallmadge proved relentless in his attacks on slavery, even professing willingness to risk disunion rather than surrender antislavery principles.[6] His Dutchess County constituents, meanwhile, followed the political battles in Washington closely. Gravely concerned about the threat slavery presented to free institutions and the "happiness and the safety of the country," the *Dutchess Observer* "gladly yielded" its columns to the matter "in the hopes that public attention might be aroused."[7]

Having legislated the end of slavery in the state, white New Yorkers proceeded to explore ways to exclude and remove their black neighbors—both literally and figuratively. Agents of the American Colonization Society discovered sympathetic audiences when they traveled throughout the Hudson Valley during the 1820s. Founded in late 1816, the American Colonization Society was a national organization that offered a solution to the dilemma of slavery and race in the Early Republic in the guise of expatriating liberated slaves to Africa. As an 1824 colonizationist address printed in the *Poughkeepsie Journal* explained, the "humane and philanthropic plan" to remove African Americans to the "land of their fathers" would encourage manumission, remove a degraded and troublesome population from the United States, provide people of African descent a refuge from oppression, and "pour the lights of civilization, science, and religion upon long benighted and degraded Africa."[8] Although colonization schemes remained attractive to some Americans as late as the Civil War, the combination of prohibitive costs, formidable logistical obstacles, and fervent opposition of many black Americans ultimately doomed the movement. Given the impracticality of colonization, white New Yorkers devised other mechanisms to separate and subordinate the state's free black population. The state's constitutional convention of 1821 provided an opportunity to restrict the political lives of black New Yorkers. By the second decade of the nineteenth century, dramatic economic development and explosive population growth in New York City and upstate regions had shifted the balance of political power in the state. As delegates convened in Albany in the late summer of 1821, populist "Bucktail" Republicans led by Martin Van Buren sought to challenge the Clintonian faction of their party and their Federalist allies who had long dominated state politics. Arguably the most important constitutional reform sought by the convention's Republican delegates was the expansion of the franchise. The state's original constitution of 1777 imposed property requirements on New York voters but no racial restrictions on suffrage. The convention's Committee on Suffrage introduced a proposal that vastly expanded the electorate by extending the franchise to all *white* men twenty-one years or older who met a six-month residency requirement and either paid taxes on real or personal estate or performed service on public roads or in the militia—virtually every white male of age in the state. The insertion of the word "white" and corresponding disqualification of black voters precipitated contentious debate. Proponents of disfranchisement argued that black New Yorkers were not fellow citizens but a "peculiar" people whose natural depravity and ignorance disqualified them from suffrage. Long antagonized by political alliances between African Americans and opposition Federalists sympathetic to abolition, Republican supporters of the proposal warned that corrupt elite interests would pervert the democratic process by manipulating ignorant black voters.[9] Insisting that the purpose of government was to promote the happiness and security of its citizens, proponents argued that a majority had both the moral authority and constitutional duty to exclude those who were alien and dangerous. Peter Livingston of Dutchess County, a member of the seven-man suffrage committee, characterized African Americans as a vicious and degraded population. Arguing that black New Yorkers lacked the intelligence and moral competence to exercise the ballot, Livingston exhorted his fellow delegates not to put a "weapon into their hands to destroy you." However much he personally pitied former slaves and lamented their miserable condition, Livingston could never "consent to invest them with a power that may be wielded to the destruction of all we hold dear."[10] Opponents of black disfranchisement responded with equally forceful rhetoric. Among the most outspoken defenders of the rights of black New Yorkers was Peter A. Jay of Westchester County, son of John Jay. Accusing his opponents of pandering to racial prejudice and vigorously refuting the racist arguments made by exclusion's defenders, Peter Jay attributed the inferior position of black New Yorkers not to innate inferiority but to the debilitating legacy of slavery. Humanity and justice, Jay argued, demanded the rejection of such an abominable proposal. Eloquent moral and political arguments convinced a slim majority of the convention's delegates to approve a motion deleting the word "white" from the suffrage committee's report. Nonetheless, those intent on disfranchising the state's black male residents remained undeterred. Although the word "white" was stricken from the suffrage committee's original proposal, race remained relevant to broader discussions about voter eligibility, residency requirements, registration, property qualifications, voter intelligence, and militia service—from which African Americans were barred by federal law. The creation of a special committee on the elective franchise later in the session provided opponents of black suffrage another opportunity. Attempts to reinsert the word "white" into the working draft continued to meet vehement opposition from Peter Jay and others, but debates over other criteria opened the door to a compromise. In its final form, the 1821 constitution enfranchised virtually all white male citizens twenty-one years of age and older who met specified residency requirements (one year for most men). It did not disfranchise African American men outright, but it did sharply circumscribe black voting rights by denying suffrage to any "man of colour" who was not a three-year resident of New York State who owned and paid taxes on a freehold estate valued at $250 or higher.[11]

Justified ostensibly as a means of encouraging black New Yorkers to self-improvement, the discriminatory suffrage provision of the 1821 constitution more accurately revealed New Yorkers' discomfort with their own slave past and increasing white anxiety about the presence of liberated slaves in the state. In a reprise of the role he assumed in Washington, D.C., a year earlier, James Tallmadge attempted to accelerate emancipation in the state by encouraging his convention colleagues to adopt constitutional provisions abolishing slavery and all involuntary servitude. A decisive majority rejected the proposal. Several opponents objected to including any reference to bondage lest it taint such a hallowed document; omitting even language abolishing slavery was a means by which delegates could willfully forget the state's slave past. Even Tallmadge and Peter Jay shared some of the biases and prejudices of their colleagues. Presumptions of black economic dependency and fears of the consequences of immediate emancipation compelled Jay to vote against Tallmadge's proposed constitutional prohibition of slavery. And Tallmadge for his part joined the majority of convention delegates in endorsing the stiff barriers to black suffrage.[12]

As white New Yorkers constructed new conceptions of race and citizenship in the aftermath of emancipation, African Americans in the Mid-Hudson Valley fashioned an identity as free people of color. Black residents found themselves a shrinking minority in Dutchess County during the second quarter of the nineteenth century. As Dutchess grew by more than 12,000 people between 1820 and 1850, the county's black population dropped from 2,468 to 2,026 individuals, and the proportion of black residents dropped from 5.3 to 3.4 percent. Specific areas of the county, however, experienced modest growth as the post-emancipation black population became even more concentrated in western townships. Despite modest declines in the black populations of Red Hook and Rhinebeck in the northwestern corner of the county, approximately three of every four African Americans during the second quarter of the century continued to reside in the more populous and economically dynamic regions along the river.[13] As the state's economy boomed after the completion of the Eric Canal, the Hudson remained a vital avenue of commerce. Bustling riverfront wharves and landings linked local producers to burgeoning markets in New York City and provided regional consumers access to an increasing volume of finished goods. Although manufacturing enterprises in Dutchess tended to be comparatively small in scale, the availability of water power and other resources and proximity to markets meant that the county remained attractive to manufacturers and investors. Dutchess ranked behind only Oneida County in total number of manufactories in 1836, and the county continued to boast an astounding array of manufacturing enterprises even after the Panic of 1837.[14] The towns of Fishkill and Poughkeepsie experienced the most dynamic economic growth. Manufacturers expanded operations in Matteawan, Glenham, and other localities in southwestern Dutchess, and Fishkill Landing remained an important commercial center. By virtue of its central geographic position on the river and its access to the county's interior, the village of Poughkeepsie remained the county's most important transportation hub, while the Fallkill and Wappinger's Creeks powered dozens of mills and manufactories in the village and town. Poughkeepsie experienced a period of particularly explosive growth during the 1830s as an association of prominent businessmen and political leaders known as the "Improvement Party" pursued an aggressive program of economic development. Such bustling activity attracted black and white migrants alike. Between 1820 and 1850, the proportion of the county's black residents living and working in Fishkill (and East Fishkill) and Poughkeepsie increased from more than two-fifths to more than one-half. With a population of approximately seven hundred black inhabitants, Fishkill (and East Fishkill) was home to the largest number of African Americans in the county during the antebellum period, accounting for almost one in three black county residents. Poughkeepsie experienced even more dramatic growth. The number of black town residents jumped forty percent between 1820 and 1840, from 353 to almost 500 people, while Poughkeepsie's share of the county's total African American population increased from fourteen to twenty-two percent. Poughkeepsie's black population dropped during the 1840s, but almost one of five black residents continued to reside in the county's most populous town at midcentury (see table 5.1).

In the wake of emancipation, free African Americans throughout the county increasingly congregated with other black residents. African Americans in the countryside continued to coalesce around small rural neighborhoods, including "Freemanville" in Beekman, the vicinity of Lithgow and Millbrook in central Dutchess, Baxtertown in Fishkill, and the "New Guinea" settlement near the village of Hyde Park. Larger villages were too small to permit racially segregated neighborhoods, but black residents in river communities tended to reside with or near other people of color. In Poughkeepsie, the heaviest concentration of black villagers resided in the racially mixed working-class neighborhoods on the fringes of the commercial district, including Jefferson, Montgomery, Pine, and Union Streets. Several dozen African Americans resided on Main and Cannon Streets, while a third cluster lived in the vicinity of Catharine and Cottage Streets.[15] Residential clustering was a vital step in the creation of autonomous free

Table 5.1
African American Population of Dutchess County by Town (with Proportion of Total African American Population), 1820–1850

| Town | 1820 N (%) | 1830 N (%) | 1840 N (%) | 1850 N (%) |
|---|---|---|---|---|
| Amenia | 98 (4.0) | 63 (2.5) | 50 (2.2) | 64 (3.2) |
| Beekman | 160 (6.5) | 80 (3.2) | 98 (4.3) | 55 (2.7) |
| Clinton | 282 (11.4) | 26 (1.0) | 1 (0.0) | 5 (0.2) |
| Dover | 67 (2.7) | 81 (3.3) | 35 (1.5) | 56 (2.8) |
| East Fishkill | — | — | — | 190 (9.4) |
| Fishkill | 691 (28.0) | 683 (27.5) | 722 (31.8) | 482 (23.8) |
| Hyde Park | — | 164 (6.6) | 113 (5.0) | 75 (3.7) |
| LaGrange | — | 106 (4.3) | 81 (3.6) | 73 (3.6) |
| Milan | 67 (2.7) | 54 (2.2) | 52 (2.3) | 42 (2.1) |
| Northeast | 64 (2.6) | 24 (1.0) | 41 (1.8) | 45 (2.2) |
| Pawling | 77 (3.1) | 43 (1.7) | 18 (0.8) | 48 (2.4) |
| Pine Plains | — | 51 (2.1) | 41 (1.8) | 24 (1.2) |
| Pleasant Valley | — | 134 (5.4) | 83 (3.7) | 93 (4.6) |
| Poughkeepsie | 353 (14.3) | 365 (14.7) | 492 (21.7) | 398 (19.6) |
| Red Hook | 295 (12.0) | 241 (9.7) | 168 (7.4) | 144 (7.1) |
| Rhinebeck | 142 (5.8) | 102 (4.1) | 71 (3.1) | 70 (3.5) |
| Stanford | 100 (4.1) | 92 (3.7) | 79 (3.5) | 53 (2.6) |
| Union Vale | — | 66 (2.7) | 37 (1.6) | 11 (0.5) |
| Washington | 72 (2.9) | 110 (4.4) | 87 (3.8) | 98 (4.8) |
| **Totals** | **2,468 (100.1)** | **2,485 (100.1)** | **2,269 (99.9)** | **2,026 (100.0)** |

*Notes:* East Fishkill was set off from Fishkill in 1849; Hyde Park and Pleasant Valley were set off from Clinton in 1821; LaGrange (originally Freedom) was organized from parts of Beekman and Fishkill in 1821; Pine Plains was set off from Northeast in 1823; Union Vale was organized from Beekman and part of LaGrange in 1827.

*Sources:* Population Schedules of the Fourth Census of the United States, 1820, vol. 10, roll 71, (Washington, DC: 1959); Fifth Census of the United States, 1830, microcopy no. 19, vol. 21, roll 104 (Washington, DC: 1955); Population Schedules of the Sixth Census of the United States, 1840, microcopy 704, vol. 9, rolls 278–79 (Washington, DC: 1967); Population Schedules of the Seventh Census of the United States, 1850, microcopy 432, rolls 496–97 (Washington, DC: 1963); The Seventh Census of the United States: 1850 (Washington, DC: Robert Armstrong, 1853).

African American families. Both the number of black-headed households and the proportion of the county's black residents residing in those households increased notably in the wake of emancipation. As late as 1820, just over half of all African Americans in the county continued to reside with white families. Ten years later—three years after the legal demise of slavery in the state—three of every five black county residents lived in more than three hundred independent black households. The number of African American families remained relatively constant during the subsequent two decades, but the proportion of black county residents residing in such homes increased to three-quarters by midcentury.[16] Moreover, the overwhelming majority of black families—between eighty-five and ninety percent—were headed by men during the three decades after 1820.[17]

The creation of independent black families in Dutchess County during the second quarter of the nineteenth century signified the emotional, psychological, and economic independence of African Americans from their former masters. Families socialized the younger generation, inculcated moral values, instilled cultural pride, and nurtured historical connections with the past. Separate households provided the cornerstone in the building of other community institutions. Kinship provided the foundation of mutual assistance, and stable families became the fundamental building blocks for a separate and distinct African American Christianity. The democratization of American religious life during the late eighteenth and early nineteenth centuries proved a defining moment for black Americans, who embraced the liberating dimensions of the Gospel of Christ in the aftermath of the Revolution. Bondage and suffering were not abstract theological concepts but lived realities for those who had experienced slavery. The Christian message of deliverance, redemption, and resurrection offered spiritual liberation for a subjugated people in a hostile world.[18] Black Christians in Dutchess County originally attended the same churches as did their white neighbors. Worship in the Hudson Valley countryside was informal; churchgoers often worshipped with neighbors of different denominations in shared church buildings—or in whatever spaces were available, such as schoolhouses, shops, barns, or private homes. African Americans in more densely settled communities attended the Dutch Reformed, Episcopalian, and Presbyterian Churches that predominated in the region, typically in racially segregated pews or galleries. Approximately a dozen black worshippers, for example, participated in a revival at Poughkeepsie's Dutch Reformed Church in 1814.[19] During the first half of the nineteenth century,

African Americans in Hyde Park, many belonging to the Garrison, Griffin, Jenkins, and Quackenbush families, prayed, baptized children, solemnized marriages, and commemorated deaths in the Dutch Reformed Church and St. James Episcopal Church. Griffin Griffin served as sexton of the Dutch Reformed Church, and Richard Jenkins occupied the same position at St. James.[20] Sectarian loyalties were muted; worshippers frequently attended services at churches belonging to different denominations. James Brown, the master gardener at the Verplanck estate at Mount Gulian, attended both Dutch Reformed and Episcopal Churches after arriving in Fishkill Landing in the late 1820s. Even after purchasing his own pew at Saint Anna's Episcopal Church in Matteawan in 1841, James and his wife Julia often attended different Reformed, Episcopal, Presbyterian, Baptist, and Methodist services throughout the greater Fishkill-Newburgh area.[21]

Most African Americans in the Mid-Hudson Valley, like their sisters and brothers elsewhere, embraced Methodism. The emotional fervor of worship, the simplicity of its evangelical message, its egalitarian populist appeal, its original sympathy for antislavery, and its acceptance of black preachers and exhorters attracted liberated slaves who found in Methodism a spiritual refuge.[22] Methodism, however, originally proved slow to take root in the region. Competing against well-established Reformed and Episcopal Churches and contending with the increasing appeal of Presbyterianism, Methodist circuit riders enjoyed only limited success at the end of the eighteenth century. The noted evangelist Reverend Freeborn Garrettson founded a small congregation in Rhinebeck in the early 1790s, but very small Methodist classes were not established in Poughkeepsie until 1805 and in Fishkill until 1810; the handful of Methodists in Poughkeepsie did not even have a resident pastor until 1814. After very modest beginnings, however, Methodism in Dutchess County flourished as a series of revivals precipitated explosive growth during the subsequent decades. The Poughkeepsie church increased to 157 white and 10 black members by 1823; three years later the congregation erected a larger building on Washington Street to accommodate its growing numbers. Membership soared to 449 by 1833 and continued to increase. By 1836, the Methodist Church on Washington Street provided a spiritual home for more than 600 Poughkeepsie residents, including almost 60 black members.[23]

Local black Methodists did not long remain in racially mixed congregations. The establishment of separate black churches in Dutchess County was the fruit of intensive labor on the part of both local residents and black

Figure 5.1 Richard Jenkins, sexton of St. James Episcopal Church in Hyde Park. Courtesy of St. James Episcopal Church.

Methodists from New York City. As the African American population of the seaport soared after the Revolution, black Methodists in the city secured from the episcopate permission to conduct separate religious meetings in 1796; five years later, members formally incorporated the African Methodist Episcopal Zion Church (AMEZ) under the rules and governance of the larger Methodist Episcopal Church. After almost two decades of conflict with the Methodist General Conference over governance and property ownership, black Methodists formally withdrew from the parent church in 1820 and established a separate denomination, ordaining its first minister in 1822. AMEZ itinerants from New York City were active in the Hudson Valley at least as early as the 1820s. Reverend George Matthews established a congregation in Newburgh and organized a station across the river in Fishkill Landing in 1827. Reverend Jacob Matthews, a close associate of Bishop James Varick, assumed pastorship of the new congregations; by 1834, the Newburgh church numbered fifty-one members, while twenty-three people worshipped at the Fishkill station. Poughkeepsie likely constituted another station; Reverend Charles Gardner was present in Poughkeepsie by 1834, and Nathan Blount was ordained sometime in the mid-1830s.[24] It was within this context—and during a revival at Poughkeepsie's Washington Street Methodist Church—that an unknown number of the church's fifty-eight black members formally withdrew from the predominately white congregation in 1836. The bolters began to conduct worship services in the room used as a colored school by the Lancaster School Society; in December, the black worshippers incorporated themselves as the "African Methodist Episcopal Church of Poughkeepsie."[25] The three local AMEZ congregations experienced modest growth in the years that followed; by October 1837, fifty-two people in Poughkeepsie and twenty-four in Fishkill attended AMEZ services in those villages, while the Newburgh church numbered sixty-one souls.[26] The Poughkeepsie congregation purchased a lot and building on Catharine Street between Mansion and Cottage Streets in 1840 and reincorporated itself as the "First African Methodist Episcopal Church of Poughkeepsie." That same year, black Methodists in Fishkill Landing, who had been conducting services at the homes of James Gomer and Adam Atkins, formally incorporated themselves as "Zion's Pilgrams [*sic*]." In the spring of 1844, members of the church—who at that point were holding services in the district schoolhouse—obtained a lot and proceeded to erect their own building. They reincorporated themselves as an AMEZ congregation, and Bishop Christopher Rush came up from New York City to dedicate the new structure in September. Approximately fifty worshippers attended services at the church on a weekly basis. Although the building had seating capacity for 150 people, the Fishkill Landing church alone could not meet the spiritual needs of the area's sizeable but dispersed black population. Residents of the Baxtertown neighborhood a couple of miles to the north organized their own congregation a few years later.[27]

The creation of independent black churches in the central Hudson Valley had profound significance for black life in the region. Religion permeated the lives of black Christians; local ministers conducted as many as three services every Sunday (in addition to Sabbath school instruction), and members dedicated at least two other nights during the week to prayer meetings and catechism.[28] Faith provided an explanation for the vicissitudes of life and provided a sense of meaning and purpose in an otherwise hostile world. The black church provided refuge from white supervision and a forum where members could express to God and to each other their deepest spiritual yearnings in a style distinctly their own. While adhering to the fundamental tenets of the Christian faith, African Americans appropriated and transformed Christianity, adapting it and creating a distinctive religious subculture. Black theology expressed the deepest spiritual needs and strivings of African Americans. Israel's anguish in ancient Egypt, the exodus to the Promised Land, Christ's Passion, the Second Coming, and hope in divine justice lay at the core of black Christian faith. African American Methodism in particular provided opportunities for self-expression. Drawing on diverse folk traditions, black Methodists employed ecstatic prayer, calls and shouts, spiritual songs, music, and dance to express both anguish and hope. Even black Christians in the county who attended predominately white congregations retained a distinctive religious identity rooted in a shared cultural heritage. A dozen African American men in Upper Red Hook, for example, organized a separate black cemetery association in October 1849; farther south, James Brown actively solicited contributions for an African burial ground in Fishkill Landing and served as a trustee of the burial association.[29] In translating Christianity in racial terms, African American Christians mounted spiritual, psychological, and cultural resistance to oppression.[30]

The significance of the African American church in the Mid-Hudson Valley, however, lay beyond its spiritual impact. Shared spiritual experience and distinctive cultural expression solidified communal bonds, nurtured a sense of collective consciousness, and constructed a sense of nationhood.[31]

Although local AMEZ congregations were too few and too small to accommodate the region's dispersed black population, the black church was a focal point for all African American residents. Members of St. Anna's Episcopal Church, James and Julia Brown also attended services at AMEZ churches in Fishkill Landing and Newburgh—occasionally on the same day.[32] The couple included among their personal friends Daniel and Mary Varick of New York City, the eldest son and daughter-in-law of AMEZ bishop James Varick, who maintained close ties to the Fishkill-Newburgh area.[33] James Brown actively engaged himself in local AMEZ affairs; he recorded in his diary both the presentation of the lot to the Fishkill AMEZ congregation in May 1844 and the church's dedication four months later, underlining his September 8th entry to underscore the significance of the event.[34] AMEZ church gatherings and meetings provided opportunities for expressing solidarity and fellowship. Gaius Bolin recalled that the "great institution" of the Quarterly Meeting in Poughkeepsie always made for a "banner day" at the Catharine Street church. According to Bolin, "on that day every member and every attendant at the church made it his or her business to be present at the services," and participants "from all around the surrounding country" converged on the village. It was common practice for Poughkeepsie families to host out-of-town guests for dinner on Quarterly Meeting Sunday, and virtually every member of the Poughkeepsie congregation "expected it, welcomed it, [and] enjoyed it to the full."[35] Quarterly and camp meetings drew participants from beyond the immediate region, linking local black residents with free blacks across eastern New York State. African Americans from New York City took a steamboat up the river to attend the Newburgh circuit meeting in Fishkill in September 1837.[36] A camp meeting three years later outside of the village of Newburgh drew more than four thousand worshippers, white as well as black. Under the direction of Reverend John N. Mars of Poughkeepsie and Reverend William Serrington of Newburgh, the 1840 meeting lasted several days and included prayers and sermons delivered by Mars, Serrington, Bishop Rush, and other distinguished clergymen and community leaders. The meeting left an indelible impression on those who experienced the event. When several of the "lower class of white people," "violently led on by alcohol," arrived with the intention of disrupting the proceedings, they purportedly turned and walked away "astonished and confused" at the sight of so impressive an assembly. A contributor to the *Colored American* marveled at the peace and order that prevailed at such a large meeting and concluded that the event was "the best that I ever attended."[37]

The independent black church served as a powerful institution of social activism. Ministers were outspoken community leaders, and churches served not only as houses of worship but also as social halls, recreational centers, schools, dispensaries of material assistance, and political meeting houses. The lines distinguishing the secular from the sacred were blurred, and religion permeated every dimension of daily life. For black Christians, economic, social, educational, and political uplift were central to the spiritual mission of the church. As elsewhere in the North, the black congregations in the Mid-Hudson Valley dedicated themselves to community improvement and moral reform. Temperance represented one of the most important means of social uplift. The alarming increase in alcohol consumption throughout the nation during the 1820s and 1830s had devastating social consequences. Abstinence provided a powerful means by which African Americans could refute white prejudices of black vice and insobriety. A black temperance society established in Newburgh quickly grew to include sixty members by the spring of 1833.[38] Across the river in Dutchess, Reverend C. W. Gardner led an African American temperance organization in Poughkeepsie that purportedly included almost half of the village's black residents.[39] The campaign against alcohol made notable progress within the black community. Writing in the *Poughkeepsie Telegraph* in November 1837, "A Friend of All" wagered that a greater proportion of the village's African American residents were "on the side of temperance and piety" than "among the whites here or elsewhere." The contributor reasoned, "If that can be taken as a test of their moral character, it certainly speaks favorably in their behalf and ought to encourage every Christian to do more for that cause he has so solemnly espoused."[40]

For free people of color across the North, only education rivaled temperance as the principal means of self-improvement. The evangelical mission to spread the Gospel rested on the ability to read and interpret Scripture, and educational improvement was central to the church's mission on earth. The 1820 *Doctrines and Discipline* of the AMEZ Church expressly directed pastors to preach on the importance of education and meet regularly with children in Sabbath schools to instruct them in doctrine and reading.[41] After a slow start, attendance at Poughkeepsie's Sabbath school increased to the point that Sunday services were "attended by nearly the whole mass" of the village's colored population.[42] The institution of the Sabbath school was vital in the crusade for moral improvement. As one contributor to the *Colored American* put it, education was the "handmaid of religion" and "the best foundation which we can possibly lay for our children, if we wish for them a holy life, a happy death, and a blessed immortality."[43] Education, however, promised more than spiritual enlightenment; the Sabbath school not only instructed students in moral and religious truth but also taught reading, writing, and more practical knowledge that could be applied to the workplace. In an economy undergoing significant change, African Americans embraced education as the principal means of acquiring virtue, overcoming ignorance, and achieving upward mobility. The *Weekly Advocate* stated the matter succinctly: "Give a people knowledge and they will be free"—"Knowledge is POWER."[44]

Exhortations to intellectual improvement, however eloquent and impassioned, rang hollow for those denied educational opportunities. While law did not bar black New Yorkers from institutions of learning, prejudice and poverty often did. Public instruction in New York State during the early decades of the nineteenth century was exceptionally informal and rudimentary. Poughkeepsie's elite private seminaries and academies earned the village renown as the "city of schools," but instruction for the vast majority of less affluent children was virtually nonexistent. Public hostility, social stigma, inadequate resources, poor facilities, erratic attendance, and incompetent instructors plagued the common school system two decades after its founding in the 1810s.[45] The poor state of public education forced the county's black inhabitants to rely largely on their own resources. As early as 1829, a private African School opened its doors in the village of Poughkeepsie, modeled after the African Free School in New York City established forty years earlier by New York Manumission Society. The institution's directors originally installed Reverend Isaac Woodland of Baltimore as the school's first teacher, but Nathan Blount, a graduate of a black Presbyterian school in New Jersey, replaced him one year later.[46] Blount was a formidable man; he so impressed Arnold Buffum during the abolitionist's speaking tour of the Mid-Hudson region in September 1833 that Buffum singled out the Poughkeepsie teacher to the readers of the *Liberator* as "a colored young man of great merit and respectability." Born a slave, Blount procured his freedom and made his way northward. Resisting pressure to emigrate to Liberia, Blount instead resolved to dedicate his life to assisting fellow men and women of color in his native land.[47] Although he did not learn to read or write until adulthood, Blount became a particularly successful schoolmaster and then minister after his ordination in the mid-1830s. In addition to teaching at the African School in Poughkeepsie and conducting the village's Sabbath school, he instructed African American children at St. James Episcopal Church in Hyde Park.[48] The private Lancaster School Society retained Blount to teach its "colored department" after it took over the African School and assumed exclusive control of public education in the village of Poughkeepsie.[49] In April 1839, the society's trustees certified Blount to be a "respectable citizen" and "well-qualified, competent, and thorough teacher of youth" who was "worthy of the notice and patronage of an enlightened community." That assessment was echoed by the local Inspectors of Common Schools, who examined Blount and found him "qualified as to moral character, learning, and ability to teach a Common School."[50] The gifted educator and zealous minister, moreover, did not shrink from political protest and activism. An ardent abolitionist, Blount was a founding member of the Poughkeepsie Anti-Slavery Society and served on the executive committee of the county abolitionist organization. When Blount resigned his position in 1839 to assume other pastoral duties, the trustees of the Lancaster School Society hired Samuel Ringgold Ward, a graduate of the African Free School in New York City, to teach students in the colored department. Ward also replaced Blount on the executive committee of the Dutchess County Anti-Slavery Society. After a brief year or so in Poughkeepsie, Ward moved upstate and went on to become one of the most outspoken black abolitionists of the antebellum period.

Community leaders like Blount and Ward were so vocal in part because of the support they received from a small number of white allies in the larger community. The fact that the "chief manager" of the Lancaster Society was "a flaming abolitionist" undoubtedly played a significant role in Blount's and Ward's tenures at the colored school.[51] In defiance of prevailing racial sentiment, local white abolitionists openly professed their commitment to assisting their black neighbors in their campaign for moral and intellectual improvement. Drafted in 1835, the constitution of the Poughkeepsie Anti-Slavery Society committed its members to promoting the "intellectual, moral, and religious improvement of the colored people thereby endeavoring to remove all that prejudice which makes color and not intellectual and moral worth the criterion of character and respectability."[52] The founding document of the Dutchess County Anti-Slavery Society expressed similar sentiments. The executive committee of the county organization even explored the prospect of establishing a black manual labor school, going so far as to commission one of its members to visit black leaders in New York City to confer about the project.[53]

Working with a small number of sympathetic white neighbors, black Poughkeepsie residents sponsored activities to promote moral uplift and intellectual improvement. A lecture series organized by local abolitionists during the winter of 1836–1837 was particularly well received. In January, an audience of more than 150 black residents reportedly listened in "silence and fixed attention" to a lecture on "Mental Improvement" presented by local educator and editor Isaac Harrington. Doctor McClellan, the principal of the Poughkeepsie Female Academy and a member of the Poughkeepsie Anti-Slavery Society, delivered February's address.[54] Community members also organized a black Phoenix society sometime before 1837. No formal records have survived, but the local organization likely resembled that in New York City, which sponsored circulating libraries, lectures, recitals, readings, classes, vocational programs, and charitable events.[55] Local activities were almost certainly more modest in scope, but literary clubs and libraries, however small, provided forums for intellectual debate and discussion. Uriah Boston, a prominent member of Poughkeepsie's black community, carried one such discussion to a much broader audience in 1841. Sharing an excerpt from "Dr. Dick's work on society" with readers of the *Colored American*, Boston suggested that the text's recommendations for self-reflection and self-examination would lead to the most beneficial moral results.[56]

The notable progress made by the village of Poughkeepsie's black residents captured the attention of the larger community. It was with "gratification" that the *Poughkeepsie Telegraph* in January 1837 assessed the "great moral improvement" of the village's African American residents. Recalling a time when the "abandoned of both sexes" allegedly wandered the village streets "exhibiting human nature in the most degrading form," the editor extolled the work of "a school and regular religious worship" under the "pious and intelligent" Nathan Blount, whose "work of reform" had transformed the community. According to the *Telegraph*, the "morals of that class of society" had undergone such a "radical change" that there was no "more orderly portion of our whole community than they."[57] However patronizing and disparaging in its characterization of African American life, the journal could not help but be impressed by the dynamism of the black community. The *Telegraph* returned to the subject nine months later. Again marveling at how educational and religious institutions had radically transformed supposedly intemperate, "vicious," and "wretched" black residents into "attentive listeners to the holy truths of religion," the paper appealed to its readers to support ongoing black efforts.[58]

Despite the enterprise and resourcefulness of Poughkeepsie's black residents and their allies, the struggle for educational improvement suffered in the wake of the Panic of 1837. The economic depression strained financial resources and left parents unable to pay rate bills. Unspecified dissension within the African American community exacerbated the school's problems. Facing the potential closure of the Lancaster Society's colored department, black residents rallied to keep the school's doors open. Women assumed vital roles. The Colored Female United Assistant Sewing Society distributed as many as two hundred garments to needy children otherwise unable to attend school for want of decent clothing. The Colored Children's Improvement Society sponsored lectures and public exhibitions to raise funds. After attending one such poetry recitation in late 1837, the editor of the *Telegraph* reported that he was "highly gratified" by what he heard.[59] Such efforts, however, proved barely adequate to meet the pressing need; attendance at the colored department dropped to as few as twenty-five pupils by the spring of 1839.[60] A wider call went out in April for a public meeting to address the need for a "more general and thorough education" of the village's African American population. Presuming that "the wretched condition of the colored people" made it "too clearly obvious that they need instruction," the notice appealed to "friends of Education" and all Christian-minded people "favorable to the improvement of mankind" to attend.[61] Community support managed to keep the colored department operating, but the school hardly flourished. An 1841 report indicated that the school was conducted in an "irregular manner" due to the teacher's poor health and persistent "sectional differences" among black villagers; while fifty students had attended the school during the previous summer, average daily attendance during the winter never exceeded sixteen or eighteen pupils.[62]

The difficulties encountered by Poughkeepsie's black residents during the late 1830s and early 1840s were part of a larger educational crisis in Dutchess County as a whole. Despite the continued and well-publicized success of elite private institutions, the common school system had deteriorated to the point that an incensed public demanded fundamental changes in public instruction. The weaknesses of the Lancaster system compounded the educational crisis in Poughkeepsie. In 1840, the state superintendent of common schools cited the village as an example of a community that earned little return on tax dollars invested in education. Although the village's Lancaster Society received more than $1,000 in public money in 1840, barely 200 of the village's 1,778 school-age children attended the Lancaster School regularly; as many as one-quarter to one-third had never set foot in a schoolroom.[63] Concerned citizens filled the pages of the local press with letters demanding improvements and convened meetings throughout the county to address the crisis. Educational reform, however, proved to be an explosive public issue. In Poughkeepsie, defenders of the status quo consistently pointed to the remarkable success of the community's private academies; reformers responded by arguing that it was precisely the popularity of those elite institutions that siphoned off resources for the large majority of less affluent students. Proponents of educational reform and their critics engaged in acrimonious debate on the pages of the local press. The *Telegraph* and *Eagle* provided forums for those who advocated a new system of tax-supported free schools open to all village children comparable to those created in New York City, Brooklyn, Buffalo, Albany, Rochester, and Hudson. Rival papers, the *Journal* and *Free Press* served as organs for those who bristled at the prospect of free schools funded by public money. Condemning an indiscriminate levy on all taxpayers as unjust, critics stoked fears of spiraling costs and the despotic power wielded by a politicized board of education. In the end, however, opponents were waging a losing battle. After more than three years of public debate and political wrangling, village voters in May 1843 ratified a plan establishing a system of free schools that the state legislature had approved the preceding month.[64]

The village's African American residents almost certainly participated in the debates over education, but they must have greeted the creation of a public school system with some ambivalence. The sixteenth section of the act approved by voters authorized the establishment of a separate school for colored children, but many parents might have entertained doubts about the quality of instruction or worried about sending their children to a segregated institution administered by a popularly elected white school board.[65] Moreover, the actions of the new board—or more accurately its inaction—must have aggravated fears. Busily engaged in the construction of a new grammar school and identifying spaces for three white primary schools, board members demonstrated little interest in opening a black school.[66] After waiting and watching patiently for several months, black residents acted to demand access to the new system. The board had taken no formal action on a school for colored students when in October Nathan Blount petitioned the body to do so and offered his services as teacher. By that time, the trustees of the Lancaster School had closed its colored department, and the plight of black children in the village had grown desperate. Blount pressed the issue again at the board's November meeting. This time the board agreed to establish a school for black pupils "as soon as the means of the board" would permit and appointed a three-man committee that included local abolitionists Ira Armstrong and David Starr to examine the question. The resignations of Starr and another board member shortly thereafter, however, deferred the matter yet again. By the time the school board issued its first annual report, three primary schools were operating in the village and a large grammar school was under construction, but "insufficient means" had allegedly prevented the opening of a separate school for African American children. Undeterred, black residents continued to press the board. In February 1844, the AMEZ Church not only proposed to lease a room for a colored primary school at the very modest rent of $35 per year but also offered to pay expenses for renovating and equipping it. More than two months elapsed, however, before a black school finally opened its doors in the village; thirty-five pupils entered the school on May 6th—not at the AMEZ Church, but at the Primitive Methodist Church at a higher rent of $50 per year. Nonetheless, black residents gradually asserted a degree of control over the school. Helen Mars, a black woman, replaced Thomas Brewer, a white man, as the school's teacher in July 1845; her sister Harriett assumed teaching responsibilities at the school a few months later. The following summer, the school moved to the AMEZ Church. By 1850, enrollment at the colored school numbered as many as seventy-nine pupils.[67]

While black residents in Poughkeepsie battled successfully to gain access to the village's public school system, children of color elsewhere in the county struggled to achieve even a rudimentary education. If not ostracized by their white neighbors, black youngsters in the countryside attended the same schoolhouses as white pupils; state law permitted local districts to establish schools for African American children, but their small numbers typically did not warrant separate institutions.[68] The quality of common school instruction varied greatly throughout the county. Superior schools rivaled any in the state, but the condition of inferior schools was in some cases abysmal. Most schoolhouses in the countryside were in disrepair, and many schools lacked textbooks, slates, and other essential materials. A few remote underpopulated districts failed to maintain any schools at all. Few districts could attract and retain qualified teachers; as the county's deputy commissioner of education reported in 1842, several instructors were "an honor to the profession," but a "numerous class" was "totally unfit to teach."[69] Irregular attendance plagued district schools. Poverty left many families unable to pay rate bills or purchase books and other supplies. Apathy further undermined the common school system in the countryside. Too many families questioned the utility of education beyond instruction in the rudiments of reading, writing, and arithmetic. Such indifference actually kept the doors of a few schoolhouses shut. One contributor to the *Poughkeepsie Telegraph* summarized the state of education in rural Dutchess in a June 1849 letter. Lamenting the "miserable" state of common schools readily apparent to even the "most careless observer," the writer argued that incompetent teachers, irregular attendance, "improper textbooks," "ill-looking, ill-arranged, uncomfortable, and unhealthy rooms" all contributed to a "miserable apathy" among many parents and children in Dutchess County.[70]

Racial prejudice compounded the plight of African American children. Black students who attended integrated schools suffered harassment and myriad "petty annoyances" on a daily basis.[71] In some instances, blatant discrimination barred black youngsters from even entering local schoolhouses. L. M. Arnold, the superintendent for the county's southern district, reported in 1844 that local school trustees typically refused to waive the payment of rate bills for such students as permitted by law. Observing that an inordinate number of black children came from poor families who could not afford to send them to school, Arnold claimed that children in such "sorrowful cases of distress" suffered serious and "permanent" injury.[72] When faulting local officials two years later for providing inadequate information on black pupils in their districts, the state superintendent acknowledged that the limited data reflected "extremely limited" attendance; as few as one-quarter of African American children were enrolled in local schools. The superintendent was candid in identifying the principal reason for such poor attendance rates; despite the civil rights guaranteed black citizens by the State of New York, social conventions "excluded" black New Yorkers "from all social intercourse, as equals."[73]

The African American campaign for improvement challenged prevailing racial sentiment. Black community leaders embraced racial uplift as a means of refuting the emerging ideology of white supremacy. By proving black capacity and demonstrating achievement, Americans of African descent attempted to dispel pejorative stereotypes and prove their worth as equal citizens. Practically, however, such efforts just as frequently incensed white observers in the Mid-Hudson Valley who continued to perceive their black neighbors as a servile caste. As one speaker at a meeting of African Americans in Newburgh pointed out in August 1833, it was precisely the liberating power of education that whites found most threatening.[74] In some instances, hostile opponents of black uplift specifically targeted the very institutions dedicated to self-improvement. During the summer of 1842, a group of young men disrupted a benefit concert for the Poughkeepsie AMEZ Church performed by the Colored People's Sacred Music Society. An outraged contributor to the *Telegraph* considered it shameful that "our colored citizens, who are professors of religion" should be so disturbed by a "gang of rowdies" and demanded that the perpetrators be brought to justice.[75] Both the *Telegraph* and *Poughkeepsie Eagle* condemned the incident, but the *Eagle* betrayed the latent prejudice of the larger community when it commented that anyone responsible "showed that he had much more of the real *negro* in his composition than the blacks he had turned out so gratuitously to insult and abuse."[76] Even sympathetic white residents supportive of black improvement disavowed any desire to disrupt the prevailing racial order. While heralding the uplift of Poughkeepsie's African American community and calling for wider popular support of such efforts, the *Telegraph* reassured its readers that moral and intellectual improvement would not cause their black neighbors to forget their proper place as proverbial "hewers of wood and drawers of water." Indeed, as the paper proceeded to explain, knowledge tempered with "the meek and humiliating spirit of the gospel" would enable people of color to "respect those whom circumstances have rendered superior" and "perform the functions of their respective stations under the guidance of correct principles of right and wrong."[77] Some white allies expressly dissociated themselves from the incendiary doctrine of abolitionism. Educational reformers disclaimed any radical intent when issuing their call for a public meeting on black education in April 1839. Their announcement insisted, "This is exclusively an education movement and has no connection with the abolitionist society. Our effort is purely and distinctly instruction, and all who are favorable to the improvement of mankind may safely unite with us without fear of committing themselves for or against any other object."[78] While black residents embraced self-improvement as a means of achieving upward mobility, their white neighbors either opposed such efforts or regarded them as means of reinforcing the status quo. However, the campaign for uplift represented far more than a failed attempt to refute white supremacy. Even if black achievement proved woefully inadequate in dispelling racial prejudice, moral and intellectual improvement were empowering in their own right. As historians such as Patrick Rael and Erica Ball have demonstrated, the struggle for uplift proved indispensable in the creation of both individual and collective identity. The development of character, personal integrity, and self-respect provided the means by which self-made men and virtuous women defined and empowered themselves as individuals and transformed their communities.[79]

Poughkeepsie's public school celebration in September 1845 illustrates the unique space African Americans occupied in Dutchess County during the antebellum era. The celebration actually entailed two different ceremonies. The larger event took place on the afternoon of the nineteenth, as students and teachers from the white public schools marched in grand procession through village streets to the Presbyterian Church, where they joined in a community prayer service. A smaller exhibition the day before was sponsored by parents, teachers, and students of the colored school. On the one hand, the segregated events symbolize the hardened racial order that had crystallized in the Mid-Hudson Valley during the decades after emancipation. Having eliminated slavery, white New Yorkers constructed new mechanisms to control and subordinate their black neighbors. A bourgeois ethic of respectability extolled moral and intellectual improvement as the principal avenues of achievement, but prejudice and poverty sharply curtailed educational opportunities for African Americans in rural Dutchess County. Even in Poughkeepsie, one of only six villages in the state to maintain a colored school, erratic attendance suggests that few families were capable of sending their children to school on a daily basis.[80] When not barred from public educational institutions altogether, black children were clearly set apart, whether in racially integrated schoolhouses in the countryside or in Poughkeepsie's segregated school. The village's board of education never regarded the colored school a priority, and black parents struggled to gain equal access to education for their children. The village school board flatly rejected Jared Gray's petition to allow his daughter to attend the female department of the village grammar school. The board did organize a committee to explore ways of providing students in the colored school with instruction equivalent to that in the white grammar school, but apparently little came of the matter; just a few years later, Harriett Mars was again petitioning the board for desperately needed books for her students.[81]

Nevertheless, if Poughkeepsie's segregated public school celebration reflected the marginalization of the county's black residents after slavery, the ceremony at the colored school also signified the flowering of a self-conscious and active African American community in the wake of emancipation. After annual examinations and an exhibition at the school on Church Street, pupils, teachers, and community members proceeded to the AMEZ Church on Catharine Street, the spiritual and social center of the village's black community. There, they listened attentively to an "excellent and appropriate" address delivered by Reverend Henry Highland Garnet of Troy, who had been invited to speak for the occasion. Garnet, who had emerged as one of the most outspoken and militant of black abolitionists of his era, shared with the Poughkeepsie audience his own experience at the African Free School in New York City and highlighted the achievements of several fellow graduates. Refuting racist beliefs in the natural inferiority of African Americans with arguments of "ingenuity and force," the abolitionist explained how prejudice fell with "crushing weight" upon black children and insisted that African Americans could achieve as much as whites in all respects if only allowed equal opportunities. Garnet's eloquence impressed even the *Poughkeepsie Telegraph*, which admitted, "We do not know when we have listened to any thing more practical and useful." The newspaper concluded, "Every man who strives to elevate himself in the scale of being, and who battles manfully against adverse influences, is entitled to public respect, confidence and support. MR. GARNET has shown himself to be such a man."[82]

An expression of solidarity and racial pride, the celebration at the AMEZ Church on Catharine Street fittingly symbolized the dramatic developments that had taken place among African Americans in the central Hudson Valley during the second quarter of the nineteenth century. Finally released from the constraints of bondage, free people of color exercised their independence by abandoning the homes of former owners and employers to establish autonomous two-parent households. Black residents of Dutchess County continued to live among an overwhelming white majority, but they increasingly associated with other people of color in small rural neighborhoods and most notably in more densely populated river towns. Just a few years after the formal demise of slavery in the state, African Americans in Fishkill Landing and the village of Poughkeepsie established small black churches and other institutions dedicated to self-improvement. Rather than accommodating an increasingly antagonistic racial environment, black ministers, teachers, and residents embraced an ambitious campaign of racial uplift. Although woefully inadequate in casting off the long and ominous shadow of slavery, the forging of free institutions and an ambitious crusade of improvement empowered Dutchess County's black residents and nurtured a collective identity. As African Americans in the central Hudson Valley grew increasingly conscious of themselves, their needs, and their aspirations, they came to embrace abolitionism and political protest.

# 6

# Abolitionism, Protest, and Black Identity

During the decades before the Civil War, African Americans in the Mid-Hudson Valley assembled in towns and villages the first of every August to commemorate the end of slavery in the British West Indies. Drawing hundreds of participants, Emancipation Day celebrations featured processions, communal prayer, music and song, religious sermons, and rousing political orations that attacked slavery and indicted white supremacy. Hailing British emancipation as "one of the greatest achievements in the annals of history," participants in Newburgh's 1839 celebration thanked God for "raising up" abolitionists on both sides of the Atlantic who fearlessly testified against the "unmanly and abominable sin of slavery" and championed the cause of the "oppressed and downtrodden." Celebrants denounced slavery "at any time, in any place, or in any circumstances whatever" and rejected discrimination "on account of color of the skin and the texture of the hair" as inconsistent with "reason, Christianity, and an enlightened understanding."[1] Similar commemorations in Poughkeepsie in 1840, 1841, and 1842 began with grand processions through village streets to the AMEZ Church, the spiritual center of the community. After opening with prayer and hymns, participants listened to readings of such hallowed documents as the Declaration of Independence and heard impassioned speeches by community leaders and antislavery activists. Among the orations delivered at the 1842 celebration was "an interesting and animating address" by village resident Uriah Boston that examined the root causes of racism and laid down "a heavy hand upon the monster, prejudice." Highlighting the achievements of several distinguished people of color, Boston exhorted his neighbors to self-improvement and racial uplift. Song and music interspersed

Emancipation Day activities, and recitations by school children added "vivacity" and "merriment" to the proceedings. Incorporating virtually all members of the African American community, Emancipation Day festivities reinforced communal bonds, constructed a collective memory, and provided African Americans a forum for political protest.[2]

Free African Americans engaged in Emancipation Day celebrations and other public festivals across the Northern states during the antebellum era, but such celebrations in the central Hudson Valley were rather remarkable. Concentrated predominately in towns and villages along the river, fewer than 2,500 former slaves in Dutchess County led comparatively more isolated lives than free African Americans in New York City who enjoyed economic, social, and cultural opportunities unavailable in the rural Hudson Valley. Moreover, black residents in the Mid-Hudson region lived and worked in an unusually hostile racial climate. When reporting on an anti-abolitionist riot in Poughkeepsie in 1837—a mere decade after the official end of slavery in New York State—the antislavery journal *Friend of Man* reminded its readers that "Poughkeepsie is in Dutchess County," where clergymen had imposed gag rules on "evangelists and anti-slavery lecturers."[3] Itinerant abolitionist agents quickly learned to concentrate their energies on the far more fertile—and safer—ground of the "burned over district" of upstate New York. Nevertheless, the region's political conservatism and racial hostility failed to derail the freedom struggle waged by black residents. Rather than constraining protest or undermining abolitionism, violent opposition nurtured and intensified black activism. Having played important roles in hastening the demise of slavery in the Mid-Hudson Valley, African Americans represented the vanguard of the local abolitionist movement during the antebellum period. Dutchess County's black residents engaged in a struggle that was both part of but also separate from that waged by white abolitionists. Black abolitionists in the central Hudson Valley collaborated with white allies, but they ultimately pursued an independent course of political protest. While demanding an end to slavery in the South and agitating for their own rights as citizens, African Americans in Dutchess County during the second quarter of the nineteenth century constructed and embraced a distinctive identity as *black* Americans.

While radical abolitionism transformed the antislavery struggle elsewhere in the North during the early 1830s, it made only halting progress in the Mid-Hudson Valley. Arnold Buffum, an agent of the New England Anti-Slavery Society, enjoyed limited success when he toured the region in the late summer of 1833. Although he addressed sympathetic audiences in three different Poughkeepsie churches, Buffum encountered strong opposition from most residents. Denied access to any of the meeting houses in Newburgh, the abolitionist was forced to rent a hall where he managed to deliver only a single lecture to a very small audience. After crossing the river again, Buffum encountered fierce opposition from the minister of Fishkill's Dutch Reformed Church, who vowed to do everything in his power to thwart Buffum's efforts.[4] Perhaps learning from Buffum's experience, antislavery agents Charles Denison and William Goodell bypassed the Mid-Hudson region entirely during their respective tours the following year.[5] Many residents remained largely ignorant of the emerging abolitionist movement. Reporting on Denison's visit to Peekskill, the *Peekskill Sentinel* conceded "that we were not before fully acquainted with the views and plans" of abolitionism.[6] Ignorance bred suspicion. Alarming reports of antislavery agitation and anti-abolitionist violence elsewhere intensified fears. The *Poughkeepsie Journal* and *Poughkeepsie Telegraph* reprinted detailed accounts of anti-abolitionist riots that convulsed New York City and Philadelphia in 1834. Expressing shock and disgust at the outrages, both local newspapers blamed not rioters but their "fanatical" abolitionist victims who recklessly demanded immediate emancipation "without regard to the incapacity of the slaves, or the rights of their masters" and who advocated racial equality and the scandalous amalgamation of the races.[7]

However effective, anti-abolitionism did not silence abolitionist activity in Dutchess County altogether. Persistence on the part of abolitionist agents and local activists slowly began to bear fruit. Arnold Buffum detected some "liberality" of sentiment among residents in the village of Poughkeepsie during his otherwise frustrating tour in 1833; two years later, after a visit from Amos A. Phelps of the American Anti-Slavery Society, more than one hundred male residents of Poughkeepsie assembled to organize an auxiliary to the national organization. The constitution of the local society boldly affirmed abolitionist principles. Echoing the Declaration of Independence and asserting that all men were born equal, the document proclaimed slavery to be an abominable sin and a stain on the nation's character. Declaring that silence and inactivity amounted to "tacit assent" to slavery's "perpetual existence," members vowed to abolish slavery through nonviolent "moral influence" and remove racial prejudice through the encouragement of the intellectual, moral, and religious improvement of the local African American population.[8] Events outside the region, however, quickly undermined the credibility of the new organization. Both the *Poughkeepsie Journal* and *Poughkeepsie Telegraph* expressed alarm at the American Anti-Slavery Society's aggressive campaign to inundate the nation's mails with abolitionist propaganda; the *Telegraph* warned its readers that abolitionists were "calculated to work evil" and would stop at nothing to "push their incendiary designs."[9] The *Journal*, meanwhile, closely followed events leading up to the anxiously anticipated state antislavery convention in Utica in October. Reprinting articles from the *Albany Argus*, the Poughkeepsie newspaper voiced support for those residents of the upstate community who opposed the planned event and printed disclaimers from Poughkeepsie residents who claimed to have been falsely accused of endorsing the proposed convention. When anti-abolitionists violently broke up the Utica meeting, the *Journal* (again reprinting an account from the *Argus*) lauded the "spirited and praiseworthy cause of the citizens of Utica" who had "strangled the monster at its birth."[10] Such popular antipathy took a toll on radical antislavery in the region during the 1830s. By 1837, abolitionists had established nineteen different county antislavery societies across upstate New York, but no such organization existed in the Hudson Valley; of approximately 175 delegates who attended an antislavery convention in Albany in early 1838, not one hailed from the Hudson Valley.[11]

Anti-abolitionist violence erupted in Poughkeepsie itself during the winter of 1837, when Samuel Gould, an agent of the American Anti-Slavery Society, arrived in the village in February. On Thursday the 23rd, the abolitionist addressed a small audience of two dozen people at the village's Baptist Church, most of whom were members of the local antislavery society. Gould proceeded to deliver a second lecture before a slightly larger audience at the Second Presbyterian Church two days later. Both events passed without incident, but the rather "incendiary" lecture at the Presbyterian Church reportedly met with "much disapprobation" among some in the community. Advertisement of a third lecture stirred critics to action. Printing and posting handbills that condemned Gould as an "ABOLITIONIST, of the most revolting character," opponents appealed to residents to attend the event in order to put down "this tool of evil and fanaticism." A large audience assembled in the First Presbyterian Church on the appointed evening of the 27th. All remained quiet during the opening prayer, but a group of predominantly young men and boys in the galleries shouted Gould down once the abolitionist began his address. After several attempts to resume his lecture met with similar interruptions, the speaker reportedly confronted his hecklers. Although what Gould actually said remains unclear, the abolitionist's response provoked an incensed assembly to rush upon the pulpit where Gould stood, crying "hustle him out," "ride him on the rail," "tar and feather him," and "out with the nigger." Managing to escape the grasp of his assailants, Gould fled the church with the aid of Reverend Eaton and rushed to the home of his local host, Dr. Hammond, with his pursuers close behind. Upon arriving at Hammond's home, the angry mob pelted the house with snowballs, breaking several windows. With their target beyond reach, the crowd proceeded to roam the streets of the village, engaging in "considerable riotous conduct" for at least a half hour after the church's closing.[12]

Public response to the incident was immediate. Although condemning the disruption of law and order, the local press uniformly placed blame for the episode on Gould himself. The *Literary Casket* went so far as to defend the mob, denying any intent on the part of the crowd "to injure the person of the obnoxious individual."[13] The *Poughkeepsie Telegraph* criticized the mob for chasing Gould and attacking Dr. Hammond's home but likewise refused to censure those who disrupted the agent's lecture.[14] The *Journal* proved scarcely more sympathetic. The paper did concede the "abstract" right of abolitionists to speak freely and reminded its readers that "free discussion and an unshackled press" were the "strongest barriers against tyranny and despotic power." However, it also criticized abolitionists for brazenly imposing "measures so decidedly in the face of public opinion" and faulted Gould for inflaming the volatile situation by lashing out at his hecklers. The *Journal* expressed regret that residents had not acted sooner to prevent Gould from speaking in the first place, since riotous behavior only drew attention to the movement. "Unhelped by mobs and unaided by excitements," the newspaper predicted, abolitionists "would pass quietly into forgetfulness."[15]

The *Journal* proved perceptive. The mobbing of Gould only galvanized the county's small abolitionist minority. Two prominent local activists courageously defied public sentiment in an open letter to the citizens of Poughkeepsie printed only days after the episode. Claiming to speak on behalf of "a large portion of the community," Samuel Thompson and Ira Armstrong condemned the abridgment of free speech by "mob law and violence" and appealed to local residents to accord abolitionists an honest and "dispassionate" hearing. If their doctrines were "wild" and "enthusiastic," the writers reasoned, then they would "perish with their authors"; if rooted in liberty, however, they would "bear rich fruits of peace and prosperity."[16] Antislavery activists from outside the region offered support and encouragement. Noted abolitionists Gerrit Smith, Angelina Grimke, and Sarah Grimke visited Poughkeepsie just over a month after Gould's ill-fated visit.[17] Meanwhile, the unfolding sectional crisis between North and South sensitized local residents to the potential threat of slavery to the national union. That spring, as many as 269 citizens signed a petition for the abolition of slavery in the District of Columbia.[18] County abolitionists must have been encouraged by local criticism of Congress' notorious "gag rule" suspending the hearing of abolitionist petitions as an abridgement of the right of free speech. Poughkeepsie newspapers expressed outrage at the 1837 murder of abolitionist Elijah P. Lovejoy in Alton, Illinois, and warned readers about the prospective admission of Texas to the Union as a slave state.[19] Taking advantage of a slightly less hostile public climate, local abolitionists seized the opportunity to expand their organizing efforts elsewhere in the county. During the spring of 1838, as many as 252 individuals from across Dutchess issued a call for a mass meeting at the county courthouse for the purpose of organizing a county antislavery society.[20] The public call, however, also mobilized opponents. When the meeting convened in Poughkeepsie on Tuesday, April 24th, an anti-abolitionist crowd disrupted the proceedings and forced the assembly to suspend its deliberations. This time, the local press expressed a measure of sympathy for those who had answered the public call. "However much we may differ with the abolitionists in opinion as to the propriety of their policy and measures," the *Telegraph* opined, "we must, on all occasions . . . deprecate the influence of the dangerous spirit of mobocracy."[21] Antislavery activists quickly reassembled to complete their unfinished business, and the executive committee of the new Dutchess County Anti-Slavery Society convened its first meeting on May 29th.

Battles over abolitionism and free speech raged elsewhere in the county. Attempts to create an antislavery organization in Pleasant Valley galvanized opposition during the summer of 1838. According to one account, as many as forty "inhabitants of respectability" visited the home of Stephen Flagler on June 23rd to demand that Flagler and fellow abolitionists desist in their activities. Condemning abolitionists for sowing "discord and disunion," opponents pledged to employ "all reasonable means to prevent the discussion of slavery" in the community. Local abolitionists, however, were not easily intimidated. Tensions that produced "a state of excitement . . . altogether unrivalled in the annals of Pleasant Valley" exploded when abolitionist opponents disrupted an antislavery meeting on the evening of July 3rd. Accounts of the incident diverged greatly. In a letter to the *Poughkeepsie Journal*, "W" claimed that villagers who interrupted the event included the most respected, "sober, reflecting, moral and religious men" of the community who recognized that abolitionism was "productive of evil" and who acted to ensure that the "hitherto quiet village" would not be "made the rendezvous of a party whose express object is to infringe upon the laws of our Sister states." Another observer painted a very different portrait of the disturbance. Refuting the "grotesque and ludicrous" misrepresentation of events provided by "W" (who was deserving of the "silent contempt of an indignant and outraged community"), an anonymous writer insisted that the lecture delivered by Reverend J. M. Blakesly of the New York Anti-Slavery Society was well received by fifty to sixty of the most respected and intelligent members of the community. Moreover, the writer continued, those who took to the streets were hardly "inhabitants of respectability" but in fact a "lawless rabble" and "motley group" of "notorious" adolescent "inebriates" who vandalized property and menacingly roamed village streets.[22] After printing divergent accounts of the episode, the Poughkeepsie newspapers attempted to put the controversy to rest by refusing to publish additional correspondence on the matter. However, the conflict in Pleasant Valley continued to fester. In August, a village minister supportive of colonization delivered a scathing anti-abolitionist sermon that attacked abolitionists for their self-righteous fanaticism. In this instance, the ferocity of anti-abolitionism seems to have backfired. The fiery sermon was allegedly filled with errors and falsehoods so egregious that abolitionist Benjamin Wiles wrote a detailed response that was promptly published by the antislavery Oneida Institute. In a sixty-page review of the sermon, Wiles refuted each of the minister's flagrant misrepresentations in detail and laid out logically reasoned arguments in defense of abolitionism.[23] Local abolitionists meanwhile found support among allies elsewhere in the county. The Dutchess County Anti-Slavery Society held its convention in Pleasant Valley that November at Stephen Flagler's home. The organization's secretary reported that the convention enjoyed "good attendance" from neighboring towns and a "real turn-out of the citizens of Pleasant Valley" in particular.[24]

The 1838 convention in Pleasant Valley provided an opportunity for the fledgling organization to lay out a blueprint for abolitionism in the county. Inaugural meetings of the society's executive committee revealed sharp disagreements over strategies and tactics that plagued the wider movement. Insisting that emancipation required moral conversion and conviction of the sinfulness of slaveholding, advocates of moral suasion warned that involvement in the political process would lead to the compromise of moral principle. Conversely, proponents of political action argued that effective change was possible only through the adoption of antislavery laws and public policies. Political abolitionists themselves, moreover, were divided between those who advocated working within the existing party system and those who insisted on endorsing antislavery third-party candidates.[25] After "stormy debate," the majority at the convention concluded that only "the proper exercise of the elective franchise" could eliminate slavery and instructed members to cast ballots only for candidates firmly committed to abolition. However, in a nod to moral suasionists, the society also reaffirmed its commitment to nonviolence and spoke boldly on behalf of racial equality. The convention resolved to elevate the "character and condition" of their black neighbors through the promotion of "intellectual, moral, and religious improvement" and pledged to remove "public prejudice" and procure "civil and religious" equality for all black Americans. Hoping to capitalize on recent successes and disseminate their message to a wider audience, the convention resolved to publish a local abolitionist newspaper. Abolitionist James G. Birney closed the convention with an address that provided "a grand outline of the principles of abolitionism" "to the entire satisfaction" of some who had previously opposed the movement.[26]

With the creation of a county organization and the prominence of slavery as a national issue, antislavery activists in Dutchess County began to express themselves more openly. Abolitionists from the region participated in state and national antislavery meetings. The eight Poughkeepsie delegates in attendance at the sixth annual convention of the American Anti-Slavery Society comprised the largest state delegation after that from New York City.[27] When the national organization fractured over questions of goals, strategies, and tactics, abolitionists in Dutchess reaffirmed their commitment to political action. In October 1839, the county society endorsed an independent abolitionist "Free Party" and nominated Ira Armstrong of Poughkeepsie, Solomon Sleight of LaGrange, and Thomas Hammond of Dover as antislavery candidates for New York State Assembly. The organization also resolved to hold regular weekly meetings "to discuss the political duties of abolitionists."[28] Local abolitionists struck a yet more assertive tone at their second anniversary meeting in Poughkeepsie in May 1840. Among its resolutions, the Dutchess County Anti-Slavery Society resolved to "use all the means in our power, by printing, writing, speaking and subscribing money, to forward the Anti-Slavery cause in this county." For the first time, the organization publicly identified itself with the plight of fugitive slaves. The convention boldly resolved to do "all in our power to assist those of our brethren, coming through this county, that may have thus far escaped the iron grasp of tyranny, by giving them, meat, money and clothes, to enable them to prosecute their journey to a LAND OF LIBERTY."[29] Central and western New York provided the most direct routes to freedom for Southern fugitives, but the Hudson River Valley provided an important avenue of escape for runaways who made their way up the eastern seaboard. Fugitives who managed to make their way to New York City found refuge among David Ruggles and members of the city's Committee of Vigilance, who provided material assistance to runaways before dispatching them northward to Albany. From there, members of the underground network led by Stephen Myers sent fugitives to Canada either directly northward or across upstate New York via Syracuse and Rochester. River sloops, steamboats, ferries, and barges offered the quickest, cheapest and most direct means of travel, but fugitives making their way through the central Hudson Valley traveled overland as well as on water. Underground Railroad networks were neither formal nor fixed, but runaways traveling along the river's eastern bank likely followed one of two principal routes. The first essentially followed the river itself, where many different landings and spots along the shoreline provided points for landing and embarkation. In 1840, a group of as many as thirty girls were at play next to their Poughkeepsie schoolhouse when a panicked young fugitive ran in among them with a slave catcher close behind. The girls assisted the young runaway in eluding capture by hiding him behind some boards and sending his pursuer in the wrong direction. They then gathered food and a small sum of money for the boy before he resumed his journey.[30] The second major route essentially followed the long chain of Quaker communities along the Connecticut border. Runaways arriving in southeastern Dutchess from Putnam and Westchester Counties conceivably headed in two primary directions. From the vicinity of the Oblong Friends Meeting House in Quaker Hill, some fugitives continued due north along the border to Massachusetts and Vermont. Others made their way through central Dutchess toward the river. From Quaker Hill, escaped slaves headed in a northwesterly direction toward Freedom Plains and the Oswego Friends Meeting House at Moore's Mills and then on toward the Nine Partners

Meeting House and Boarding School near Millbrook before continuing on through Pleasant Valley and Clinton to Hyde Park and Poughkeepsie. Homes, farms, and shops belonging to Friends and other white abolitionists served as station stops, but fugitive slaves also found refuge among local black residents. Inhabitants of Freemanville and Lithgow conceivably served as conductors along the overland route that meandered through central Dutchess, and members of the Crum Elbow Meeting in Hyde Park likely coordinated activities with their black neighbors in the nearby "Guinea" settlement. The AMEZ Church in Baxtertown purportedly served as a stop on the Underground Railroad, and escaped slaves likely found haven among the sizeable black populations of Fishkill Landing and Poughkeepsie. African American dockworkers and river men secreted fugitives on river vessels. Joe Collis, a Fishkill boatman and fish peddler, transported fugitives across the river from Newburgh, supposedly communicating with station masters on shore by horn blasts and lamps.[31]

At first glance, antislavery prospects in Dutchess County in 1840 appeared bright. During the 1830s, local activists had established antislavery societies in Fishkill, LaGrange, Pleasant Valley, and Poughkeepsie, while a county organization united abolitionists from across Dutchess.[32] The village of Poughkeepsie remained the heart of antislavery in Dutchess County. In a letter to the *Emancipator*, "J.S.G." boasted that community leaders could not keep abolitionism out of the schools, claiming that the majority of teachers were "uncompromising" abolitionists.[33] Abolitionist George LeRow of Poughkeepsie concurred. Observing that abolitionists came from "all ranks and grades of society" and were no longer timid or fearful, LeRow commented that "our cause is fast becoming popular."[34] Black residents shared the optimism of their white allies. Writing to the *Colored American* in late 1840, "A Friend" declared that abolitionists were "springing up like mushrooms" and that antislavery principles were "spreading like . . . a green bay tree by the water's side" and "sprouting up like the cedars of Lebanon."[35] Nevertheless, despite the burst of abolitionist activity during the late 1830s and early 1840s, a powerful undercurrent of anti-abolitionist hostility persisted in the Mid-Hudson Valley. The doctrine of abolitionism that emerged during the 1830s constituted a radical assault on the prevailing order. Rooted in the evangelical revival of the Second Great Awakening and other intellectual and cultural movements of the era, abolitionism embraced a perfectionist vision of society that demanded both the immediate and uncompensated emancipation of more than two million slaves and the recognition of black Americans as equal citizens. The democratic and egalitarian impulses of abolitionism threatened conservative ruling elites—"gentlemen of property and standing"—who feared the disruption of traditional social relations. The very public roles women and African Americans assumed within the movement were especially provocative. To the majority of Northerners, abolitionists were self-righteous fanatics who challenged the fundamental right to property, threatened the Union, attacked the family, and promoted racial amalgamation.[36] In New York, the Hudson Valley and downstate region remained particularly hostile to antislavery. Ironically, economic and political ties to the Slave South strengthened during the decades after emancipation. The economy of the Hudson Valley was bound even more tightly to the burgeoning metropolis of New York City, which emerged as the principal commercial center for raw cotton and other commodities from the South. New York's mercantile elite largely underwrote the expansion of the Cotton Kingdom; New York bankers, brokers, investors, and agents courted intimate economic, personal, and political relationships with the planter aristocracy.[37] Politically, the coalition between Northern Democrats led by Martin Van Buren and Jacksonians from the South and West dominated national politics for more than a decade. In response, their Whig challengers forged their own competing political alliance that united Northern and Southern commercial interests. In state politics, downstate counties remained the most socially and politically conservative in the state, and religious revivals and cultural movements that convulsed the "burned-over" district and fueled moral reform in upstate New York had a far more muted impact on the Hudson Valley.[38]

The region's history and culture continued to weigh heavily on local abolitionists. In late 1839, the executive committee of the Dutchess County Anti-Slavery Society requested pastors in the village of Poughkeepsie to announce antislavery prayer meetings in their respective churches. Abolitionist Reverend Underwood of the newly organized First Congregational Church eagerly complied; founded after the mobbing of Samuel Gould in 1837, the congregation provided a spiritual home for several Poughkeepsie abolitionists. Four other pastors, however, flatly refused the society's request. Reverend Eaton of the Presbyterian Church initially attempted to avoid the question altogether, claiming that he already read too many notices from the pulpit. When pressed, he admitted that he was intent upon keeping abolitionism out of his church; having witnessed the mobbing of Gould only a couple of years earlier, Eaton refused to risk a similar incident. While disavowing any personal objections to the request, the pastor of the Dutch Reformed Church refused to cooperate ostensibly for the sake of his congregation. Reverend Babcock of the Baptist Church expressed concern that the society's prayer meetings would conflict with those at his own church. When pressed, Babcock retorted angrily that he "hoped the reasons he gave would be satisfactory." Reverend Carpenter, claiming to have witnessed the "bad influence of abolitionism on the church," and the "unkind feeling" it engendered among members, insisted that he would "have nothing to do with it."[39] Meanwhile, antislavery lecturers fortunate enough to find public forums open to them continued to risk harassment and even bodily harm. Tensions continued to simmer in Pleasant Valley, where a "considerable disturbance" broke up an abolitionist meeting at the Presbyterian Church in April 1844.[40] Antislavery political candidates, meanwhile, fared miserably in the Mid-Hudson Valley. In 1840, Gerrit Smith garnered merely thirteen of more than ten thousand Dutchess County votes for governor, while James G. Birney, Liberty Party candidate for the presidency, received a scant sixteen votes. The three local "Free Party" candidates for the state assembly each received only 29 of more than 29,000 votes cast in 1839, a paltry 4 of 27,554 votes in 1841, and merely 22 of 25,260 ballots cast in 1842.[41] Although successful in establishing local antislavery organizations, abolitionists struggled to expand their appeal and mobilize grassroots activism. A "mass" anti-slavery meeting of abolitionists from throughout the central Hudson region advertised for weeks in 1841 drew only a handful of participants who found themselves mired in contentious debates over strategies and tactics.[42] Meanwhile, the Dutchess County Anti-Slavery Society's long-awaited newspaper, the *Bow of Promise*, proved short-lived. In August 1839, the executive committee authorized the publication of 500 copies of the journal to be circulated throughout the county to solicit subscriptions; four months later, the journal numbered merely 131 subscribers—only 17 of whom had actually paid their bills.[43] In fact, evidence of abolitionist activity in Dutchess County during the two decades preceding the Civil War remains thin. The Poughkeepsie Anti-Slavery Society disappears from the historical record. Minutes of the executive committee of the Dutchess County Anti-Slavery Society end abruptly in May 1840, and there is no record of another convention after the organization's June meeting. Local newspapers remained largely silent on antislavery agitation in the region, while references to the Hudson Valley in the abolitionist press were few. A small number of committed abolitionists remained active in the county, but radical abolitionism remained a minority movement clearly at odds with prevailing public sentiment. Indeed, the region's anti-abolitionist reputation extended as far as the South itself. Relating his experiences on a tour of the Southern states in a letter to the *National Anti-Slavery Standard* in 1843, a writer from Pleasant Valley recorded a conversation with a Southern gentleman who remarked, "We understand they mob at Poughkeepsie those who talk against slavery."[44]

Far from being silenced by such a hostile climate, African Americans in Dutchess County embraced abolitionism and political protest. While agents from the New England and American Anti-Slavery Societies struggled to attract audiences in the Mid-Hudson region during the early 1830s, several black residents had already established themselves as active participants in the national antislavery movement. Poughkeepsie pastor and teacher Nathan Blount served as an agent for both the *Liberator* and *Emancipator*. He and Poughkeepsie shopkeeper Jared Gray—whom abolitionist lecturer Arnold Buffum considered to be "equally persevering and meritorious"—each pledged ten dollars to the New England Anti-Slavery Society's school fund in 1833.[45] Reverend Blount also attended the 1834 national meeting of the American Anti-Slavery Society—a full year before the establishment of the Poughkeepsie organization. One of at least seven black founding members of the Poughkeepsie Anti-Slavery Society, Blount also served on the executive committee of the county abolitionist organization.[46] Samuel Ringgold Ward became a member of both societies when he arrived in Poughkeepsie in early 1839, replacing Blount on the county body's executive committee. Ward was welcomed by the antislavery First Congregational Church, where he was ordained by the Congregational Association when it met in Poughkeepsie in May 1839.[47] Other prominent members of Poughkeepsie's small black community publicly identified themselves with the antislavery cause. Barber Uriah Boston and proprietor Jared Gray, for example, penned their names to the call for the mass abolitionist meeting during the summer of 1841.[48] Antislavery sentiment was expressed not only by community leaders. Only a month after the mobbing of Samuel Gould in Poughkeepsie, as many as three hundred black residents assembled to hear Gerrit Smith and the Grimke sisters speak at the village's Lancaster School. Confessing that it was the first time she had spoken to a "promiscuous assembly" of both sexes, Angelina Grimke reported that the meeting proved "very satisfactory" to "all parties" present.[49]

If cooperation with white allies was essential for the comparatively small number of black abolitionists in Dutchess County, African American activists ultimately relied on their own resources and strove to meet their own unique needs as people of color in the central Hudson Valley. While participating in predominately white organizations, local black residents forged bonds with free African Americans elsewhere in the North. Delegates from Dutchess County attended the early National Conventions for the Improvement of the Free People of Color. George Richardson and New York City abolitionist David Ruggles, an associate of Nathan Blount's who likely spent time in Dutchess County, represented Poughkeepsie at the Third Annual Convention in 1833; Blount himself joined Jared Gray in attending the subsequent meeting a year later.[50] Organized by black leaders in Baltimore, Philadelphia, and New York, the early National Negro Conventions provided a forum for free blacks from across the North to debate emigration, antislavery, and the future of black Americans in the United States. Local representatives joined the majority of participants in denouncing the colonization movement and exhorting free people of color to moral uplift and educational improvement.[51] Black residents in the Mid-Hudson Valley followed the proceedings closely. African Americans assembled in the village of Newburgh in August 1833 to consider "the necessity of general improvement" and educational uplift, and they formally endorsed the resolutions adopted by the convention held in Philadelphia that June.[52] Religious and community leaders explicitly linked moral and intellectual improvement with the antislavery cause. Demonstration of black moral virtue and accomplishment struck at the very foundation of the proslavery argument that justified slavery on the grounds of black degeneracy and moral inferiority. As Erica Ball has argued, respectable black men and women who strove to improve themselves morally, intellectually, and economically *lived* "antislavery lives."[53] Clergymen committed to moral and intellectual improvement were in the forefront of the antislavery struggle. Reverend Gardner explicitly linked moral reform to anti-colonization and abolitionism in a letter to the *Emancipator* in the spring of 1834. Refuting allegations of black incapacity made by specific clergymen at a recent meeting of the American Colonization Society in Washington, D.C., the Poughkeepsie preacher pointed to the work of countless black churches, educational institutions, benevolent societies, and temperance organizations across the North; Gardner vowed that black Americans would remain "decidedly hostile" to the organization until it demonstrated "proof of its good will and philanthropy."[54] Noting that "moral elevation" and opposition to African colonization went "hand in hand," the *Emancipator* followed the publication of Reverend Gardner's letter with a detailed account of an

April 1834 meeting of Poughkeepsie's black temperance organization. After taking a strict abstinence pledge, members affirmed their status as citizens of the United States and condemned colonization as an unholy, racist, and "anti-republican" conspiracy to exile Americans of African descent to a "heathen land." Extolling abolitionists as "the true friends of mankind" and affirming abolitionist principles as the "only true safeguards of the union of the republic," members pledged to support the abolitionist movement with all "that lies in our power."[55]

While agitating for the liberation of Southern slaves, black abolitionists simultaneously focused on the unique needs of free African Americans in the North. The black antislavery struggle was infinitely more immediate and urgent than that waged by their white allies. While white abolitionists—however sincere—related to slavery on an abstract ideological and moral plane, African Americans as victims of bondage and racial discrimination defined the freedom struggle in far more personal and concrete terms. Black abolitionists were not content to indict slavery as a moral abomination. For African Americans, the campaign to destroy Southern slavery and the struggle to achieve political, economic, and social justice in the North constituted but two fronts in one common war against white supremacy and racial oppression. No person of color in the North was truly free and secure as long as the overwhelming majority of black Americans remained in bondage in the South and white skin remained a principal criterion of citizenship.[56] Questioning the efficacy of moral suasion in the face of intensifying anti-abolitionist opposition and the sincerity of some white abolitionists in combatting racial prejudice in the North, black activists in the central Hudson region joined African American abolitionists across the state in a more aggressive strategy of political protest to demand equal citizenship for black New Yorkers. The struggle for political rights centered on the campaign for equal suffrage. The franchise represented far more than simple access to the political process. The ballot represented an expression of power and served as a poignant symbol of membership in the political community; the formidable restrictions imposed on black voting in 1821 largely excluded African Americans from the body politic.[57] After black abolitionists in New York City proposed an aggressive statewide petition campaign to demand the removal of the property restrictions, Philip Bell toured Hudson River towns during the late summer of 1837 to "excite" African Americans in the Hudson Valley "in regard to their political rights."[58] As grassroots organizing accelerated during the late 1830s, some black abolitionists proposed convening a meeting of African Americans from across the state to address the suffrage question. The call for a black state convention precipitated debate in the wider free black community. The prospect of a racially exclusive forum posed troubling questions that struck at the very core of black identity. Maintaining that Americans of African descent shared a distinctive cultural heritage that set them apart from their white neighbors, proponents of an independent course argued for the importance of exercising political, social, and cultural autonomy. Opponents, however, feared antagonizing powerful white allies and argued that separate action in an all-black organization only reinforced white supremacy by perpetuating the very racial distinctions that black abolitionists sought to overcome.[59] Growing disillusionment with an increasingly fractious abolitionist movement generated increasing support for a black state convention. The influential editor of the *Colored American*, Charles B. Ray, originally resisted endorsing a black state convention but admitted in early May 1840 that "our mind has become somewhat changed" on the question. The journal explained, "While we believe that, being of the American nation, we ought to identify ourselves with the American people," there would always be "special interests for us to attend to, so long as American caste exists, and we have not equal rights, in common with the American people."[60]

African Americans in Dutchess County boldly embraced a separate course. "A Friend" in Poughkeepsie engaged in contentious debates over strategy and black identity and citizenship on the pages of the black press. The contributor resoundingly endorsed a black state convention in a letter to the *Colored American* in the spring of 1840. Believing such an endeavor to be "loudly called for at the present time," "A Friend" predicted that such a meeting would attract the "wisest and best men among us" and accomplish "that which cannot be accomplished in any other way, or by any other means." However, "A Friend" went beyond simply endorsing a separate convention to advocate the establishment of a black high school or college taught exclusively by black teachers. The writer anticipated objections of critics who argued that separate institutions only perpetuated racial distinctions. "A Friend" reasoned that black educational institutions would provide employment for intelligent and talented people of color otherwise denied professional positions on account of their race who in turn would serve as role models and encourage students "to aspire after such stations." Rather than perpetuating racial distinctions, stellar black achievement could only dispel white racial prejudice. "A Friend" went farther than even Ray was willing to go. Although concurring with the call for a state convention, the *Colored American* equivocated on the matter of a black college, noting that an independent school "would, in one respect, abstractly considered, be wrong in principle, but in another respect, practically considered, would be right."[61]

By early June 1840, popular momentum for a state meeting prompted a committee of black New Yorkers to issue a formal call for a convention to consider the "political condition" of African Americans in the state and demand the "unrestricted use of the elective franchise." Jared Gray, Milber Francis, Uriah Boston, and H. Johnson of Poughkeepsie, and Adam Adkins of Fishkill served as the local committee of correspondence charged by the state committee to mobilize their respective communities "to adopt such measures . . . as will further the object of the convention."[62] Local residents convened a "large and respectable" meeting in Poughkeepsie on June 21st. After selecting Uriah Boston as chair and joining in prayer "fervently offered by Reverend Blount," the assembly enthusiastically endorsed the convention. Proclaiming that the elective franchise was "the birthright of every man" and that "the long deprivation of this right" had "inflicted a wound upon our soul" that could be healed only by "full and complete enfranchisement," residents expressed "gratitude to God" for the call for a state convention and pledged their "hearty cooperation" in the effort.[63] "A Friend" meanwhile continued to argue for the propriety of independent action on the pages of the *Colored American*. Pointing to the "large and extensive field open before us ready for harvest," the writer insisted "if the peculiar circumstances of our people require separate action, let it come, the sooner the better until the time when the political and religious condition of the colored man shall be the same as that of the white man."[64] In Poughkeepsie, black village residents commissioned three of the community's most capable leaders—Reverend John Mars, Uriah Boston, and John N. Gloucester—to attend the convention when it opened in Albany on August 18. Having recently arrived in Poughkeepsie to assume pastorship of the Catharine Street Church, Reverend John Mars had already established himself as a minister of "considerable ability" and "antislavery agitator" while serving in the Berkshires and the upper Hudson Valley. Like Nathan Blount and Samuel R. Ward, Mars assumed a leadership position in the Dutchess County Anti-Slavery Society, serving on the organization's Board of Managers.[65] Uriah Boston's personality and economic success made him a logical choice. A man of aristocratic bearing, Boston assumed a "polite," "suave and courtly" demeanor and appeared "faultlessly attired" whenever in public. One of the region's few independent proprietors, the Pennsylvania native operated a combination barbershop and variety store in Poughkeepsie. Actively engaged in church affairs, Boston served as one of the original trustees of the Poughkeepsie AMEZ congregation.[66] Mars and Boston each played active roles during the August convention in Albany. Reverend Mars served with Alexander Crummel of New York City and James W. Duffin of Geneva on a committee that drafted an important report on the petition campaign. Boston labored on no fewer than three committees and joined Henry Highland Garnet, Alexander Crummel, Charles B. Ray, and others in "spirited" debates on property ownership and the rights of citizenship.[67] Upon their return from Albany, representatives organized a local committee that launched a particularly successful petition campaign, garnering 101 signatures for equal suffrage; of more than a dozen communities from across the state, only New York City and Rochester secured more names than Poughkeepsie.[68] Local black residents resoundingly endorsed the work of a second state convention in Troy the following year. Women and men assembled in the village of Poughkeepsie on September 14, 1841, to hear the report of the convention's delegates. After listening to a reading of the proceedings and the convention's address to the "colored inhabitants of the State," participants formally approved of the "high-spirited, dignified and patriotic sentiments embodied" at Troy and ratified the convention's appeal to "'agitate, agitate' unceasingly until the odious, proscriptive, and invidious property qualification is removed from the statute book of the State."[69]

The petition campaign for equal suffrage bore little fruit during the early 1840s in the face of hostile white opinion and the opposition from the state's Whig and especially Democratic Party organizations. However, the state's second constitutional convention in twenty-five years provided a new opportunity to remove the discriminatory property requirement. By the 1840s, the state's explosive population growth, rapid economic development, and the emergence of the second party system had rendered the 1821 constitution inadequate.[70] Debates over black suffrage during the 1846 constitutional convention echoed those made twenty-five years earlier. Hailing predominately from upstate counties, delegates who advocated the elimination of the discriminatory restriction grounded their arguments in moral and political principle. Opponents insisted that the franchise was not an inalienable right but a privilege that few black New Yorkers were capable of exercising. Characterizing people of color as unassimilable aliens, some critics appealed to prejudice by stoking fears of racial amalgamation.

Opponents of equal suffrage dominated the convention's committee on the elective franchise, which originally proposed to disfranchise black voters altogether by restricting the ballot to white citizens. Dutchess County Whig James Tallmadge opposed the effort, first joining colleagues in an unsuccessful attempt to remove the word "white" from the committee's report, and then supporting a subsequent (similarly unsuccessful) motion to reduce the property requirement imposed on black voters. Dutchess County's two other delegates, Democrats Peter K. Dubois and Charles H. Ruggles, remained decidedly hostile to black suffrage. Although Ruggles ultimately agreed to the final compromise measure retaining the $250 property requirement, Dubois consistently opposed the black franchise in any form.[71] In the end, convention delegates decided to submit the question of black suffrage to the state's voters as a separate ballot measure; a popular referendum allowed politicians from both major parties to avoid taking a decisive stand on a politically volatile issue.

The submission of equal suffrage to the state's voters mobilized abolitionists to garner public support for the referendum. While members of the Dutchess County suffrage committee labored to educate voters on the ballot initiative, "A Colored American" appealed to the electorate in the columns of the local press.[72] The contributor specifically addressed opponents of equal suffrage who justified racial qualifications on the grounds of alleged black incapacity and innate racial inferiority. In the first of two letters to the *Poughkeepsie Telegraph* published in the spring of 1846, "A Colored American" presented a detailed history of African achievement and civilization in the ancient world. The second letter refuted popular perceptions of the supposed ignorance and degradation of free African Americans. Far from being godless and immoral, "A Colored American" argued, people of color were a profoundly religious people. Providing statistics on African American churches, church attendance, temperance organizations, benevolent institutions, literary societies, schools, and property holding, the writer concluded that "no well-informed Christian man" could believe in the moral and intellectual degeneracy of black Americans in light of such evidence.[73] In the end, however, arguments made by "A Colored American" and others fell upon deaf ears. New Yorkers resoundingly defeated the ballot measure in the November elections by a ratio of 2.6 to 1. The Hudson Valley and downstate counties proved especially antagonistic to the proposition. Dutchess County voters rejected equal suffrage by a ratio of almost 8 to 1, a margin three times as large as that for the state as a whole. However respectful, well-reasoned, and eloquent, arguments in favor of equal suffrage ultimately failed to placate white racial fears.[74]

Although the protracted political battle to remove the discriminatory suffrage restriction ultimately resulted in bitter defeat, the spirited campaign for equal suffrage politicized African Americans in the Mid-Hudson Valley. Engagement in political protest incorporated black residents of Dutchess County into a wider racial community. Local representatives to state and national conventions expressed the voices of the region's black residents to broader audiences and educated their neighbors at home about important developments in the state and nation. Antislavery and African American newspapers similarly nurtured a political consciousness and linked the central Hudson region with other parts of the nation. Although not all black residents were fully literate and perhaps even fewer could afford subscriptions, access to such newspapers had a far-reaching impact; a single copy of an issue could have easily made its way throughout local neighborhoods or have been read from the pulpit or discussed in Uriah Boston's barbershop or Gray and Jennings' grocery. The *Colored American* was especially important. Philip Bell endeavored to procure subscriptions to the newspaper during his summer 1837 tour of the valley; Nathan Blount, Reverend Mars, and Uriah Boston each served as local agents. Black county residents fully recognized the importance of the journal for themselves and for all people of color across the North. Community members who assembled in Poughkeepsie in June 1840 to voice support for a black state convention simultaneously endorsed the *Colored American*; although the newspaper was "a new acquaintance" to many in the region, the assembly "bid it welcome" and resolved that it should "ever merit . . . our entire confidence and support."[75] When community members gathered the following year to hear the report from the Troy convention, they readily complied with the convention's request to create a local committee to solicit donations for the journal.[76] A month after "A Friend" from Poughkeepsie wrote to the paper to chastise readers for failing to pay their subscriptions, Uriah Boston explained the importance of the *Colored American* to readers in a November letter. Rejoicing that "we have an organ through which we can communicate with each other, and correspond upon all different subjects which demand our attention," Boston explained how the journal promoted political activism and provided a vital a forum for self-expression for African Americans "from Maine to Georgia." Boston proclaimed, "Let our motto be ACTION, ACTION, energetic, untiring, and continued action; let us nail it to the mast head of our noble ship, and by a strict adherence to it, we will come off triumphant."[77] The black press allowed African Americans in the Mid-Hudson Valley to become active members of a racial community that transcended geographic space. Local contributors to the *Colored American* engaged in at times contentious debates among black abolitionists on the pages of the newspaper. In addition to promoting the movement for a black state convention, "A Friend" from Poughkeepsie explored the merits of passive resistance and nonviolence and criticized Charles B. Ray for the editor's endorsement of the Liberty Party.[78] Nor did "A Friend" shrink from more contentious philosophical and ideological debates. Having already argued for separate black schools when endorsing a black state convention in the spring of 1840, "A Friend" did not hesitate to jump into the "names controversy," the particularly fierce debate among free blacks across the North on the propriety of identifying African Americans and black institutions as "colored." In correspondence to the *Colored American* in early 1841, "A Friend" responded directly to Philadelphia's William Whipper, the most outspoken critic of black separatism. The Poughkeepsie contributor argued that it was not color but the historical experience of slavery and "wicked prejudice" that were responsible for the degraded position of African Americans in the United States. Rather than apologize for his ancestry, "A Friend" proudly embraced identification as a man of color; "having suffered under this name and color," explained the Dutchess County resident, "I want to raise [*sic*] by the same."[79]

While contributors such as "A Friend" and Uriah Boston engaged in spirited dialogue on the pages of the black press, hundreds of other African Americans in the Mid-Hudson Valley expressed their voices in vibrant community celebrations. Conventions of the national African American Delevan Temperance Union provided forums for collective expression and political protest. As many as five thousand people of color from across the Northeast converged on the village of Poughkeepsie for the organization's annual meeting in July 1846. "Throngs" of well-dressed and "respectable" colored citizens began to assemble at village streets and in public houses early on the "uncommonly fine" morning of July 7th. Participants "began to pour in from the country" before nine o'clock, and by eleven-thirty no fewer than seven steamboats had arrived at village wharves carrying passengers from New York City, Albany, and elsewhere. Around noon, Poughkeepsie resident William Jennings, the grand marshal for the day's festivities, led one of the "grandest and most imposing" processions the village had ever seen. The marchers, with six full bands and fourteen large and "magnificent" banners, proceeded through the heart of the village, "up Main Street to Washington, through Washington to Mill, up Mill to Hamilton, through Hamilton to Church, down Church to Academy, down Academy to Noxon, down Noxon to Market, up Market to Main, up Main to Catharine, and through Catharine" to a large pavilion that had been erected for the occasion. There participants engaged in prayer, worship, and song before listening with "deep attention" to a series of speeches delivered by such notables as Henry Highland Garnet, Charles B. Ray, and Horace Greeley that rivaled any oration heard in "the halls of legislature or Congress." The day's events concluded in the evening, when participants proceeded to different hotels and houses for a "splendid dinner."[80] The grand convention of 1846 was not an exceptional event. After similar celebrations in Newburgh in 1847 and Kingston in 1848, the organization returned to Poughkeepsie in 1849. The 1849 meeting was no less impressive than the convention three years earlier, attracting sizeable delegations from New York, New Jersey, Pennsylvania, Vermont, Massachusetts, Connecticut, and Long Island as well as the Hudson River counties. Festivities again included a grand procession with a band and marchers in "handsome" regalia, musical performances, prayers, stirring speeches on temperance and reform, and a grand dinner. Although the evening session was reportedly marred by "wrangling and quibbling," the convention proved to be a "glorious" moment for African Americans throughout the Northeast.[81]

Like Emancipation Day commemorations, temperance conventions politicized ordinary men and women and allowed them to construct and express a common racial and political identity. Participation in such grand public events allowed African Americans in the central Hudson Valley opportunities to transcend those geographic barriers that otherwise isolated them from each other. Public celebrations solidified communal bonds by blurring lines of gender, age, occupation, education, and color that potentially divided the free African American community. Song, music, prayer, parades, picnics, fine dress, banners, flags, and orations were all powerful means by which participants recalled a common cultural heritage and constructed a shared historical memory. Celebrations infused political protest with powerful religious overtones. Explicitly linking the lives of participants with those of free blacks across the nation and Southern slaves, communal events transformed ordinary men, women, and children into political actors. Indeed, the very presence of such large congregations of African Americans in public spaces frequently hostile to them was politically significant. The *Journal and Eagle* reported that white residents watched the 1846 celebration in Poughkeepsie with "deep interest and admiration" and "gazed with wonder and astonishment" at the respectability and gentility "among a class they had been long accustomed to despise." Marveling at the decorum of such a large assembly, the newspaper declared "without extravagance" that "a body of people more respectable in manners, appearance, and orderly behavior, have [*sic*] never visited us."[82] An expression of cultural autonomy, communal celebrations allowed participants to celebrate a unique racial heritage while simultaneously affirming an American identity and asserting claims to equal citizenship.[83]

By midcentury, African Americans in Dutchess County had embraced political protest and cultivated a distinct racial consciousness in a particularly inhospitable climate. The historical experience of slavery cast an ominous shadow over the Mid-Hudson Valley. Outspoken abolitionists in Dutchess County courageously defied popular sentiment, but the region as a whole remained decidedly unsympathetic to the antebellum antislavery movement. Paradoxically, however, racial hostility promoted political activism among the county's black residents. Black abolitionism predated the establishment of local antislavery societies, and leading black citizens played conspicuous roles in local abolitionist organizations. Interracial cooperation with white allies, however, did not preclude separate action. African Americans in Dutchess County resoundingly supported the black state convention movement, and local black abolitionists played active roles in state and national forums. Active participation in the black convention movement, engagement in the statewide petition campaign for equal suffrage, active support of the black press, and participation in grand public celebrations politicized black residents of the Mid-Hudson region and integrated them into a broader imagined racial community. By midcentury, the fate of Dutchess County's black residents was increasingly tied to ominous national events.

# 7

# Black Dutchess County at Midcentury

It is difficult to imagine the intense anxiety John Bolding must have felt in the summer of 1851. Having fled bondage in South Carolina a few years earlier, John, his brother David, and a young woman named Susan had made their way to Dutchess County and assumed new identities. Susan married Francis Moore, a Poughkeepsie tailor, and the Bolding brothers moved into the Moore household. John assisted Francis in the tailoring trade and quickly earned a reputation as a "first rate workman" in his own right. Early in 1851, John married Henrietta, a local woman of mixed racial ancestry in her early twenties. Despite his success, however, Bolding found himself in increasingly grave danger. The Fugitive Slave Act of 1850, an integral component of the famous Compromise of 1850 that narrowly averted the dissolution of the Union, dramatically strengthened a slaveowner's authority to retrieve runaway slaves. The statute enlisted federal authorities in the pursuit and capture of fugitives, severely circumscribed the legal rights of accused runaways, and imposed stiff penalties on anyone who assisted fugitives or impeded the execution of the law. Bolding's apprehension must have only intensified in January 1851, when a party of slave catchers arrived in Poughkeepsie in pursuit of another runaway whom they had tracked to the village. The fugitive, like Bolding, had assumed a new identity, supporting a family as a carpenter. After an attempt to seize the fugitive failed, the man simply disappeared.[1]

Bolding's greatest fears were realized several months later. By chance, a Southern woman who had been staying in Poughkeepsie for an extended period recognized Bolding and informed one of his owners, Robert Anderson of Columbia, South Carolina. Anderson promptly procured a warrant from the United States Commissioner in New York City for

Bolding's arrest. United States Marshal Henry F. Tallmadge planned the fugitive's capture carefully. Federal marshals procured a carriage upon their arrival in Poughkeepsie on Monday, August 25th; claiming to be in pursuit of a counterfeiter, they insisted that the curtains of the carriage be drawn lest they be detected. The unsuspecting Bolding was hard at work when the carriage pulled up to his shop. The officers jumped from the carriage, seized the startled Bolding, and raced directly to the rail station, having carefully timed their operation so that they boarded the two o'clock train to New York City only minutes before its scheduled departure. Events transpired so quickly that no one in Poughkeepsie had an opportunity to react to what was happening. Once the facts became known, Bolding's supporters sprang into action to redeem the fugitive. After two failed attempts to procure a writ of habeas corpus, Bolding's case came before Mr. Nelson, the US commissioner in New York City. Denied the right to testify on his own behalf by the federal statute, Bolding's defense fell to attorneys Mr. Culver and Mr. Upton, who pursued a two-pronged strategy. The first was to challenge the validity of the original arrest warrant. The second principal argument focused on Bolding's racial ancestry. Culver and Upton brazenly argued that the very light complexioned Bolding—"as white as a great many white men"—was in fact not of African descent at all and therefore could not be a slave. Bolding's wife Henrietta, her mother, and several other relatives and friends from Poughkeepsie sat near the accused when the commissioner delivered his decision in the crowded courtroom. After quickly dismissing the defense's procedural objections, Mr. Nelson took up the question of Bolding's racial identity and legal status. Despite the testimony of Reverend Levi Waldo of Poughkeepsie and different doctors and phrenologists who denied Bolding's African ancestry, the commissioner found the weight of contrary evidence overwhelming and remanded Bolding to his owners. A stoic Bolding reportedly listened to the decision with "great equanimity," while "not the least emotion was perceptible on the countenance of his friends." The complicated decision in fact left the fugitive and his supporters some ground for hope. Although finding that Bolding's owners had met the legal threshold to prove their claims as stipulated by federal law, Nelson refused to provide a definitive judgment on Bolding's legal status. The commissioner even suggested that defense counsel could file suit in a South Carolina court for Bolding's freedom. Bolding's owners, however, had had enough. Eager to avoid additional litigation, they readily entered into negotiations with unidentified parties who had made overtures to purchase the fugitive even before the conclusion of the trial. Citizens from Poughkeepsie and the surrounding region, with help from residents in Albany and New York City, quickly raised funds to meet the $1,500 purchase price and the additional $500 his owners demanded in compensation. The *Poughkeepsie Journal and Eagle* bristled at the outrageous sum but admitted that public sympathy for the fugitive and his traumatized wife "caused the demand, exorbitant as it was, to be submitted to." Bolding returned to Poughkeepsie within a month of his arrest, where he lived as a free man until his death in 1876.[2]

Bolding's ordeal demonstrates the precarious position African Americans in the central Hudson Valley occupied in the decade before the Civil War. By midcentury, the fate of Dutchess County's black residents was increasingly tied to disturbing national events. Although the 1850 Fugitive Slave Law targeted black Southerners who had escaped bondage, no free person of color in the North was truly safe after the passage of the statute. Merritt Green of Fishkill was so tormented by the fear of being kidnapped by slave catchers that he attempted to slit his own throat, vowing that "he was a free man, and that he had rather die than be enslaved."[3] Moreover, Dutchess County's black residents had few white allies to whom they could turn. The unfolding sectional crisis sensitized their white neighbors to the expansion of slavery into the western territories, but local abolitionists continued to confront popular hostility to radical abolitionism. Immigrant newcomers from Europe, who were arriving in the Mid-Hudson region in increasing numbers, vied with local black residents for housing and employment. Increasing political insecurity, racial antipathy, and deteriorating economic fortunes at midcentury confronted African Americans in the Mid-Hudson Valley with a painful crisis of identity. However, as the nation inched closer to civil war, Dutchess County's black residents continued to cling to a proud racial consciousness as men and women of color.

The War with Mexico sensitized residents of the central Hudson Valley to the threat of slavery to the national union. Frederick Douglass visited Poughkeepsie in early October 1847. Lecturing at Reverend Levi Waldo's Congregational Church, the black abolitionist impressed even the Democratic *Telegraph*. Although claiming that Douglass "said some things that might as well have been omitted," the paper admitted that "as a whole, his address left a strong impression upon the minds of the large audience who listened to him."[4] Congressman David Wilmot arrived in the village only two weeks later. The Pennsylvania Democrat precipitated a national political crisis the year before when he introduced an amendment in the House barring slavery in any territory the United States should acquire from Mexico. While visiting Poughkeepsie, Wilmot delivered an "enthusiastic" speech on free soil.[5] Abolitionists in the Mid-Hudson Valley attempted to capitalize on growing popular fears of the territorial expansion of Southern slavery. Antislavery activists from throughout the region assembled in Washington Hollow for a "mass" antislavery meeting during the autumn of 1849. In addition to local figures such as Poughkeepsie's Congregational minister Levi Waldo, speakers at the November 14th assembly included prominent Garrisonians James and Lucretia Mott, Stephen S. and Abby Kelley Foster, and Parker Pillsbury. Reporting that the meeting attracted more participants than anticipated, Abby Kelley Foster detected "a much greater readiness . . . to taking the ultra ground of the American [Anti-Slavery] Society than we had supposed . . . possible." Encouraged by "the present aspect of the affairs in this county," Foster predicted that the ground was "now prepared for a new crop."[6]

Foster's assessment of the prospects of abolitionism in Dutchess County proved overly optimistic, to say the least. The legacy of slavery continued to weigh heavily in the central Hudson Valley. While abolitionists might have been encouraged by heightened attention to the national crisis over slavery in the western territories, free soil ideology was hardly radical abolitionism.[7] A "mass" abolitionist convention the preceding year that had been advertised for weeks drew only a handful of participants, prompting the editor of the *Telegraph* to thank his antislavery "friends" for the "amusement" they afforded.[8] When fewer than two dozen residents attended a local free soil meeting in August 1849, the *Journal and Eagle* suggested that the county's free soilers "may now as well hang up their fiddles, for their cake is dough."[9] Conceivably, Abby Kelley Foster saw so much potential precisely because antislavery had made so little progress in the region. She herself conceded that the majority of those who attended the November 1849 meeting in Washington Hollow had "never given a thought to our principles and measures" previously.[10] Parker Pillsbury provided a more critical assessment of local antislavery sentiment. Writing from the town of Clinton only weeks after the event in Washington Hollow, Pillsbury reported that the region lay in a "state of moral petrification" comparable to "what our whole country presented twenty years ago." "To lecture and labor among such a people, and under such circumstances," Parker bemoaned, "is a calling not surely to be desired."[11] The local press meanwhile continued to ridicule the radical antislavery movement. The Poughkeepsie papers excoriated an 1850 abolitionist convention in Cazenovia as a "crazy" and fanatical "amalgamation affair."[12] Closer examination of the community's response to John Bolding's ordeal is particularly revealing. The significance of the episode lay not only in what transpired but also in what did *not* happen. Despite the excitement generated by the incident and an outpouring of sympathy for the fugitive and his new wife, Bolding's arrest did not produce the furor comparable to that precipitated by the apprehensions of Shadrach Minkins and Thomas Sims in Boston months earlier. Nor did it provoke violent resistance comparable to that of the "Christiana Riot" in southeastern Pennsylvania or in the forcible rescue of William "Jerry" McHenry in Syracuse weeks later. The community's measured response to the incident reflected the inherent conservatism of the region. Popular support for the fugitive slave law and the Compromise of 1850 was strong in the Hudson Valley. The local press characterized the compromise as an equitable and reasonable solution to the sectional crisis. As the *Rhinebeck Gazette* put it, "Our predilections are for Free Soil, but we prefer to have the question coolly and deliberately discussed."[13] The *Poughkeepsie Telegraph* placed blame for the controversial fugitive slave law on abolitionists, even suggesting that "the colored race would be at this moment much nearer the blessings of liberty than they are now" had it not been for the "intemperate ardor of northern agitators." The paper insisted that preservation of the Union was far more important than the "rescue of a few slaves from their bondage" and commended the compassionate but "law-abiding" citizens of Poughkeepsie for purchasing Bolding's liberty rather than defy the law.[14] Indeed, public outcry at Bolding's apprehension arose as much from the surreptitious nature of the arrest as the seizure itself. The *Poughkeepsie Journal and Eagle* maintained that the capture "caused a good deal of indignation" precisely because the measures taken were "unnecessarily harsh in a community where he [Bolding] might have been detained for a week without the least danger of disturbance" while the legal parties attended to the necessary arrangements.[15]

Facing an insecure political future, African Americans also occupied an uncertain and increasingly tenuous position in the regional economy. Farming at midcentury remained lucrative only for commercial growers who could adjust to a rapidly changing market. Unable to compete with an increasing volume of superior quality wheat from upstate New York, Hudson Valley farmers were forced to rely even more heavily on stock raising, dairying, and the production of coarser grains, fruits, and vegetables. While larger farmers marshaled resources to adapt to the changing marketplace, small farmers struggled to compete.[16] In 1850, a handful of black county residents, including Anthony Williams of Milan in northern Dutchess and Jonathan Heady of East Fishkill, enjoyed modest success as freeholders; owning an estate valued at $3,500, Williams was one of the two largest black property holders in the county.[17] However, Williams and Heady were truly exceptional; merely fifteen of more than five hundred black men in Dutchess County whose occupations were recorded in the 1850 census were identified as farmers who maintained independent households.[18] The majority of black residents in the countryside either worked very small parcels as tenants or sharecroppers or labored for others as hired hands.[19]

Commercially oriented river towns offered greater economic opportunity. Several black residents earned their living in the robust river trade, including a dozen young men explicitly identified as boatmen in the 1850 census. Seventeen-year-old Henry Johnson of Fishkill worked as a crewman on a steamboat operated by Solomon Hopkins and William Bishop; sixty-year-old James Brown served as the vessel's cook.[20] Hotels, private homes, and river estates of affluent families provided employment for coachmen, cooks, servants, and waiters.[21] Skilled workers were more likely to ply their trades in villages than in the countryside. All but one of the county's black craftsmen in 1850—Morris Quarters, an iron molder in Amenia—resided in towns along the river. John S. Loun, a mulatto carpenter, and Anthony Churchill, a blacksmith, lived and worked in Red Hook.[22] The greatest occupational diversity existed in the commercial and manufacturing center of Poughkeepsie, where six tailors, four carpenters, three barbers, and three pot bakers plied their trades.[23] Skilled laborers in the town of Fishkill included tailor Charles Hardenburgh, barbers L. S. Pelham and Theodore Delili, tinman Andrew Morrison, and master gardener James F. Brown.[24] Brown's story was rather remarkable. Born a slave in Maryland, Brown acquired skills and hired out his own time in Baltimore, where he ultimately earned enough to purchase his wife's freedom. Frustrated in his attempts to negotiate his own manumission, in 1827 James fled to New York City. There, Brown found employment as a domestic in the household of judge and former congressman Daniel Verplanck, who assisted James in purchasing his freedom. James came to spend more and more of his time at Mount Gulian, the Verplanck home at Fishkill Landing, where he devoted increasing attention to the care of the estate's grounds. The former Maryland slave ascended to the position of master gardener within a few short years, assuming responsibility not only for maintaining the estate's exquisite gardens but also for making purchases, marketing produce, conducting estate business, and supervising the racially mixed garden staff. His income, supplemented by his wife Julia's earnings as a domestic, afforded the couple a modest but comfortable middle-class lifestyle. Brown's horticultural expertise earned him unique access to an exclusive craft guild. Color barred him from membership in professional organizations, but James cultivated personal and professional relationships with renowned horticulturalists. Under the patronage of Daniel's daughter Mary Anna Verplanck, he engaged in his own botanical experiments and participated in horticultural exhibitions.[25]

While Brown carved out a semblance of middle-class respectability as a master gardener, a handful of black men achieved success as small proprietors. One Poughkeepsie businessman who enjoyed a period of notable success was Jared Gray, who purchased a lot on Main Street in 1842 for the sizeable sum of $5,500. The 1845 village directory listed Gray as proprietor of a "barber and fancy store" at 290 Main; Thomas Green sold clothing at his shop immediately next door at 290½ Main Street. After William Jennings took over the clothing business, the two establishments became known collectively as "Gray and Jennings." In addition to Uriah Boston, who operated his own "hair dressing and variety store," black shopkeepers in 1840s Poughkeepsie included Francis Legg, a cloth dresser, and Moses Humphrey, who operated a fish market.[26] Erastus Kimball of Red Hook, a mulatto merchant who employed a black clerk named Philip Peeler, was the only African American so designated in the 1850 census. Owning $3,500 in real property, Kimball ranked with farmer Anthony Williams of Milan as the largest black property holder in the county.[27]

Despite notable examples of individual success, most African Americans in the Dutchess countryside and county villages experienced declining economic fortunes at midcentury. Comparatively few had entered the expanding manufacturing sector; the two dozen men engaged in skilled trades comprised less than ten percent of the county's African American workforce. Reverend Noah Brooks of Fishkill and Reverends John A. Williams and William Decker of Poughkeepsie were the only black professionals in the entire county. The overwhelming majority of black workers engaged in menial labor and service occupations. The most common occupational designation for African Americans in the 1850 census by far was "laborer," which accounted for four of every five black men for whom occupations were listed (see table 7.1). Census takers identified another forty-seven men as coachmen, cooks, domestics, servants, stable hands, and waiters, who collectively comprised nine percent of the county's black male workforce; adding to that figure those in white households for whom no occupation was listed, the actual number of domestics was likely greater. In total, at least nine of ten black men in Dutchess County in 1850 earned livelihoods as menial laborers and servants.[28]

Admittedly, in the diverse economy of the Mid-Hudson Valley, the designation "laborer" or "farmer" can obscure as much as it reveals. Farming, rural manufacture, and even domestic service continued to demand an array of skills. Moreover, several black laborers in the county lived in modest comfort; as many as forty laborers in the 1850 census were listed as owning real property.[29] Even men engaged in domestic service, including waiters

**Table 7.1**
**Occupational Distribution of African American Males in Dutchess County, 1850**

| Category | N | % |
|---|---|---|
| Laborer[a] | 417 | 79.9 |
| Unskilled/Domestic[b] | 47 | 9.0 |
| Semiskilled[c] | 14 | 2.7 |
| Farmer | 15 | 2.9 |
| Skilled[d] | 24 | 4.6 |
| Proprietor[e] | 2 | 0.4 |
| Professional[f] | 3 | 0.6 |
| **Totals:** | **522** | **100.1** |

*Notes:*
[a]Includes 409 laborers and 8 farmers in white-headed households
[b]Includes 19 coachmen, 16 waiters, 1 domestic, 6 servants, 3 cooks, and 2 "livery stable"
[c]Includes 12 boatmen, 1 cartman, and 1 woolen spinner
[d]Includes 7 tailors, 5 carpenters, 5 barbers, 3 pot bakers, 1 iron molder, 1 blacksmith, 1 gardener, and 1 tinman
[e]Includes 1 merchant and 1 clerk
[f]Includes 3 clergymen

*Source:* Population Schedules of the Seventh Census of the United States, 1850, New York, Dutchess County, microcopy 432, rolls 496 and 497 (Washington, DC: 1963).

Theodore Thomas of Rhinebeck and Robert Sackett of Poughkeepsie, and Poughkeepsie coachmen Abraham and Thomas Bradford acquired property sufficient to qualify them for suffrage.[30] For the most part, however, the socioeconomic position of the least-skilled laborers in the rural economy had eroded during the first half of the nineteenth century. Seasonal cycles, mechanization, and the increasing specialization of agricultural labor allowed farmers to hire workers by the month, week, or even day. Labor contracts sometimes included provisions for room and board, but the surplus of workers in the countryside kept wages low. For most farm laborers, meager earnings, irregular employment, and a rising cost of living effectively closed off opportunities for independent property ownership and upward mobility.[31] The small number of black workers engaged in manufacture confronted similar challenges. Mechanization of the workshop and the specialization of labor eroded craft skills and depressed wages for mechanics and operatives. As cheap machine-made goods displaced custom-made items produced by craftsmen, the number of artisans in the countryside declined; journeymen were forced either to migrate elsewhere or accept employment as wage laborers or farmhands. Mass production also changed the nature of skilled work, reducing artisans to repairing and maintaining items rather than producing them. Some mechanics prospered, but the incomes of most skilled workers in Dutchess County were modest. While the most successful master craftsmen rose to become manufacturers and merchant-capitalists, many more were reduced to the position of wage laborers.[32] A few black artisans in Dutchess County remained dependents in white households. Eighteen-year-old Andrew Morrison lived and worked with three other young apprentice journeymen under Fishkill tinsmith Isaiah Van Kleeck. Morris Quarters worked for iron founder Joseph Bassett in Amenia; in Red Hook, Anthony Churchill labored in Edward Vanbradenbergh's blacksmith shop.[33] Work for semiskilled and unskilled laborers remained uncertain and insecure. Many laborers and domestics were transients who relocated according to the seasons. Migrant farmhands found employment during planting and harvest but searched for other means of supporting themselves during slack times. Domestics left home for weeks or months at a time to work at resorts and hotels during peak tourist seasons. James Brown's wife Julia worked predominately in local homes but occasionally took jobs in resort communities like Saratoga and more distant locations.[34] Meager earnings, impermanent work, and transiency left a sizeable number of black residents largely propertyless. Black property owners in Dutchess

County were comparatively few and their estates modest; as many as four of five black residents in 1855 did not hold taxable property.[35] Property ownership, moreover, did not ensure security. Economic success could be fleeting. One successful business enterprise conducted by a particularly "reputable colored citizen" in the village of Poughkeepsie—possibly Jared Gray—failed in 1849 much "to the astonishment of all."[36] George Frisch experienced similar hardship when attempting to establish a small business in the village. A Vermont native, Frisch made his way to the Mid-Hudson region from Virginia and set up a shoe shop in Newburgh. Frisch moved to Poughkeepsie in 1840 to open a shoe-blacking business, but unidentified "colored rowdies" allegedly forced him to abandon his efforts.[37]

In the daily struggle to make ends meet, the contribution of women to the household economy was vital. A far higher proportion of African American women in Poughkeepsie labored outside of the home than did either their native or foreign-born white sisters. Opportunities for employment, however, remained sharply limited. As many as ninety percent of black women labored as domestics. Many of those who did not reside in white homes earned income providing domestic services such as washing, child care, and cooking.[38] Boarding provided yet another potential source of income. Augmented households continued to provide material assistance and emotional support to newcomers, single men and women, the elderly, and orphaned children. In 1844, the Schuyler household on the south side of Union Street near Church Street in the village of Poughkeepsie included family members and "others." Jane and William Gaston, both natives of Virginia, could have been among several unidentified African Americans who resided at the home of Nathaniel and Elisabeth Townsend.[39]

While residential clustering created social networks that provided emotional and material support, poverty and prejudice confined many African Americans to crude and ramshackle dwellings in undesirable and unhealthy locales. Black inhabitants in the countryside occupied less productive soils. The Baxtertown neighborhood in Fishkill, for example, rested on stony, low-lying, swampy terrain. The Beekman holdings of the Freeman family and their black neighbors were hilly and comparatively marginal.[40] In Poughkeepsie, the predominately working-class neighborhood surrounding Jefferson and Union Streets that was home to many African American families was among the "filthiest" sections of the village. Cholera ravaged the neighborhood in 1832 and proved even deadlier when it returned seventeen years later, claiming the lives of 250 village residents. Public attention in

1849 focused on the poor crowded vicinity of Jefferson and Church Streets. According to one account, the "unduly filthy" section of the village was dangerously overcrowded; sixteen families and thirty-two boarders allegedly resided in one building alone. The stench from wastewater and refuse that accumulated in the streets made it difficult even to breathe.[41] Village residents also associated the neighborhood with vice and criminal activity. A suspicious fire in August 1850 destroyed a vacant Jefferson Street residence that had once been used as a brothel.[42]

Many black residents in Poughkeepsie lived among those who shared their economic plight, most notably newly arrived Irish immigrants who had fled destitution in their native land. Construction of the Hudson River Railroad during the 1840s brought hundreds of Irish laborers to Poughkeepsie, Fishkill, Hyde Park, Rhinebeck, and other river communities. These newcomers often lived in uneasy proximity with native black residents. In November 1850, a suspicious fire in Poughkeepsie consumed a couple of buildings "of small value" near the intersection of Church, Union, and Clover Streets that had been occupied by colored and Irish families.[43] Such spatial intimacy inflamed both racial anxieties and nativist fears. During the late 1840s and early 1850s, the local press regularly carried accounts of drunken brawls, fistfights, riots, and even murders among Irish railroad workers, and militia units such as the Poughkeepsie Guards mobilized on more than one occasion to quell violent uprisings.[44] Such outbreaks stemmed principally from conflicts among immigrants themselves, but Irish workers targeted Poughkeepsie's African American community during the winter of 1850. Trouble in the village's multiracial working-class neighborhood began on Saturday, January 26th, when an argument escalated into a brawl between armed Irish and black residents at the foot of Church Street. Several victims emerged from the fight "terribly mangled," but the police—perhaps accustomed to such behavior—dismissed the incident "as of no account." Several Irishmen, however, vowed to exact vengeance. On Monday evening, January 28th, a group of approximately fifteen to twenty Irish "maddened by liquor" rioted at the corner of Church and Jefferson Streets. The sheriff arrived on the scene only to be attacked by the rioters. Fleeing for his life, the sheriff rushed to the courthouse and rang the village bell to spread the alarm. As the Poughkeepsie Guards and local rifle company mobilized, Irish gangs terrorized local black residents. One group fell upon an African American couple on Union Street. The man managed to escape to a nearby house, but the assailants beat his female companion so savagely that she was not expected to survive the attack. A bystander, Peter Cramer, was shot in the chest. Recrimination, however, was swift. The guards and rifle company, assisted by as many as three hundred armed citizens, descended on the neighborhood and arrested seventy Irish. The following day, authorities and vigilantes rounded up dozens of other immigrants—in some cases literally dragging them from their beds—and ransacked Irish homes in search of weapons.[45] The community's decisive response to the riot, however, provided small consolation to the village's black residents. Focusing almost exclusively on the behavior of the Irish rioters and depicting black residents largely as hapless victims, newspaper accounts suggest that most villagers acted not out of sympathy for their black neighbors but out of nativist fears and alarm at the breakdown of social order.[46] Conflicts between African Americans and white residents over housing and employment only intensified over time. As Clyde and Sally Griffen have demonstrated, a clear occupational hierarchy was beginning to emerge in mid-nineteenth-century Poughkeepsie, as European immigrants and native-born whites marginalized black workers in an increasingly competitive labor marketplace.[47]

The small number of African American artisans and shopkeepers in the county assumed important roles in their respective communities. Economically secure craftsmen and proprietors supported community institutions and provided financial assistance to those in need. James Brown, for example, aided black neighbors in Fishkill Landing in purchasing property and paying their tax bills.[48] Barbers Uriah Boston, Jared Gray, and the Vermong brothers in Poughkeepsie and L. S. Pelham and Theodore Delili in Fishkill served a variety of economic and social roles; "hair dressing and variety stores" offered patrons an array of goods as well as services. Barber shops provided places to socialize, catch up on gossip, advertise community events, and discuss politics. One of the very few trades dominated by African Americans during the nineteenth century, barbering provided rare opportunities for self-employment and avenues toward middle-class respectability. However, barbers occupied a peculiar and often awkward space in antebellum America. Black critics objected to the servile role barbers assumed. Catering to a largely white clientele, barbers had to accommodate racial prejudice. The self-effacing barber who routinely exercised forbearance in the face of condescension or ridicule only perpetuated demeaning racial stereotypes. Barbers themselves, however, developed a strong craft consciousness and cultivated a powerful sense of pride.[49] Among them was Uriah Boston, who responded forcefully to a perceived attack on his vocation on the pages of *Frederick Douglass' Paper.* Douglass laid out the deteriorating position of free African American workers in a controversial editorial series entitled "Learn Trades or Starve" during the spring of 1853. Lamenting intensifying racial discrimination in the workplace and the increasing concentration of black workers in menial occupations, the abolitionist editor exhorted African American men to learn skilled trades. Only by proving their worth as mechanics and independent farmers, Douglass argued, would black men assert their manhood and escape pauperism. Hard work, perseverance, and sacrifice were creative and empowering; conversely, idleness and low expectations bred degeneracy. The waiter who only set tables, the porter who carried a few pieces of baggage early in the day but spent the afternoon relaxing at the steamboat or rail station, and the barber who "shaved a half dozen faces in the morning" but spent the rest of the day napping or playing guitar not only failed to improve themselves but also led themselves into temptation and vice. Douglass concluded that parents' responsibility was clear: to make their sons "mechanics and farmers—not waiters, porters and barbers."[50]

Douglass' provocative letter exposed painful class tensions that had been long simmering within the free black community. For decades, predominately middle-class leaders who promoted racial uplift walked a fine line between exhorting black workers to economic improvement and disparaging those who actually occupied menial and unskilled occupations. An outraged Boston was among many readers who responded to Douglass' controversial editorial. The Rochester abolitionist seems to have been taken aback by the intensity of Boston's response; Douglass refused to publish Boston's letter and provided two reasons for doing so. The first was obvious—there was simply no need to do so because Douglass had made no "attack" on barbers or barbering. The second reason Boston must have considered particularly humiliating. Claiming that the letter's "chirography and grammar" were so poor that his staff simply did not have time to correct it, Douglass returned the letter, noting that he would consider additional correspondence from the Poughkeepsie barber if it were written "more carefully and intelligently."[51] Drawn out on a national stage, Boston took up the challenge and fired off a second letter. The Poughkeepsie barber held his ground. Insisting that readers could do nothing but interpret Douglass' language as a denigration of barbering as a servile occupation, Boston vigorously defended his vocation. Property ownership and business success were practical and real measures of economic independence, and barbers were "as intelligent and respectable as any class of businessmen, and much more so than some others." The Poughkeepsie resident also took Douglass to task for unnecessarily and unfairly ridiculing him before his readers—an affront more humiliating than the quiet return of his letter would have been. After all, Boston pointed out, the paper's readers would hardly have blamed Douglass for any poor grammar on his part. Closing his correspondence with "This is all I have to say," the Poughkeepsie barber respectfully requested the publication of his second letter.[52]

If Boston reacted personally to Douglass' perceived slight on his trade, he did not shrink from confronting the prominent editor on a national stage. By the 1850s, the Poughkeepsie barber had established himself as an outspoken abolitionist in his own right. A community leader and one of Dutchess County's leading black citizens, Boston had championed the black press and played active roles in the black state convention movement. Colleagues at the 1853 Convention of Colored People in Rochester paid Boston tribute when they selected the Poughkeepsie delegate to serve as a state councilor.[53] Noting Boston's conspicuous absence at the Troy meeting two years later, "Cosmopolite" commented, "There is a vacancy in our Conventions when Uriah Boston is not present."[54] During the 1850s, Boston grappled with questions of race, national identity, and citizenship in other correspondence to *Frederick Douglass' Paper*. The Poughkeepsie abolitionist was uncompromising in his denunciations of white supremacy. Boston did not hesitate to admonish Horace Greeley of the influential *New York Tribune* for allegedly presuming the inferiority of black Americans in an 1853 article on African colonization. Rejecting Greeley's assertion that African Americans needed to demonstrate their equality with whites, Boston dismissed popular pseudoscientific racial theories as "humbug phrenology."[55] The Poughkeepsie abolitionist explored the question of race and prejudice in yet greater detail in a subsequent letter to *Frederick Douglass' Paper* in early 1855. Rejecting the notion that color was the source of racial bigotry, Boston argued that a natural inclination to perceive different peoples with suspicion—a "national prejudice of race"—was found in all cultures. The virulence of American racism, Boston argued, was attributable to the juxtaposition of the "abject and deeply degraded" position of the African continent devastated by the slave trade on the one side and the uniquely "enlightened" and "exalted" position of the United States on the other. Boston reasoned that since American racism stemmed from the inferior geopolitical position of Africa in global affairs, equality "with the Anglo-Saxon and Gaelic races" would be achieved once Africa ascended to the position of a "great, powerful, Christian, commercial and industrial nation" that commanded the respect of the world. Powerful religious overtones infused Boston's millennial vision. Although the end of slavery was yet far off, the Poughkeepsie abolitionist expressed unabashed confidence in God's providential design. Boston exhorted "all true patriots and Christians" to "labor, live, and die in faith," fully assured of the future "glorious consummation" of God's divine plan.[56]

For Boston, an "African" consciousness did not preclude claims to American citizenship. A trustee of Poughkeepsie's AMEZ congregation, staunch advocate of racial uplift, active participant in the black state convention movement, and supporter of the African American press, Boston also cautioned against identifying exclusively with black institutions. The Poughkeepsie abolitionist expressly rejected a separatist vision of black nationhood in a subsequent letter to Douglass' paper. Criticizing the separatist positions of "Ethiop" (William J. Wilson) and "Communipaw" (James McCune Smith), Boston noted sarcastically that had he not known the two men personally he would have suspected them of being "colonizationists in disguise." For Boston, the construction of a tiny, separate black nation *within* the United States was not only impractical but also dangerous. Boston warned that three million "Africans" contending with "24 millions of Americans" would have disastrous consequences "more fatal to the colored race" than the suicidal charge of the British Light Brigade at Balaclava in Crimea. No one could be a citizen of two nations. "We are American citizens by birth, by habit, by habitation, and by language," Boston insisted. "Why, then," Boston asked rhetorically, would black Americans "wish to be considered Africans [?]" The "true policy," Boston continued, was not the establishment of a separate black nation—whether in the United States or elsewhere—but the *lessening* of distinctions between white and black Americans. Identification as "*Colored* Americans" was acceptable in the United States but identification as "Africans" was not. "For my part," Boston asserted, "I claim to be an American citizen, and also claim to be a man."[57]

While Boston expressed an American identity and demanded equal citizenship, his loyalty to a national government that recognized slavery was tenuous. In the wake of the Kansas crisis, Boston dared to contemplate how the breakup of the nation would accelerate emancipation. An August 1855 letter argued that the dissolution of the union would free the federal government from the "enormous" expense of promoting slaveholding interests, release the North from its "heart-sickening" complicity in Southern slaveholding, and so seriously debilitate the "Slave Power" to encourage wars of liberation among slaves. Once slavery had been destroyed, a new purified Union could be restored. Boston's argument proved to be too much for Douglass, who dismissed the ludicrous proposal as "unsafe, unsound, and unwarrantable."[58] An unchastened Boston, however, continued to press his case, insisting on the practicality of a large-scale slave revolution and expressing fervent confidence in God's judgment of the "incorrigibly wicked." In defending his argument for disunion to Douglass, Boston again reiterated his complicated views of racial and national identity. As a matter of principle, Boston preferred not to see "distinctive organizations of 'colored people'" but reasoned that since they already existed, there was "no reason why they should not be improved." Ultimately, however, contentious debates about identity remained theoretical. Boston continued, "The only result that I at present cheerfully acquiesce in, and heartily desire, is the grand final result—the destruction of slavery. The others are the means to an end."[59]

On the eve of Civil War, the national and cultural identity of black Americans in Dutchess County had become inextricably interwoven with the destruction of Southern slavery and the fate of the Union. Accustomed to indifference and hostility, abolitionists found slightly more receptive audiences as the furor over Kansas and the proslavery Dred Scott decision sensitized residents of the central Hudson Valley to the machinations of the Southern "Slave Power." An impressive slate of agents from the American Anti-Slavery Society that included Parker Pillsbury, Aaron Powell, Susan B. Anthony, and black abolitionist Charles Lenox Remond visited Pleasant Valley, Clinton Corners, and Clinton Hollow during the spring of 1857.[60] Frederick Douglass visited Poughkeepsie twice in 1858. Remarking on a series of lectures the Rochester abolitionist delivered to large audiences at the Universalist Church in January, the *Poughkeepsie Eagle* reported that Douglass "handled all his subjects with marked ability and thrilling power."[61] Douglass' eloquent two-hour address "Freedom in the West Indies" was only one of several orations delivered at Poughkeepsie's Emancipation Day celebration seven months later. Local public commemorations of West Indian emancipation during the late 1850s were no less impressive than they had been the preceding decade, drawing literally thousands of participants and including elaborate processions, brass bands, stirring orations, music, prayer, and opportunities for recreation and refreshment.[62] In its own account of the 1859 celebration, the *Weekly Anglo-African* of New York City observed that abolitionism had finally made an impression on the central Hudson Valley and predicted that it would "eventually triumph in spite of all opposition."[63] A Poughkeepsie resident echoed a similar sentiment in a letter to the newspaper's editor at the very end of the year. Noting that African Americans in the region had grown "a little jealous" reading about news from other communities, "Romeo" boasted of the village's own black organizations and reported on moving local commemorations of John Brown's raid at Harper's Ferry.[64]

In many respects, the African American experience in the Mid-Hudson Valley after 1850 blends with the larger historical narrative. During the Civil War, black men from Dutchess County and the wider Hudson Valley enlisted in black regiments to preserve the Union and destroy Southern slavery. At home, black residents persisted in their political battle for equal suffrage—which was achieved only with the ratification of the Fifteenth Amendment in 1870. Local activists joined other black New Yorkers during the Reconstruction period and beyond to battle segregation and advocate for equal access to schools and other public facilities. Meanwhile, the contours of regional black life and culture began to change. As the nation began to industrialize, many native residents left for New York City and other urban centers to be replaced by an infusion of black immigrants from the South. However, if the experience of black Dutchess County after 1850 began to resemble a familiar national story, the freedom struggle in the central Hudson Valley before the Civil War had proven more arduous and painful than that waged by African Americans in the urban North. African Americans in rural Dutchess County could not isolate themselves from their white neighbors or escape into the relative anonymity of a larger urban environment. Small-scale slavery in the countryside and river villages was extraordinarily oppressive, and the painfully slow, piecemeal process of abolition in Dutchess County took a formidable toll on black life during the long transitional period between slavery and freedom. The historical experience of racial slavery left an indelible mark on the people and culture of the Mid-Hudson Valley. In the wake of emancipation, white New Yorkers continued to perceive liberated slaves as an inferior servile caste and constructed new mechanisms and ideologies to subordinate and marginalize people of color. Free African Americans enjoyed comparatively fewer economic opportunities in a predominately rural county like Dutchess. Slaves proved their value and versatility as laborers and craftsmen during the colonial era, but the Market Revolution, changes in the workplace, the decline of Hudson Valley agriculture, and intensifying job competition eroded the economic position of the region's black laborers during the antebellum period. The political conservatism of the region and economic dependency ultimately presented formidable obstacles to free black community formation during the opening decades of the nineteenth century. While free African Americans in New York City and other urban centers forged an identity as free people of color rooted in independent families, churches, and charitable organizations, liberated slaves in Dutchess County struggled in a stultifying social, political, and economic climate.

Ultimately, however, the conservatism of emancipation and the legacy of slavery in the Mid-Hudson Valley delayed but did not prevent the formation of autonomous, self-conscious, and politically active free black communities in Dutchess County. Black residents deftly navigated multiple worlds. A small minority economically dependent on white employers and patrons, African Americans in the central Hudson Valley worked alongside whites, often attended the same churches, and sometimes lived in white households. Yet people of African descent in Dutchess County clearly identified with each other and constructed lives distinct from those of their white neighbors. Lacking social, cultural, and economic resources available to free blacks in urban environments, African Americans in the rural Hudson Valley literally built communities from the bottom up. During the eighteenth and early nineteenth centuries, enslaved and free black residents partly overcame isolation of the countryside by forging informal social networks that provided a foundation for the establishment of separate black institutions during the antebellum period. Finally released from the constraints of bondage, African Americans in Dutchess County congregated with black neighbors in small rural neighborhoods and larger towns and villages like Poughkeepsie and Fishkill Landing, where they established independent black churches and communal organizations dedicated to uplift. A fragmentary historical record—notably advertisements for fugitive slaves and references to cultural celebrations such as Pinkster—suggest the persistence of African cultural forms in the Hudson Valley. However, the construction of a distinct racial consciousness among Dutchess County's black residents was largely a political creation. The dark shadow of slavery stifled radical abolitionism in the Hudson Valley as a whole, but an increasingly antagonistic racial climate paradoxically fostered political activism among the region's small African American population. Local black abolitionists aggressively championed the antislavery cause and demanded the rights of equal citizenship but embraced a separate course of black protest. Uniting themselves with free people of color across the North and with slaves in the Southern states, Dutchess County's black residents became active members of an imagined racial community that extended far beyond the geographic confines of the central Hudson Valley. Local communities were not free from discord or conflict. Sectarian differences divided Poughkeepsie's free black community during the 1830s, and a temporary split in the wider AMEZ Church fractured the Poughkeepsie congregation shortly before the Civil War.[65] Some residents apparently found the courtly Uriah Boston a bit overbearing; during the mid-1850s, the local black suffrage organization experienced conflict over leadership and Boston's role.[66] Practically, only a minority of black residents throughout the county were outspoken activists. Preoccupation with the demands of daily life, indifference, and fear undoubtedly tempered communal and political activism.[67] Abolition was almost certainly among the "isms" that initially polarized the local black community. However, appreciation for the formidable obstacles to community formation and political activism only casts black achievement in greater relief. The emergence of small but vibrant, politically active, and racially self-conscious free black communities in Dutchess County after a painfully long transition from slavery to freedom was striking. When providing an account of Emancipation Day festivities in Poughkeepsie in 1841 that drew as many as six hundred celebrants, Uriah Boston justifiably boasted, "although Poughkeepsie was not mentioned among those places from which you expected great things, I am of the opinion that she has shown herself not least among the towns, villages, and cities of the Union in celebrating that day."[68]

# Notes

## Introduction

1. Ira Berlin provides a comprehensive overview of the evolution of slave societies in *Many Thousands Gone: The First Two Centuries of Slavery in North America* (Cambridge: Belknap Press of Harvard University Press, 1998). See especially chaps. 2, 7, and 9 on the northern experience.

2. Scholarship on slavery, emancipation, and the construction of race in the North is extensive. For an introduction to slavery and its aftermath in New York, see Ira Berlin and Leslie M. Harris, eds., *Slavery in New York* (New York: New Press, 2005). Joanne Pope Melish provides a provocative interpretation of abolition and northern racial thought in *Disowning Slavery: Gradual Emancipation and "Race" in New England, 1780–1860* (Ithaca: Cornell University Press, 1998). For a somewhat different perspective, see James J. Gigantino II, *The Ragged Road to Abolition: Slavery and Freedom in New Jersey, 1775–1865* (Philadelphia: University of Pennsylvania Press, 2015).

3. Ira Berlin, "The Revolution in Black Life," in *The American Revolution: Explorations in the History of American Radicalism*, ed. Alfred Young (DeKalb: Northern Illinois University Press, 1976), 349–82.

4. Histories of the free African American experience in the North include James Oliver Horton, *Free People of Color: Inside the African American Community* (Washington, DC: Smithsonian Institution Press, 1993); James Oliver Horton and Lois E. Horton, *In Hope of Liberty: Culture, Community, and Protest among Northern Free Blacks, 1700–1860* (New York: Oxford University Press, 1997); Leon F. Litwack, *North of Slavery: The Negro in the Free States, 1790–1860* (Chicago: University of Chicago Press, 1961); Harry Reed, *Platform for Change: The Foundations of the Northern Free Black Community, 1775–1865* (East Lansing: Michigan State University Press, 1994); and Julie Winch, *Between Slavery and Freedom: Free People of Color in America from Settlement to the Civil War* (New York: Rowman & Littlefield, 2014).

5. Billy G. Smith, *The "Lower Sort": Philadelphia's Laboring People, 1750–1800* (Ithaca: Cornell University Press, 1990), 200.

6. Leslie M. Harris, *In the Shadow of Slavery: African Americans in New York City, 1626–1863* (Chicago: University of Chicago Press, 2003), 8–9.

7. Horton, *Free People of Color*, 1–19, 198–200; Clarence E. Walker, *Deromanticizing Black History: Critical Essays and Reappraisals* (Knoxville: University of Tennessee Press, 1991), xi–xviii.

8. Horton and Horton, *In Hope of Liberty*, xi–xii.

9. See "Of Our Spiritual Strivings," in W. E. B. Du Bois, *The Souls of Black Folk*, ed. David W. Blight and Robert Gooding-Williams (Boston/New York: Bedford Books, 1997), 37–44.

10. Leslie M. Alexander, *African or American? Black Identity and Political Activism in New York City, 1784–1861* (Urbana: University of Illinois Press, 2008); Craig Steven Wilder, *In the Company of Black Men: The African Influence on African-American Culture in New York City* (New York: New York University Press, 2001).

11. Elizabeth Rauh Bethel, *The Roots of African-American Identity: Memory and History in Free Antebellum Communities* (New York: St. Martin's Press, 1999); Patrick Rael, *Black Identity and Black Protest in the Antebellum North* (Chapel Hill: University of North Carolina Press, 2002).

12. See, for example, Leonard Curry, *The Free Black in Urban America, 1800–1850: The Shadow of a Dream* (Chicago: University of Chicago Press, 1981). For New York City and environs, see Berlin and Harris, *Slavery in New York*; Harris, *In the Shadow of Slavery*; Graham Russell Hodges, *Root and Branch: African Americans in New York and East Jersey, 1613–1863* (Chapel Hill: University of North Carolina Press, 1999); Shane White, *Somewhat More Independent: The End of Slavery in New York City, 1770–1810* (Athens: University of Georgia Press, 1991); and White, *Stories of Freedom in Black New York* (Cambridge: Harvard University Press, 2002). Gary Nash examines black Philadelphia in *Forging Freedom: The Formation of Philadelphia's Black Community, 1720–1840* (Cambridge: Harvard University Press, 1988). New England studies include Robert J. Cottrol, *The Afro-Yankees: Providence's Black Community in the Antebellum Era* (Westport: Greenwood Press, 1982); and James Oliver Horton and Lois E. Horton, *Black Bostonians: Family Life and Community Struggle in the Antebellum North* (New York: Holmes & Meier, 1979). Graham Hodges examines African Americans in rural New Jersey in *Slavery and Freedom in the Rural North: African Americans in Monmouth County, New Jersey, 1665–1865* (Madison: Madison House, 1997), but Hodges expands his analytical scope to include New York City and its environs.

13. In 1790, sixty percent of the state's slave population resided in the counties of Albany, Columbia, Dutchess, Orange, Ulster, and Westchester. At the time of the first federal census, more than four of every five black New Yorkers resided outside of Albany, Brooklyn, and New York. See Evarts B. Greene and

Virginia D. Harrington, eds., *American Population before the Federal Census of 1790* (New York: Columbia University Press, 1932), 105.

14. Curry, *The Free Black in Urban America*, 239.

15. See, for example, David N. Gellman, *Emancipating New York: The Politics of Slavery and Freedom, 1777–1827* (Baton Rouge: Louisiana State University Press, 2006); Gigantino, *The Ragged Road to Abolition*; Gary B. Nash and Jean R. Soderlund, *Freedom by Degrees: Emancipation in Pennsylvania and Its Aftermath* (New York: Oxford University Press, 1991); White, *Somewhat More Independent*; and Arthur Zilversmit, *The First Emancipation: The Abolition of Slavery in the North* (Chicago: University of Chicago Press, 1967).

16. Putnam County remained part of Dutchess until 1812.

## Chapter 1. Slaves and Slavery in the Mid-Hudson Valley

1. *New York Packet and American Advertiser*, July 17, 1783. Hereafter, *New York Packet*.

2. Joyce D. Goodfriend examines the significance of the black presence in colonial New York and the challenges of historical interpretation in "Merging the Two Streams of Migration to New Netherland," in *The Worlds of the Seventeenth-Century Hudson Valley*, ed. Jaap Jacobs and L. H. Roper (Albany: State University of New York Press, 2014), 237–52. General histories of slavery in New York include Berlin and Harris, *Slavery in New York*, and Edgar McManus, *A History of Negro Slavery in New York* (Syracuse: Syracuse University Press, 1966). For slavery in New York City, see Thelma Louise Foote, *Black and White Manhattan: The History of Racial Formation in Colonial New York City* (New York: Oxford University Press, 2004); Joyce D. Goodfriend, "Slavery in Colonial New York City," *Urban History* 35, no. 3 (2008): 485–96; Harris, *In the Shadow of Slavery*, chap. 1; Hodges, *Root and Branch*, chaps. 1–4; and White, *Somewhat More Independent*, chap. 1. For the Mid-Hudson Valley, see William P. McDermott, *Dutchess County's Plain Folks: Enduring Uncertainty, Inequality, and Uneven Prosperity, 1725–1875* (Tolland: Kerleen Press, 2004), chap. 7; McDermott, "Slaves and Slaveowners in Dutchess County," *Afro-Americans in New York Life and History* 19 (January 1995): 17–41; Helen Wilkinson Reynolds, "The Negro in Dutchess County in the Eighteenth Century," *Yearbook*, Dutchess County Historical Society 26 (1941): 89–100; Eric J. Roth, "'The Society of Negroes Unsettled': A History of Slavery in New Paltz, New York," *Afro-Americans in New York Life and History* 27 (January 2003): 27–54; A. J. Williams-Myers, "The Arduous Journey: The African-American Presence in the Mid-Hudson Region," in *The African-American Presence in New York State History: Four Regional History Surveys*, ed. Monroe Fordham (Albany: State University of New York Press, 1990), 19–49; and Williams-Myers, *Long Hammering: Essays on the Forging of an African-American Presence in the Hudson River Valley to the Early Twentieth*

*Century* (Trenton: Africana World Press, 1994). Dennis Maika provides an illuminating glimpse of slaveholding in one prominent New York family and the evolution of slavery in the lower Hudson Valley in "Encounters: Slavery and the Philipse Family: 1680–1751," in *Dutch New York*, ed. Roger Panetta (Yonkers: Hudson River Museum/Fordham University Press, 2009), 35–72.

3. See Berlin, *Many Thousands Gone*, chap. 2; Joyce D. Goodfriend, "Burghers and Blacks: The Evolution of a Slave Society at New Amsterdam," *New York History* 59, no. 2 (April 1978): 125–44; Hodges, *Root and Branch*, chap. 1; McManus, *History of Negro Slavery*, chap. 1; Christopher Moore, "A World of Possibilities: Slavery and Freedom in Dutch New Amsterdam," in Berlin and Harris, *Slavery in New York*, chap. 1.

4. McDermott, *Dutchess County's Plain Folks*, 1–2; James H. Smith, *History of Dutchess County, New York* (Syracuse: D. Mason & Company, 1882), 47–55.

5. Greene and Harrington, *American Population*, 95–97; McDermott, *Dutchess County's Plain Folks*, 1–2; Smith, *History of Dutchess County*, 56–57. For the settlement and development of English New York, see Patricia Bonomi, *A Factious People: Politics and Society in Colonial New York* (New York: Columbia University Press, 1971); Michael Kammen, *Colonial New York: A History* (New York: Oxford University Press, 1975); and Milton M. Klein, ed., *The Empire State: A History of New York* (Ithaca: Cornell University Press, 2001), especially chap. 9. Sung Bok Kim explores tenancy in *Landlord and Tenant in Colonial New York: Manorial Society, 1664–1775* (Chapel Hill: University of North Carolina Press, 1978).

6. See Kammen, *Colonial New York*, 161–72, and Samuel McKee, Jr., "The Economic Pattern of Colonial New York," in *History of the State of New York*, ed. Alexander C. Flick, vol. 2 (New York: Columbia University Press, 1933), 249–68.

7. Greene and Harrington, *American Population*, 96–104.

8. See Martin Bruegel, *Farm, Shop, Landing: The Rise of a Market Society in the Hudson Valley, 1780–1860* (Durham: Duke University Press, 2002), chaps. 1 and 2; and Thomas Wermuth, *Rip Van Winkle's Neighbors: The Transformation of Rural Society in the Hudson River Valley, 1720–1850* (Albany: State University of New York Press, 2001), chaps. 2 and 3.

9. J. Hector St. John de Crevecoeur, *Sketches of Eighteenth-Century America*, ed. Henri L. Bourdin, Ralph H. Gabriel, and Stanley T. Williams (New Haven: Yale University, 1925), 82–83.

10. A. Leon Higginbotham, Jr., *In the Matter of Color: Race and the American Legal Process: The Colonial Period* (New York: Oxford University Press, 1978), 115–16; Samuel McKee, "A Century of Labor," in Flick, *History of the State of New York*, 305–07; McKee, *Labor in Colonial New York, 1664–1776* (Port Washington: Ira J. Friedman, 1963; originally published 1935), 93–94.

11. E. B. O'Callaghan, ed., *Documents Relative to the Colonial History of the State of New York*, vol. 5 (Albany: Weed, Parsons & Company, 1855), 136.

12. Berlin, *Many Thousands Gone*, 182; McManus, *History of Negro Slavery in New York*, 25. James G. Lydon examines the New York slave trade in "New

York and the Slave Trade, 1700 to 1774," *The William and Mary Quarterly*, Third Series, 35, no. 2 (April 1978): 375–94.

13. Greene and Harrington, *American Population*, 96–104. On the eve of the Revolution, more than 3,200 slaves lived and worked in Dutchess and Ulster Counties, comprising almost ten percent of the regional population. In Dutchess, 1,360 slaves comprised six percent of the population in 1771; the proportion of slaves was notably higher in Ulster County, where almost 2,000 slaves comprised fourteen percent of Ulster's population. More than 4,700 slaves resided in the two counties nineteen years later. Thomas Davis explores the demography of New York's eighteenth-century slave population in "New York's Black Line: A Note on the Growing Slave Population," *Afro-Americans in New York Life and History* 2 (January 1978): 41–59. See also McManus, *History of Negro Slavery in New York*, 24–25, 42–46.

14. The town of Fishkill was home to almost one-third of all slaves in the county (601), followed by the towns of Rhinebeck (421 slaves, or almost one-quarter of the county's slave population), Poughkeepsie (199 slaves), and Clinton (176 slaves). *Heads of Families at the First Census of the United States Taken in the Year 1790: New York* (Baltimore: Genealogical Publishing Company, 1976); Population Schedules of the First Census of the United States, 1790, microcopy 637, roll 6, New York, vol. 2 (Washington, DC: 1965). In 1790, Clinton included the current towns of Clinton, Hyde Park, and Pleasant Valley; Fishkill included Fishkill, East Fishkill, part of LaGrange, and Wappinger; Rhinebeck also included Red Hook. The black population was smallest in the eastern townships bordering Connecticut and the more mountainous southern towns (now Putnam County): Amenia (52 slaves), Beekman (106 slaves), Frederickstown (63 slaves), Northeast (80 slaves), Pawling (42 slaves), Philipstown (25 slaves), Southeast (13 slaves), and Washington (78 slaves). In 1790, Beekman included the current towns of Beekman, Union Vale, and part of LaGrange; Northeast included Milan, Northeast, and Pine Plains; Pawling also included the town of Dover; Washington also included the town of Stanford.

15. The proportion of slaves in other county townships ranged from four percent in Clinton and three percent in Beekman to between one and two percent in southern towns.

16. Twenty-two percent of households in Fishkill and Poughkeepsie and twenty-four percent of households in Rhinebeck included slaves. Enslaved men, women, and children resided in almost one in ten households in Clinton and Beekman. Slaveholding households were least common in eastern and southern Dutchess: Amenia (five percent), Frederickstown (four percent), Northeast (seven percent), Pawling (three percent), Philipstown (four percent), Southeast (four percent), and Washington (five percent).

17. McKee, "A Century of Labor," 291–98. See also McDermott, *Dutchess County's Plain Folks*, 112–18; McDermott, "Slaves and Slaveowners," 20–22; Roberta Singer, "The Livingstons as Slave Owners: The 'Peculiar Institution'

on Livingston Manor and Clermont," in *The Livingston Legacy: Three Centuries of American History*, ed. Richard T. Wiles (Annandale-on-Hudson: Bard College, 1987), 72–75; and A. J. Williams-Myers, "Hands That Picked No Cotton: An Exploratory Examination of African Slave Labor in the Colonial Economy of the Hudson River Valley to 1800," *Afro-Americans in New York Life and History* 11, no. 2 (July 1987): 33–43.

18. *New York Packet*, July 31, 1777. See also *New York Journal and General Advertiser*, September 4, 1780; *New York Packet*, September 7, 1780.

19. *Poughkeepsie Journal*, June 13, 1797.

20. For examples of slaves engaged in milling and skilled trades, see *New York Journal and General Advertiser*, January 17, 1780; *Poughkeepsie Journal*, January 15, 1794; November 21, 1797. Several millers in the town of Clinton owned slaves. See Eleanor Rogers, "Mills of the Old Clinton Precinct," in *Clinton, Dutchess County, New York: A History of a Town*, ed. William P. McDermott (Clinton Corners: Clinton Historical Society, 1987), 57–69.

21. *Poughkeepsie Journal*, May 11, 1802; *Political Barometer*, January 27, 1808. Another seller suggested that his healthy and able-bodied twenty-five-year-old farm laborer "would be a very good hand on board a sloop in the river." *New York Packet*, March 20, 1783.

22. *New York Packet*, January 24, 1782. For similar examples, see *New York Packet*, September 16, 1779; *Poughkeepsie Journal*, August 17, November 30, 1802; March 6, 1804; February 11, 1806; June 13, 1810; April 15, 1818.

23. *Poughkeepsie Journal*, May 30, 1797; *New York Packet*, June 27, 1779; *Poughkeepsie Journal*, May 26, 1791; April 13, 1802. See also *New York Packet*, May 3, 1781; July 18, 1782; January 9 and August 14, 1783; *Poughkeepsie Journal*, May 26, 1791; February 6, 1793; July 2, 1799; February 18, 1800; April 13, 1802; June 7, 1803; May 8, 1804; June 10, 1807; January 8, 1812; *Political Barometer*, December 21, 1808.

24. *New York Packet*, August 14, 1783. Some sellers specified that their female slaves were adaptable to both town and country. Henry Livingston suggested that the woman he offered for sale was "well calculated for a tavern," being familiar with "plain cooking, washing, ironing, and baking." *Poughkeepsie Journal*, December 21, 1796.

25. *New York Packet*, August 14, 1783. Henry Livingston noted that the "strong and healthy" woman he offered for sale in 1795 was "accustomed to work in haying and harvesting." *Poughkeepsie Journal*, October 7, 1795.

26. Sojourner Truth, *Narrative of Sojourner Truth*, ed. and intro. Margaret Washington (New York: Vintage Books, 1993), xv, 20.

27. *New York Packet*, February 14, 1782.

28. *New York Packet* June 27, 1782.

29. *Poughkeepsie Journal*, December 5, 1810.

30. *Poughkeepsie Journal*, June 8, 1814.

31. *New York Journal and General Advertiser*, October 11, 1779; June 5, 1780; *New York Packet*, October 21, 1779; *Poughkeepsie Journal*, June 5, 1798; May 25, 1808. See also *Dutchess Observer*, June 1, 1825; *New York Packet*, September 4,

September 11, November 27, 1777; June 28, 1781; *Political Barometer*, July 22, 1806; *Poughkeepsie Journal*, July 24, 1804; June 11, October 8, 1805; June 3, 1807.

32. *New York Packet*, October 30, 1777; July 29, 1779; *Poughkeepsie Journal*, February 12, 1799; *Poughkeepsie Journal*, August 26, 1812; *Republican Herald*, August 26, 1812. Other injuries and distinguishing physical characteristics included missing teeth and vision loss. See *Dutchess Observer*, September 13, 1822; *Political Barometer*, February 4, 1806; March 21, 1810.

33. Berlin, *Many Thousands Gone*, 95–108, 177–94.

34. *Colonial Laws of New York from the Year 1664 to the Revolution*, vol. 1 (Albany: James B. Lyon, 1894), 597–98; McManus, *History of Negro Slavery in New York*, 60–66.

35. "Court Case of Thom, Accused of Murder," 1696. *Hudson River Valley Heritage*, Southeastern New York Library Research Council, accessed January 4, 2016, http://www.hrvh.org/cdm/compoundobject/collection/hhs/id/516/rec/78.

36. "Court of Sessions, September 3, 1707." *Hudson River Valley Heritage*, Southeastern New York Library Research Council, accessed January 4, 2016, http://www.hrvh.org/cdm/compoundobject/collection/hhs/id/338/rec/56. Slave statutes appear in *Colonial Laws*, vol. 1, 519–21, 597–98, 761–67; vol. 2, 310–11, 679–88. For an overview of slave law in New York, see McManus, *History of Negro Slavery in New York*, chap. 5; Carl Nordstrom, "The New York Slave Code," *Afro-Americans in New York Life and History* 4 (January 1980): 7–25; and Edwin Olson, "The Slave Code in Colonial New York," *Journal of Negro History* 29 (April 1944): 147–65.

37. *Colonial Laws*, vol. 1, 582–83; vol. 3, 448–49; McManus, *History of Negro Slavery in New York*, 90–91.

38. *Colonial Laws*, vol. 1, 631.

39. The 1712 law also required a slaveowner to make payments of twenty pounds each year for the duration of the freed slave's life. *Colonial Laws*, vol. 1, 761–67. Subsequent legislation rescinded the annual payment but retained the sizeable two-hundred-pound security. *Colonial Laws*, vol. 1, 922–23; vol. 2, 683.

40. J. Hector St. John de Crevecoeur, *Letters from an American Farmer* (New York: E. P. Dutton, 1912), 164.

41. Hodges, *Root and Branch*, 41–42, 83, 106–10; McKee, *Labor in Colonial New York*, 129–30; McManus, *History of Negro Slavery in New York*, 49–54; White, *Somewhat More Independent*, 149–52.

42. Record of the Overseers of the Poor, Poughkeepsie, New York, 1807–1815, Adriance Memorial Library, Poughkeepsie, New York, 396. Hereafter, Overseers of the Poor.

43. Overseers of the Poor, 130, 322.

44. Overseers of the Poor, 233–34, 327–29.

45. Truth, *Narrative of Sojourner Truth*, xxii–xxiv, 5–9; Carleton Mabee, *Sojourner Truth: Slave, Prophet, Legend* (New York: New York University Press, 1993), 3; Nell Irvin Painter, *Sojourner Truth: A Life, a Symbol* (New York: W.W. Norton & Co., 1996), 11–13.

46. See Greene and Harrington, *American Population*, 96–105.

47. Only fourteen slaveholders in the entire county—comprising merely two percent of slaveowners—owned ten or more slaves. There was little variation in the median size of slaveholdings across towns. The estimate of the proportion of those separated from family members comes from Vivienne L. Kruger, who arrived at comparable figures in the six downstate counties of New York. Kruger, "Born to Run: The Slave Family in Early New York, 1626 to 1827" (PhD dissertation, Columbia University, 1985), 139, 167–76.

48. Truth, *Narrative of Sojourner Truth*, 4.

49. McManus, *History of Negro Slavery in New York*, 66; William D. Piersen, *Black Yankees: The Development of an Afro-American Subculture in Eighteenth-Century New England* (Amherst: University of Massachusetts Press, 1988), 35–36, 93–95.

50. Truth never saw Robert again; the young man died shortly after his marriage, and Isabella herself married a man likely of her master's choosing. Truth, *Narrative of Sojourner Truth*, 22–24; Mabee, *Sojourner Truth*, 5–7; Painter, *Sojourner Truth*, 18–19.

51. Gilbert ostensibly withheld the particulars "from motives of delicacy, and others, because the relation of them might inflict undeserved pain on some now living, whom Isabel remembers only with esteem and love." Truth, *Narrative of Sojourner Truth*, 18. Historians have speculated about the nature of the abuse Truth suffered. See Mabee, *Sojourner Truth*, 8–9; Painter, *Sojourner Truth*, 14–18.

52. Melvin Patrick Ely, *Israel on the Appomattox: A Southern Experiment in Black Freedom from the 1790s through the Civil War* (New York: Alfred A. Knopf, 2004).

53. De Crevecoeur, *Sketches*, 148. Graham Hodges examines community life in the rural environs of New York City in *Root and Branch*, 48–51, 115–16, 220–23. See also Piersen, *Black Yankees*, 25–36.

54. Several advertisements for fugitive slaves included references to musical instruments, notably fiddles and violins. See *New York Journal and General Advertiser*, June 8, 1778; June 5, September 4, 1780; *New York Packet*, January 24, 1782; *Poughkeepsie Journal*, November 17, 1791; October 21, 1795; November 23, 1802; June 11, 1805; February 4, 1806; July 22, 1807. John Pearsall's twenty-one-year-old slave Amos was supposedly "very fond of singing and dancing." *Poughkeepsie Journal*, September 12, 1810.

55. McManus, *History of Negro Slavery in New York*, 97–98.

56. Document 4976, Ancient Documents Collection, 1732–1800, Dutchess County Archives, Poughkeepsie, New York; Henry Noble MacCracken, *Old Dutchess Forever! The Story of an American County* (New York: Hastings House, 1956), 127–28.

57. De Crevecoeur, *Sketches*, 148. See also McManus, *History of Negro Slavery in New York*, 66–67.

58. Stephen sought damages in the amount of two hundred dollars. Document 4185, Ancient Documents Collection.

59. Ancient Documents Collection, October 1792.

60. McManus, *Slavery in New York*, 61–63, 145; Piersen, *Black Yankees*, 29–31; White, *Somewhat More Independent*, 49, 106–11, 149–52.

61. "Abstracts of Wills," *Collections of the New-York Historical Society*, vol. 7 (New York: The Society, 1898), 458–59. Eighteenth-century wills are on file in the New York State Archives in Albany and recorded in *Collections of the New-York Historical Society for the Years 1892–1908*, vols. 1–17 (New York: The Society, 1893–1909).

62. Will Book A, Dutchess County Surrogate's Court, Poughkeepsie, New York, 211; "Abstracts of Wills" (1896), 99–100. Although bequeathed to his master's heirs, Philip Cinceboe's slave Prince enjoyed the right to initiate his own sale if he so desired. "Abstracts of Wills" (1900), 219–20.

63. "Abstracts of Wills" (1898), 429. See also "Abstracts of Wills" (1900), 262–63; (1903), 227–28; (1904), 111–12; Will Book A, 48, 211; and Will Book H, 290–91.

64. "Abstracts of Wills" (1896), 99–100; (1900), 262–63; and Will Book H, 290–91.

65. Truth, *Narrative of Sojourner Truth*, 3.

66. The "slaves' economy" is examined in Ira Berlin and Philip Morgan, eds., *Cultivation and Culture: Labor and the Shaping of Slave Life in the Americas* (Charlottesville: University Press of Virginia, 1993); Ira Berlin and Philip Morgan, eds., *The Slaves' Economy: Independent Production by Slaves in the Americas* (London: Frank Cass, 1991); Larry Hudson, *To Have and to Hold: Slave Work and Family Life in Antebellum South Carolina* (Athens: University of Georgia Press, 1997); Larry Hudson, ed., *Working Toward Freedom: Slave Society and Domestic Economy in the American South* (Rochester: University of Rochester Press, 1994).

67. Document 301, Ancient Documents Collection.

68. "Case of Slave Owners, Accused of Allowing Slaves to Meet," December 29, 1741. *Hudson River Valley Heritage*, Southeastern New York Library Research Council, accessed January 4, 2016, http://www.hrvh.org/cdm/compoundobject/collection/hhs/id/554/show/553/rec/84.

69. Document 572, Ancient Documents Collection.

70. Petition of Slaveholders of Ulster County to the Legislature of the State of New York, December, 28, 1791, Dutchess County Historical Society, Poughkeepsie, New York.

71. For Dutch-speaking slaves, see *New York Packet*, March 1, 1780; *Political Barometer*, February 4, 1806; *Poughkeepsie Journal*, January 25, 1803; July 24, 1804; June 11, October 8, 1805; June 3, 1807. English speakers are advertised in *New York Journal and General Advertiser*, December 21, 1778; May 1, September 4, 1780; *New York Packet*, September 4, 1777; August 20, 1778; September 2, 1779; May 25, 1780; June 28, July 5, August 30, 1781; *Political Barometer*, June 8, 1802; May 14, 1805; December 20, 1809; *Poughkeepsie Journal*, April 27, 1790; November 17,

December 8, 1791; October 21, 1795; June 13, November 21, 1797; June 19, August 21, 1798; July 15, 1800; October 8, 1805; *Republican Herald*, May 3, 1815.

72. *New York Packet*, March 1, 1780. Abraham J. Hardenburgh of New Paltz likewise explained that his fugitive slave Mink was "of Dutch origin" and spoke "that language considerably better than English." *Political Barometer*, February 4, 1806.

73. *Poughkeepsie Journal*, April 25, 1810. For examples of bilingual speakers, see *Country Journal and Poughkeepsie Advertiser*, October 13, 1785; *New York Journal and General Advertiser*, September 7, 1778; September 6, 1779; December 10, 1781; January 6, 1782; *New York Packet*, May 8, July 3, 1777; November 4, 1779; August 24, September 7, September 21, 1780; January 24, February 14, June 27, 1782; August 28, 1783; *Political Barometer*, July 22, 1806; November 16, 1808; April 26, 1809; October 24, 1810; *Poughkeepsie Journal*, September 9, 1788; July 6, 1796; August 20, 1799; June 14, July 19, 1803; July 22, 1807; January 20, 1808; June 22, 1814; June 12, 1816. Mary, the thirty-year-old mulatto slave of Ezekiel Garnsey of Stanford, spoke some French in addition to English. *Political Barometer*, September 12, 1810.

74. *Poughkeepsie Journal*, November 25, 1788; August 18, 1789; June 6, 1797. See also *Political Barometer*, July 22, 1806.

75. *Poughkeepsie Journal*, May 1, 1798; August 4, 1789; August 2, 1803. See also *Dutchess Observer*, July 24, 1822; *Political Barometer*, May 14, 1805; May 27, 1806; *Poughkeepsie Journal*, November 18, 1800; July 19, 1803.

76. *Poughkeepsie Journal*, August 16, 1809.

77. *New York Packet*, February 14, 1782; August 28, 1783.

78. De Crevecoeur, *Sketches*, 148. Gretchen Holbrook Gerzina explores the "negro network" in rural New England in *Mr. and Mrs. Prince: How an Extraordinary Eighteenth-Century Family Moved Out of Slavery and into Legend* (New York: Amistad/Harper Collins, 2008). See also William Piersen, *Black Yankees*. For studies of rural black communities in other settings, see Ely, *Israel on the Appomattox*, and Stephen A. Vincent, *Southern Seed, Northern Soil: African-American Farm Communities in the Midwest, 1765–1900* (Bloomington: Indiana University Press, 1999).

79. Hodges, *Root and Branch*, 53–63, 84–88, 119–28; Horton and Horton, *In Hope of Liberty*, 19–22; McManus, *History of Negro Slavery in New York*, 67–78.

80. Berlin, *Many Thousands Gone*, 182–84, 188–92.

81. *New York Packet*, September 2, 1779; *New York Journal and General Advertiser*, May 1, 1780; *Poughkeepsie Journal*, August 18, 1789. See also *New York Packet*, September 11, 1777.

82. *Republican Herald*, May 3, 1815.

83. Foote, *Black and White Manhattan*, 63–69; Hodges, *Root and Branch*, 38–40, 77–82; Lepore, "The Tightening Vise: Slavery and Freedom in British New York," in *Slavery in New York*, ed. Ira Berlin and Leslie M. Harris (New York: New Press, 2005), 61–62.

84. David Steven Cohen, "In Search of Carolus Africanus Rex: Afro-Dutch

Folklore in New York and New Jersey," *Journal of the Afro-American Historical and Genealogical Society* 5, nos. 3–4 (1984): 151–53; Horton and Horton, *In Hope of Liberty*, 19.

85. Accounts of the 1803 Albany festival come from Shane White, "Pinkster in Albany, 1803: A Contemporary Description," *New York History* 70 (1989): 191–99.

86. Conclusive evidence of Pinkster in Dutchess County does not exist, but circumstantial evidence suggests that the festival was celebrated throughout the Hudson Valley. For interpretations of Pinkster, see Alexander, *African or American?*, 6, 21–22; Berlin, *Many Thousands Gone*, 188–92; Cohen, "In Search of Carolus Africanus Rex," 148–68; Hodges, *Root and Branch*, 87–88, 221–22; Horton and Horton, *In Hope of Liberty*, 22–24, 30–36; Sterling Stuckey, *Slave Culture: Nationalist Theory and the Foundations of Black America* (New York: Oxford, 1987), 73–83; Shane White, "Pinkster: Afro-Dutch Syncretization in New York City and the Hudson Valley," *Journal of American Folklore* 102, no. 403 (January–March 1989), 68–75; White, *Somewhat More Independent*, 95–106; and A. J. Williams-Myers, "Pinkster Carnival: Africanisms in the Hudson River Valley," *Afro-Americans in New York Life and History* 9, no. 1 (1985): 7–17. While scholars such as Leslie Alexander and Sterling Stuckey interpret Pinkster and similar celebrations as inherently African, Shane White argues that the festival represented the syncretization of different cultural forms. William Piersen analyzes black culture and "resistant accommodation" in New England in *Black Yankees*, especially chaps. 10–11.

## Chapter 2. Resistance and Revolution

1. *New York Packet*, June 7, 1781.

2. For an overview of the social impact of the Revolution, see Jack P. Greene, *Understanding the American Revolution: Issues and Actors* (Charlottesville: University Press of Virginia, 1995); Hoffman and Albert, *The Transforming Hand of Revolution*; Nash, *The Unknown American Revolution*; Raphael, *A People's History of the American Revolution*; Alfred F. Young, ed., *The American Revolution: Explorations in the History of American Radicalism* (DeKalb: Northern Illinois University Press, 1976); and Young, ed., *Beyond the American Revolution: Explorations in the History of American Radicalism* (DeKalb: Northern Illinois University Press, 1993). Titles on the African American experience during the period include Herbert Aptheker, *The Negro in the American Revolution* (New York: International, 1940); Ira Berlin and Ronald Hoffman, eds., *Slavery and Freedom in the Age of the American Revolution* (Charlottesville: University Press of Virginia, 1983); Douglas R. Egerton, *Death or Liberty: African Americans and Revolutionary America* (New York: Oxford University Press, 2009); Philip S. Foner, *Blacks in the American Revolution* (Westport: Greenwood Press, 1975); Sylvia R. Frey, *Water from the Rock: Black Resistance in a Revolutionary*

*Age* (Princeton: Princeton University Press, 1991); Alan Gilbert, *Black Patriots and Loyalists: Fighting for Emancipation in the War for Independence* (Chicago: University of Chicago Press, 2012); Daniel C. Littlefield, *Revolutionary Citizens: African Americans, 1776–1804* (New York: Oxford University Press, 1997); Sidney Kaplan and Emma Nogrady Kaplan, *The Black Presence in the Era of the American Revolution*, revised ed. (Amherst: University of Massachusetts Press, 1989); Gary B. Nash, *Race and Revolution* (Madison: Madison House, 1990); and Benjamin Quarles, *The Negro in the American Revolution* (Chapel Hill: University of North Carolina Press, 1961).

3. Woolman visited Dutchess in 1747 and probably subsequent occasions. *The Journal of John Woolman* (London: Headley Brothers, 1903), 62; Warren H. Wilson, *Quaker Hill: A Sociological Study* (New York: n.p., 1907), 25. For an introduction to slavery and the Society of Friends, see Thomas E. Drake, *Quakers and Slavery in America* (Gloucester: Peter Smith, 1965) (orig. published 1950); Jean R. Soderlund, *Quakers and Slavery: A Divided Spirit* (Princeton: Princeton University Press, 1985); and Zilversmit, *The First Emancipation*, 55–83.

4. Oblong Monthly Meeting, Men's Minutes, 1757–1781, microfilm, LDS 0017315, 36, 37, 39, 41, 42, 57.

5. Oblong Monthly Meeting, 126, 127, 128, 132, 133–34, 136, 138, 140, 141, 142, 143, 144, 145, 147, 150, 155, 158–59, 163, 164, 166, 182, 185. The outcome of the case against Benjamin Lapham is unknown.

6. Oblong Monthly Meeting, 212: Drake, *Quakers and Slavery*, 80–81; Dell T. Upton, "Dutchess County Quakers and Slavery," *Yearbook*, Dutchess County Historical Society 55 (1970): 55–57; Warren H. Wilson, *Quaker Hill in the Eighteenth Century*, 2nd ed. (Quaker Hill: Quaker Hill Conference Association, 1905), 27; Zilversmit, *First Emancipation*, 80–83.

7. Oblong Monthly Meeting, 258.

8. Nine Partners Monthly Meeting, Men's Minutes, 1769–1779, vol. 1153, microfilm, LDS 17307, 4, 6, 7, 8, 9.

9. Upon appeal, the Quarterly Meeting ordered Nathan's reinstatement but upheld the judgment against his son. Oblong Monthly Meeting, 273, 274, 276, 277, 279, 280, 281, 283, 285, 286, 288, 292, 294, 295, 304–05.

10. While a few younger slaves in the record were already in their mid- to late teens, others, such as ten-year-old Isabel, nine-year-old Jane, and eight-year-old Nathaniel, had several years to serve. Nine Partners Monthly Meeting, 77, 111, 115, 176, 179, 226, 240, 242; Nine Partners Vital Records, 1769–1798, microfilm, LDS 0017311, 186–204. Manumissions are excerpted in Josephine C. Frost, comp., *Quaker Marriages, Births, Deaths, and Slaves, Nine Partners Monthly Meeting, Dutchess County, New York* (Brooklyn: n.p., 1910), and Jean D. Worden, comp., "Quaker Manumission, Nine Partners, Dutchess County, New York," *Journal of the Afro-American Historical and Genealogical Society* 3 (Fall 1982).

11. See Nine Partners Monthly Meeting, 21, 30, 35, 41, 45, 49, 53, 57, 61, 67, 75, 82, 89, 95, 101, 110, 115, 116, 126, 132, 142, 157, 166, 170, 181, 188, 190,

199, 201, 211, 218, 226, 227, 232, 234, 237, 240, 248, 257, 266, 275; Nine Partners Monthly Meeting, Men's Minutes, 1779–1783, vol. 67, microfilm, LDS 0017309, April, July, October 1779; January, April, July, October 1780; July, October 1781; January, April, July, October 1782; January, April 1783; Oblong Monthly Meeting, 162, 188, 201, 258, 263a, 272, 275, 299, 308, 315, 320, 329, 334, 338, 344, 349, 357, 374, 382, 393, 397, 411, 416, 417, 421, 427, 432, 438, 443, 448, 453, 459, 470, 485, 496, 502, 510, 519, 527.

12. Philip H. Smith, *General History of Duchess County, from 1609 to 1876, Inclusive* (Pawling: The Author, 1877), 53.

13. For a note on the geographic isolation of eastern and southern parts of the county, see Henry Noble MacCracken, *Blithe Dutchess: The Flowering of an American Community from 1812* (New York: Hastings House, 1958), 143; Wilson, *Quaker Hill: A Sociological Study*, 8–9.

14. See Zilversmit, *The First Emancipation*, 169–70.

15. In 1763, John Roon of Beekman emancipated his slave Richard and bequeathed to him a horse, saddle, bridle, and clothing. Three years later, Jonathan Austen of the Philipse Patent (in what is now Putnam County) granted liberty to his slave along with a gift of twenty-five pounds. No other testator included similar provisions in his or her will until 1783. Will Book AA, 42; "Abstracts of Wills," 134. Eighteenth-century wills on file in the New York State Archives are abstracted in *Collections of the New-York Historical Society for the Years 1892–1908*, vols. 1–17.

16. "Abstracts of Wills" (1900), 223, 287–88; Will Book AA, 51–52.

17. Edward Countryman, *A People in Revolution: The American Revolution and Political Society in New York, 1760–1790* (Baltimore: Johns Hopkins University Press, 1981), 244, 248–49; *Journals of the Provincial Congress, Provincial Convention, Committee of Safety and Council of Safety of the State of New York, 1775–1777*, vol. 1 (Albany: Thurlow Reed, 1842), 887, 889.

18. *Political Barometer*, February 15, 1809.

19. *Poughkeepsie Journal*, November 21, 1797.

20. *Poughkeepsie Journal*, January 28, 1798. Other references to alcohol abuse appear in *New York Journal and General Advertiser*, June 5, 1780; *Political Barometer*, September 12, 1810; *Poughkeepsie Journal*, September 7, 1802.

21. *Colonial Laws of New York*, vol. 1, 520.

22. Herbert Aptheker, *American Negro Slave Revolts*, 5th ed. (New York: International, 1983), 169–73; Hodges, *Root and Branch*, 63–68; Kenneth Scott, "The Slave Insurrection in New York in 1712," *New York Historical Society Quarterly* 45, no. 1 (January 1961): 43–74.

23. O'Callaghan, *Documents Relative to the Colonial History of the State of New York*, vol. 5, 461.

24. *Colonial Laws of New York*, vol. 2, 679–88.

25. The alleged 1741 conspiracy is the subject of Thomas J. Davis, *A Rumor of Revolt: The "Great Negro Plot" in Colonial New York* (New York: Free Press,

1985), and Jill Lepore, *New York Burning: Liberty, Slavery, and Conspiracy in Eighteenth-Century Manhattan* (New York: Alfred A. Knopf, 2005).

26. "Lieutenant Governor George Clarke to the Justices of the Peace for Dutchess County in General Quarter Sessions, 26 January 1741," Document 301, Ancient Documents Collection.

27. Singer, "The Livingstons as Slave Owners," 81–82.

28. MacCracken, *Old Dutchess Forever!*, 125; A. J. Williams-Myers, "The African Presence in the Mid-Hudson Valley before 1800: A Preliminary Historiographical Sketch," *Afro-Americans in New York Life and History* 8 (January 1984): 33. See also McDermott, *Dutchess County's Plain Folks*, 129–31; and Williams-Myers, *Long Hammering*, 45–48.

29. Ancient Documents Collection, January 1774.

30. William J. Allinson, *Memoir of Quamino Buccau, A Pious Methodist* (Philadelphia: Henry Longstreth, 1851), 4–5.

31. "Negro Plot in Ulster County, 1775," Kingston Senate House, Kingston, New York; Williams-Myers, *Long Hammering*, 58–59; Peter H. Wood, "'The Dream Deferred': Black Freedom Struggles on the Eve of White Independence," in *In Resistance: Studies in African, Caribbean, and Afro-American History*, ed. Gary Y. Okihiro (Amherst: University of Massachusetts Press, 1986), 173; Wood, "'Liberty Is Sweet': African-American Freedom Struggles in the Years before White Independence," in *Beyond the American Revolution: Explorations in the History of American Radicalism*, ed. Alfred Young (DeKalb: Northern Illinois University Press), 163.

32. Jonathan C. Clark, "A Government to Form: The Story of Dutchess County and the Political Upheaval in Revolutionary New York," in *From English Colony to Sovereign State: Essays on the American Revolution in Dutchess County, New York*, ed. Richard B. Morris, Jonathan C. Clark, and Charlotte Cunningham (Millbrook: Dutchess County American Bicentennial Committee, 1983), 73.

33. Williams-Myers, "The African Presence in the Hudson River Valley," 84; Williams-Myers, *Long Hammering*, 47.

34. *New York in the Revolution as Colony and State*, compiled by the Office of the State Comptroller, vol. 1 (Albany: J. B. Lyon Company, 1904), 11.

35. The military struggle for the valley is explored in Lincoln Diamant, *Chaining the Hudson: The Fight for the River in the American Revolution* (New York: Fordham University Press, 2004), and James M. Johnson, Christopher Pryslopski, and Andrew Villani, eds., *Key to the North Country: The Hudson River Valley in the American Revolution* (Albany: State University of New York Press, 2013).

36. See Countryman, *A People in Revolution*, 15–34, 47–55, 72–85, 104–16, 149–50; Thomas J. Humphrey, *Land and Liberty: Hudson Valley Riots in the Age of Revolution* (DeKalb: Northern Illinois University Press, 2004); Sung Bok Kim, "Impact of Class Relations and Warfare in the American Revolution: The

New York Experience," *Journal of American History* 69 (1982): 326–46; Staughton Lynd, *Anti-Federalism in Dutchess County, New York: A Study of Democracy and Class Conflict in the Revolutionary Era* (Chicago: Loyola University Press, 1962); Lynd, "Who Should Rule at Home? Dutchess County, New York, in the American Revolution," in Lynd, *Class Conflict, Slavery, and the United States Constitution* (New York: Bobbs-Merrill Company, 1967), 25–34, 55–61; and Thomas Wermuth, "The Central Hudson Valley: Dutchess, Orange, and Ulster Counties," in *The Other New York: The American Revolution beyond New York City, 1763–1787*, ed. Joseph S. Tiedemann and Eugene R. Fingerhut (Albany: State University of New York Press, 2005), 127–54.

37. Jonathan Clark, "The Problem of Allegiance in Revolutionary Poughkeepsie," in *Saints and Revolutionaries: Essays on Early American History*, ed. David D. Hall, John M. Murrin, and Thad W. Tate (New York: W.W. Norton & Co., 1984), 288–89; Peter Force, comp., *American Archives, Fourth Series*, vol. 1 (Washington, DC: M. St. Clair Clarke and Peter Force, 1837), 702–03. The Dutchess County Association adopted a similarly cautious position five months later. "A Number of Inhabitants of Dutchess County" committed themselves to defending life, liberty, and property but simultaneously vowed "to promote, encourage, and, when called upon, enforce obedience to the rightful authority of our most gracious Sovereign King George the Third." *American Archives, Fourth Series*, vol. 1, 1164.

38. With sword drawn, the Loyalist sheriff threatened to arrest radical town supervisor Zephaniah Platt for treason. Not to be intimidated, Platt grabbed a club and vowed to beat the sheriff if he tried. *American Archives, Fourth Series*, vol. 2 (Washington, DC: 1839), 176; Clark, "The Problem of Allegiance in Poughkeepsie," 290.

39. *American Archives, Fourth Series*, vol. 3 (Washington, DC: 1840), 596–608; Countryman, *A People in Revolution*, 150–51; Smith, *History of Dutchess County*, 130–31.

40. *American Archives, Fourth Series*, vol. 3, 457–59, 466–67, 1312–14, 1719–20; vol. 4 (Washington, DC: 1843), 187–88, 389–90, 403, 1117–18, 1719–20; vol. 5 (Washington, DC: 1844), 291, 968, 1402, 1459; and vol. 6 (Washington, DC: 1846), 1415, 1424–26, 1429; Countryman, *A People in Revolution*, 150–51; *New York in Revolution as Colony and State*, vol. 2, 137, 141–42; and Lynd, "Who Should Rule at Home?," 34–37.

41. *American Archives, Fourth Series*, vol. 5, 898; Peter Force, comp., *American Archives, Fifth Series*, 3 vols. (Washington, DC: M. St. Clair Clarke and Peter Force, 1848, 1851, 1853), vol. 1, 1542; vol. 2, 663, 697, 950; vol. 3, 215, 229, 316, 603.

42. *American Archives, Fifth Series*, vol. 1, 355–57, 360, 1408.

43. *American Archives, Fifth Series*, vol. 3, 231–32; Humphrey, *Land and Liberty*, 91–107; Cynthia A. Kierner, "Landlord and Tenant in Revolutionary New York: The Case of Livingston Manor," *New York History* 70 (1989): 133–52; Kim, "Impact of Class Relations and Warfare in the American Revolution," 326–46;

Lynd, "The Tenant Rising at Livingston Manor, May 1777," in Lynd, *Class Conflict, Slavery, and the United States Constitution* (New York: Bobbs-Merrill Company, 1967), 63–77; James Smith, *History of Dutchess County*, 130, 312–13; Philip Smith, *General History of Duchess County*, 53–56, 326.

44. "Minutes of the Committee and of the First Commission for Detecting Conspiracies in the State of New York, December 11, 1776–September 23, 1778," 2 vols., *Collections of the New-York Historical Society*, vols. 57 and 58 (New York: 1924, 1925); Countryman, *A People in Revolution*, 144, 151–54, 180–83; Humphrey, *Land and Liberty*, 107–10; James Smith, *History of Dutchess County*, 129–42, 175–76, 181–82, 312–13, 467, 510–11, 539, 546, 552, 558; Philip Smith, *General History of Duchess County*, 120–24, 141, 155, 187–91, 196–97, 219–21, 229–31, 261–64, 267–73, 326, 345, 416, 442–43; Wermuth, "The Central Hudson Valley," 135–41.

45. Runaway advertisements were extracted from the *New York Journal and General Advertiser* (1777–1783) and the *New York Packet* (1776–1783), both of which had been printed previously in New York City. In the wake of the British occupation of New York in the late summer of 1776, the *Journal and General Advertiser* resumed publication first in Kingston and then in Poughkeepsie. Samuel Loudon, printer of the *New York Packet*, fled to Fishkill in 1776. Both newspapers returned to the city at the end of the war. I have included runaways from Dutchess and Ulster Counties, as well as northern Orange and Westchester Counties and southern Albany County. For a broader context, see Billy G. Smith, "Runaway Slaves in the Mid-Atlantic Region during the Revolutionary Era," in Hoffman and Albert, *Transforming Hand of Revolution*, 199–230.

46. Slaveowners surmised the motivations and destinations of their runaway slaves in only fifteen cases, but eleven of those fugitives were alleged to have made a break for freedom. For a discussion of the complicated motivations of runways during the Revolution, see Smith, "Runaway Slaves in the Mid-Atlantic Region," in *The Transforming Hand of Revolution: Reconsidering the American Revolution as a Social Movement* (Charlottesville: University Press of Virginia, 1995), 214–24, and White, *Somewhat More Independent*, 126–31.

47. *New York Journal and General Advertiser*, June 5, 1780; *New York Packet*, June 15, 1780; *New York Journal and General Advertiser*, January 6, 1782. Nineteen of the sixty runaways in the sample (31.7%) were reported to have taken additional clothing.

48. *New York Journal and General Advertiser*, August 9, 1779.

49. *New York Packet*, October 23, 1777.

50. *New York Packet*, November 4, 1779; August 24, 1780.

51. The black Loyalist experience is explored in Gilbert, *Black Patriots and Loyalists*; Cassandra Pybus, *Epic Journeys of Freedom: Runaway Slaves of the American Revolution and Their Global Quest for Liberty* (Boston: Beacon Press, 2006); Quarles, *The Negro in the American Revolution*, 19–32, 111–81; James W. St. G. Walker, *The Black Loyalists: The Search for a Promised Land in Nova Scotia and Sierra Leone, 1783–1870* (New York: Dalhousie University Press, 1976); and Ellen Gibson Wilson, *The Loyal Blacks* (New York: G. P. Putnam's Sons, 1976).

52. *New York Journal and General Advertiser*, May 1, June 5, June 12, July 17, and September 4, 1780; *New York Packet*, September 2, November 4, 1779; May 11, May 25, 1780; June 7, June 28, 1781.

53. *New York Journal and General Advertiser*, July 17, 1780.

54. *New York Journal and General Advertiser*, May 1, 1780.

55. *New York Packet*, September 2, 1779.

56. "Minutes of the Committee and First Commission for Detecting Conspiracies," vol. 1, 57–59, 88–89, 271–72, 292; *Calendar of Historical Manuscripts Relating to the War of the Revolution*, vol. 2, 113–15, 120–25; Philip Smith, *General History of Duchess County*, 262–63.

57. "Minutes of the Committee and First Commission for Detecting Conspiracies," vol. 2, 443–44.

58. "Minutes of the Committee and First Commission for Detecting Conspiracies," vol. 1, 202; Quarles, *Negro in the American Revolution*, 105–108. For examples of African Americans arrested or incarcerated by the Committee and Commission for Detecting Conspiracies, see "Minutes of the Committee and First Commission for Detecting Conspiracies," vol. 1, 57–59, 70, 88–89, 169, 178–79, 270, 271–72, 279, 287, 292; vol. 2, 340–41.

59. Philip Smith, *General History of Duchess County*, 262–63.

60. The experience of black Loyalists in the New York City region is explored in Graham Hodges, "Black Revolt in New York City and the Neutral Zone: 1775–1783," in *New York in the Age of the Constitution, 1775–1800*, ed. Paul A. Gilje and William Pencak (Rutherford: Farleigh Dickinson University Press, 1992), 20–47; Hodges, *Root and Branch*, 139–61; Hodges, *Slavery and Freedom in the Rural North*, 91–112; and Judith L. Van Buskirk, *Generous Enemies: Patriots and Loyalists in Revolutionary New York* (Philadelphia: University of Pennsylvania Press, 2002), 129–54.

61. Raphael, *People's History of the American Revolution*, 326–41; Van Buskirk, *Generous Enemies*, 139–41.

62. "Minutes of the Committee and First Commission for Detecting Conspiracies," vol. 1, 265.

63. Henry D. B. Bailey, *Local Tales and Historical Sketches* (Fishkill Landing: J. W. Spaight, 1874), 67–69; MacCracken, *Old Dutchess Forever!*, 128; Philip Smith, *General History of Dutchess County*, 199–200; and A. J. Williams-Myers, "The African (American) in the Mid-Hudson Valley before 1800: Some Historiographical Clues," in *Transformations of an American County: Dutchess County, New York, 1683–1983*, ed. Joyce C. Ghee (Poughkeepsie: Dutchess County Historical Society, 1986), 110.

64. Aptheker, *Negro in the American Revolution*, 30–31; *Calendar of Historical Manuscripts Relating to the War of the Revolution*, vol. 1, 489; *Laws of the State of New York*, 4th Session, Chapter 32; *New York in Revolution as Colony and State*, vol. 1, 11; Quarles, *Negro in the American Revolution*, 7–18.

65. *New York in Revolution as Colony and State*, vol. 1, 145, 187–88; Quarles, *Negro in the American Revolution*, 8–9; Williams-Myers, "The Arduous Journey,"

24–28; Benjamin Myer Brink, *The Early History of Saugerties, 1660–1825* (Kingston: R. W. Anderson & Son, 1902), 349–52; Alphonso T. Clearwater, ed., *The History of Ulster County, New York* (Kingston: W. J. Van Deusen, 1907), 297.

66. Aptheker, *Negro in the American Revolution*, 30.

67. *New York Packet*, July 16, 1778.

68. Quarles, *Negro in American Revolution*, 94–100; Williams-Myers, "Arduous Journey," 28. Any member of the Dutchess County militia drafted to work on the erection of the Fishkill barracks could hire an able-bodied "Man or Negro" in his stead. *Calendar of Historical Manuscripts Relating to the War of the Revolution*, vol. 1, 489.

69. *New York Packet*, July 17, 1783.

70. Captain Archibald Anderson took out an advertisement in the *New York Packet* requesting the master of the boy to "come and pay the charges, and take him away." *New York Packet*, September 17, 1778.

71. *New York Packet*, September 5, 1782.

72. A variety of different and often competing considerations informed individual decisions. See Michael Kammen, "The American Revolution as a *Crise de Conscience*: The Case of New York," in *Society, Freedom, Conscience: The American Revolution in Virginia, Massachusetts, and New York*, ed. Richard Jellison (New York: W.W. Norton & Company, 1976), 125–89.

73. "Minutes of the Committee and First Commission for Detecting Conspiracies," vol. 2, 376–87. Jonathan Clark also discusses the episode in "A Government to Form," 73–74.

74. *New York Journal and General Advertiser*, December 21, 1778; *New York Packet*, January 21, 1779; *New York Journal and General Advertiser*, February 14, 1782.

75. *New York Journal and General Advertiser*, December 10, 1781; *New York Packet*, December 10, 1778.

76. *New York Journal and General Advertiser*, October 11, 1779.

77. *New York Packet*, June 17, 1779.

78. *New York Packet*, October 30, 1777. Charles Cullen of the Southeast Precinct described his forty-year-old fugitive as "artful and plausible." December 16, 1779.

79. *New York Journal and General Advertiser*, June 5, June 12, 1780; *New York Packet*, June 8, 1780.

80. *New York Packet*, November 27, 1777; *New York Journal and General Advertiser*, September 7, 1778; September 6, 1779; *New York Packet*, September 9, 1779.

81. *Calendar of Historical Manuscripts Relating to the War of the Revolution*, vol. 1, 642–43.

82. Hodges, *Root and Branch*, 155–56; Van Buskirk, *Generous Enemies*, 174–75.

83. Graham Hodges, ed., *The Black Loyalist Directory: African Americans in Exile after the Revolution* (New York: Garland, 1996), 18, 22, 30, 37, 50, 51, 59, 95, 98, 99, 163, 164, 174, 188, 195, 211. Although younger men comprised an

overwhelming majority of fugitive slaves during the war years, women constituted more than forty percent of black emigrants leaving the port of New York in 1783. Hodges, *The Black Loyalist Directory*, xx.

84. The ordeal of black Loyalists after the war is explored in Mary Beth Norton, "The Fate of Some Black Loyalists of the American Revolution," *Journal of Negro History* 58 (1973): 402–26; Walker, *Black Loyalists*; and Wilson, *The Loyal Blacks*.

## Chapter 3. The Ordeal of Emancipation

1. *New York Journal and General Advertiser*, September 4, 1780; *New York Packet*, September 7, 1780; Will Book A, Dutchess County Surrogate's Court, Poughkeepsie, New York, 260.

2. Arthur Zilversmit provides an overview of northern emancipation in *The First Emancipation*. For New York, see Gellman, *Emancipating New York*; Patrick Rael, "The Long Death of Slavery," in *Slavery in New York*, ed. Ira Berlin and Leslie M. Harris (New York: Free Press, 2005), chap. 4; and White, *Somewhat More Independent*. Gary B. Nash and Jean R. Soderlund analyze the Pennsylvania experience in *Freedom by Degrees: Emancipation in Pennsylvania and Its Aftermath* (New York: Oxford University Press, 1991). For New England, see Melish, *Disowning Slavery*. James J. Gigantino II explores the conservatism of emancipation in New Jersey in *The Ragged Road to Abolition*. The classic text that analyzes the paradox of slavery and freedom in the American experience is Edmund Morgan, *American Slavery, American Freedom* (New York: W.W. Norton & Company, 1975). Larry Tise examines conservative reaction and the defense of slavery in *The American Counterrevolution: A Retreat from Liberty, 1783–1800* (Mechanicsburg: Stockpole Books, 1998) and *Proslavery: A History of the Defense of Slavery in America, 1701–1840* (Athens: University of Georgia Press, 1987).

3. Gellman, *Emancipating New York*, 48–49; *Journal of the Senate of the State of New York*, 1785, Eighth Session, Second Meeting (New York: S. Loudon, 1785), 8, 15, 20–21, 22–23.

4. "Petition of the Subscribers, Freeholders, and Inhabitants of the Townships of Rochester, Marble, and Hurley, in the County of Ulster to His Excellency the Governor, the Honourable Senate and General Assembly, of the State of New York, March 31, 1785," State Senate House, Kingston, New York.

5. Four of five Dutchess County assemblymen who voted on Burr's amendment—Brinton Paine, Cornelius Humphrey, Matthew Patterson, and James Tallmadge—voted against immediate abolition. The fifth representative, "Mr. Brinckerhoff" (two Brinckerhoffs from Dutchess, Abraham and Dirck, sat in the assembly's eighth session) joined all four of his colleagues from neighboring Ulster County in voting in the affirmative as a ploy to defeat the measure.

Among the Dutchess County delegation, only Brinton Paine opposed all of the provisions that restricted the civil rights of freedpersons. On the final tally, four of the five Dutchess representatives voted for abolition with restrictions, while Mr. Brinckerhoff joined the four Ulster assemblymen in rejecting abolition in any form. See *Journal of the Assembly of the State of New York*, 1785, Eighth Session, Second Meeting (New York: S. Loudon, 1785), 14–15, 48, 49, 53–54, 55, 56, 57, 59, 62–63, 64.

6. Gellman, *Emancipating New York*, 48–53; McManus, *A History of Negro Slavery in New York*, 162–65; Rael, "Long Death of Slavery," 121–24; Zilversmit, *First Emancipation*, 146–52. In the assembly, Paine and Humphrey voted to override, but Brinckerhoff again joined his Ulster colleagues in rejecting the motion. *Journal of the Assembly*, 1785, 76, 77, 84, 119, 120; *Journal of the Senate*, 1785, 39, 42, 45, 47, 55–56, 63.

7. After 1785, any slaveholder wishing to emancipate a slave could forego paying the requisite bond if the local overseers of the poor and two justices of the peace verified that the slave was less than fifty years of age and unlikely to become a public charge. *Laws of the State of New York*, 8th Session, Chapter 68; Zilversmit, *First Emancipation*, 150–51. Until 1801, slaveowners who desired to manumit slaves older than fifty years of age had to post bond. They could avoid doing so after that date, but they or their heirs remained liable for the maintenance of former slaves in the event of illness or old age. *Laws of the State of New York*, 24th Session, Chapter 188. After 1809, a slaveholder could avoid all financial liability if the parents of a manumitted slave assumed legal responsibility for his or her care. *Laws of the State of New York*, 32nd Session, Chapter 44.

8. *Laws of the State of New York*, 9th Session, Chapter 58. See also *Laws of the State of New York*, 15th Session, Chapter 17; 39th Session, Chapter 45.

9. *Laws of the State of New York*, 11th Session, Chapter 40. David Gellman examines the New York Manumission Society and the political and legal battles of the 1780s in *Emancipating New York*, chap. 4.

10. Gellman, *Emancipating New York*, chaps. 5–8.

11. *Journal of the Assembly*, 1799, Twenty-second Session, Second Meeting (Albany: 1799), 47, 49, 77–79, 80–81, 93–95, 99; *Journal of the Senate*, 1799, Twenty-second Session, Second Meeting (Albany: 1799), 41, 43, 76, 107, 108, 109, 113, 117; Zilversmit, *First Emancipation*, 177–84.

12. The legislature revised the 1799 statute only slightly in 1801. *Laws of the State of New York*, 24th Session, Chapter 188.

13. *Laws of the State of New York*, 22nd Session, Chapter 62; Zilversmit, *First Emancipation*, 181–84; Town of Beekman Record Book, 1772–1827, Dutchess County Archives, Poughkeepsie, New York, 405–06. David Gellman has argued that the abandonment provision stemmed less from a desire to compensate slaveholders and more from mounting public anxiety over black poverty. Gellman, *Emancipating New York*, 182. The state originally remunerated local overseers of the poor up to three dollars and fifty cents for each abandoned

child. Spiraling costs quickly forced the legislature to reduce payments in 1801 and again in 1802. The state suspended such compensation altogether in 1804. *Laws of the State of New York*, 22nd Session, Chapter 62; 24th Session, Chapter 188; 25th Session, Chapter 52; 27th Session, Chapter 40.

14. See Gigantino, *The Ragged Road to Abolition*, chap. 4.

15. The decrease in the number of slaves between 1810 and 1820 is attributable in part to the organization of Putnam County from the southernmost towns of Dutchess in 1812. Excluding the five towns in 1810 that eventually comprised Putnam County, the rate of decline during the decade was thirty-six percent. The 1820 federal manuscript census, the first to delineate African Americans by sex and age, included 289 "slaves" less than fourteen years of age. Under state law, all children born of slaves after July 4, 1799, were theoretically free, but their categorization in the census as slaves suggests that their condition was not substantively different from that of their mothers.

16. Calculations do not include those towns that separated from Dutchess to form Putnam County in 1812.

17. The actual number of households with slaves in the county in 1800 was almost certainly larger. Unfortunately, the poor quality of the second manuscript census renders parts of the document illegible.

18. Eighteen of sixty-one wills dated between 1783 and 1799 and thirty-four of fifty wills dated between 1800 and 1820 mentioning slaves included articles of manumission. I have examined Dutchess County wills in the New York State Archives in Albany, which are also recorded in "Abstracts of Wills" *Collections of the New-York Historical_Society*, vols. 1–18 (New York: The Society, 1892–1909), and Will Books AA–H, Dutchess County Surrogate's Court, Poughkeepsie, New York.

19. Records of the Town of Poughkeepsie Precinct, 1769–1831, Adriance Memorial Library, Poughkeepsie, New York.

20. Will Book E, 1–2. For similar examples, see Will Book A, 189, 312; Will Book B, 239, 347, 619, 630; Will Book C, 98, 339, 389; Will Book E, 204; Will Book F, 183, 378.

21. Will Book B, 491; Will Book C, 530. The average age of emancipated slaves in records for six Dutchess County towns (Beekman, Carmel, Clinton, Poughkeepsie, Rhinebeck, and Stanford) between 1785 and 1826 was 27.2 years (28.0 years for males and 26.6 years for females). Men and women between twenty and twenty-nine years of age comprised the single largest group of emancipated slaves (forty percent of all manumissions), followed by slaves in their thirties (twenty-seven percent). Eighteen younger slaves under twenty years of age comprised just under twenty-percent of manumissions; thirteen slaves forty years and older constituted only thirteen percent. A total of 191 slaves (101 men and 90 women) appear in town records. Clerks typically recorded that a slave in question was less than forty-five or fifty years of age and capable of self-support, but they specified the ages of manumitted slaves in ninety-five

cases. Manumissions were compiled from Marilyn Cole Greene, comp., *Town Minutes, Town of Carmel, Putnam County, New York, 1795–1839* (Rhinebeck: Kinship Press, 1990); William McDermott, ed., *Eighteenth-Century Documents of the Nine Partners Patent*, compiled by Clifford Buck and William McDermott, Collections of the Dutchess County Historical Society, vol. 10 (Baltimore: Gateway Press, 1979); Records of the Town of Poughkeepsie Precinct, 1769–1831, Adriance Memorial Library, Poughkeepsie, New York; "Record of Slaves, Rhinebeck, New York," Rhinebeck Historical Society, Rhinebeck, New York; Rhinebeck Town Records, 1748–1863, microfilm, Starr Library, Rhinebeck, New York; Town of Beekman Record Book, 1772–1827, Dutchess County Archives, Poughkeepsie, New York; Town of Stanford Records, 1793–1824, microfilm, 2 reels, Stanford Free Library, Stanfordville, New York. Records break down as follows: Beekman (26 manumissions, 1785–1825), Carmel (6 manumissions, 1798–1807), Clinton (29 manumissions, 1791–1817), Poughkeepsie (82 manumissions, 1790–1826), Rhinebeck (40 manumissions, 1794–1826), and Stanford (8 manumissions, 1805–1824).

22. Slaves under twenty years of age accounted for just under one in five manumissions in town records, typically older adolescents capable of self-support or minors liberated upon the manumission of their parents. On April 21, 1800, Thomas Casey freed Prince and Countess, both in their thirties, and seven younger slaves ranging in age from two to sixteen—presumably their children. Records of the Poughkeepsie Precinct, 44. When Joseph Gregory of Carmel emancipated his female slave Angelese in 1798, he also freed Rose and Dina, aged six and three. Greene, *Town Minutes, Town of Carmel*, 10. Excluding "manumissions" of children born after July 4, 1799, that were more accurately releases from bound service, the average age of manumitted slaves would be even older. In some cases, slaveholders provided for the education or training of slave children prior to releasing them. Stephen Purdy of Fishkill instructed that his young slave Harry was to be apprenticed in a trade before being liberated at age twenty-four. Will Book C, 88. Israel Smith of Poughkeepsie similarly ordered the indenture of his slave boy Harry until his twenty-first birthday. Will Book AA, 123. Zacharias Van Voorhis of the Rombout Precinct expressed concern for his slaves' spiritual welfare as well as their temporal well-being. Explicitly commissioning his executors to serve as the moral and spiritual guardians of his "negro children," Van Voorhis instructed them to bind out five young slaves—Charles, Nick, Tom, Ab, and Peg—"to such of my relations . . . as will use them well, [and] will engage to teach them . . . to read Scriptures until such time they arrive at lawful age, when my said Negro Children . . . are to have their freedom." "Abstracts of Wills," (1903), 247–248. Van Voorhis composed his will sixteen years before the passage of the 1799 law.

23. Town of Beekman Record Book, 403.

24. Will Book C, 451–452; Will Book E, 323. Will Book B, 564.

25. Will Book C, 270.

26. Will Book AA, 148, 255–57; Will Book A, 247.

27. Will Book B, 239. For similar examples, see Will Book D, 600; Will Book F, 226; and Will Book H, 390–91.

28. "Abstracts of Wills" (1903), 247–48.

29. Will Book D, 532.

30. Will Book B, 121.

31. Will Book A, 312.

32. Rhinebeck Town Records, June, 26, 1806; January 27, 1814; Population Schedules of the Third Census of the United States, 1810, roll 30, New York (Washington, DC: 1968), 296.

33. Records of the Poughkeepsie Precinct, 61, 70, 105. See also the case of John Frear in Records of the Poughkeepsie Precinct, 26, 78.

34. Will Book C, 81–82.

35. Will Book C, 29–30. For similar examples, see Will Book AA, 123–24; Will Book A, 164–65, 392–93; Will Book B, 562–64; Will Book C, 29–30, 189–90, 339, 451–52, 530–31; Will Book E, 147–49. Even Zacharias Van Voorhis, who made such a ritual display of his magnanimity when ordering the immediate manumission of four adult slaves, did not hesitate to bequeath four others to a nephew. "Abstracts of Wills" (1903), 247–48.

36. Records of the Poughkeepsie Precinct, 27, 29, 67.

37. Will Book C, 422.

38. Records of the Poughkeepsie Precinct, 67–68, 74, 110; Population Schedules of the Third Census, 1810, 172.

39. Population Schedules of the Fourth Census of the United States, 1820, roll 71, New York, vol. 10 (Washington, DC: 1959), 123.

40. *Poughkeepsie Journal*, September 23 and October 7, 1795.

41. *Poughkeepsie Journal*, November 30, 1802.

42. *Political Barometer*, November 22, 1803. Another young woman's desire to be with her husband in Poughkeepsie compelled her owner to put her up for sale in 1812. *Poughkeepsie Journal*, January 8, 1812.

43. Will Book AA, 123; Will Book D, 192; Will Book F, 225–26. Sarah, who was lame, also received support and maintenance from Pendleton's estate.

44. *Poughkeepsie Journal*, August 6, 1799; March 25, 1800.

45. *Poughkeepsie Journal*, March 27, 1798. For similar examples, see *Poughkeepsie Journal*, March 1, 1792; August 14, 1798; and February 18, 1800.

46. *Poughkeepsie Journal*, November 8, 1803. For similar examples, see *New York Journal and General Advertiser*, April 19, 1779; March 27, June 19, 1780; November 12, 1781; *New York Packet*, July 8, August 19, 1779; August 31, September 7, 1780; January 31, May 2, November 14, 1782; August 14, 1783; *Poughkeepsie Journal*, October 13, 1785; February 18, 1795; December 21, 1796; March 8, April 19, May 30, 1797; March 13, April 3, 1798; August 6, 1799; August 12, 1800; January 5, 1802; June 7, November 8, 1803; May 8, July 31, 1804; May 21, 1805; February 4,

1806; May 10, November 15, 1809; October 14, 1812; October 13, 1813; August 31, 1814; *Republican Herald*, January 8, 1817.

47. Record of the Overseers of the Poor, Poughkeepsie, New York, 1807–1815, Adriance Memorial Library, Poughkeepsie, New York, 150–51.

48. *Poughkeepsie Journal*, August 13, 1799.

49. T. Stephen Whitman examines the complexities of slave hiring in *The Price of Freedom: Slavery and Manumission in Baltimore and Early National Maryland* (Lexington: University Press of Kentucky, 1997), chap. 3.

50. Overseers of the Poor, 192, 233–34.

51. Overseers of the Poor, 389.

52. Overseers of the Poor, 207–08.

53. Overseers of the Poor, 49.

54. Overseers of the Poor, 233–34, 327–29. T. Stephen Whitman suggests that manumission was more often the product of long and drawn-out negotiation between master and slave than an expression of humanitarian sentiment. Whitman provides a detailed examination of manumission and self-purchase in *The Price of Freedom*, chaps. 4–5. See also Herbert Aptheker, "Buying Freedom," in Aptheker, *To Be Free: Studies in American Negro History* (New York: International, 1969; originally published 1948); Sumner Eliot Matison, "Manumission by Purchase," *Journal of Negro History* 33 (April 1948):146–67; and McManus, *History of Negro Slavery in New York*, 145–55.

55. Rhinebeck Record of Slaves, March 1, 1804.

56. Records of the Poughkeepsie Precinct, 126.

57. Given the comparatively fewer opportunities available to African Americans in the countryside, T. Stephen Whitman argues that the cost of self-purchase in rural Maryland was higher than in Baltimore. Whitman, *The Price of Freedom*, 104–05, 109, 123, 130–31, 134.

58. Overseers of the Poor, 207–08; Town of Beekman Record Book, 405.

59. Overseers of the Poor, 124.

60. Overseers of the Poor, 256.

61. Smith Thompson File, Franklin Delano Roosevelt Library, Hyde Park, New York. Tom Williams worked for two and a half years before earning his manumission. Town of Beekman Record Book, 414.

62. Rhinebeck Town Records, February 21, 1810.

63. Sleght paid the required forty dollars in December 1807. Records of the Poughkeepsie Precinct, 72.

64. Overseers of the Poor, 164–65, 184, 192.

65. Overseers of the Poor, 162.

66. Overseers of the Poor, 399.

67. In either event, the slave had no legal claim to any payments already made toward self-purchase. See Whitman, *The Price of Freedom*, 87–88, 104–05, 124–29.

68. White, *Somewhat More Independent*, 147. On the growing restlessness of

African Americans in New York City during the 1790s and very early 1800s, see White, *Somewhat More Independent*, 140–46.

69. "Society of Negroes Unsettled," September 5, 1810. *Hudson River Valley Heritage*, Southeastern New York Library Research Council, accessed January 4, 2016, http://www.hrvh.org/cdm/compoundobject/collection/hhs/id/480/rec/75.

70. Advertisements almost certainly understate the number of runaways since masters did not always purchase advertisements in local newspapers. White, *Somewhat More Independent*, 125. Advertisements were compiled from the *American Farmer and Dutchess County Advertiser* (1798–1800); *Dutchess Observer* (1815–1826); *Political Barometer* (1802–1811); *Poughkeepsie Journal* (1785–1827); *Republican Herald* (1811–1823); *Republican Telegraph* (1824–1826); *Republican Telegraph and Observer* (1826–1827). Runaways came from Columbia, Dutchess, Putnam, and Ulster Counties, as well as northern Orange and Westchester, and southern Albany County.

71. *Poughkeepsie Journal*, October 18, 1809. See also *Poughkeepsie Journal*, August 18, 1789, and September 3, 1799.

72. McManus, *History of Negro Slavery in New York*, 117–18.

73. *Political Barometer*, June 8, 1802; *Poughkeepsie Journal*, June 19, 1798; February 18, 1800. See also *Poughkeepsie Journal*, August 11, 1789.

74. *Poughkeepsie Journal*, January 15, 1802.

75. *Poughkeepsie Journal*, June 1, 1808.

76. Ned wore a black wool hat, a new dark brown shortcoat, a jacket, overalls, a woolen undershirt, a white linen shirt, pale blue stockings, and a white handkerchief around his neck. *Poughkeepsie Journal*, February 12, 1799.

77. For example, see *Poughkeepsie Journal*, August 11, August 18, 1789; August 21, 1798; November 25, 1818; *Dutchess Observer*, July 24, 1822; May 28, 1823.

78. *Poughkeepsie Journal*, August 20, 1799. See also *Poughkeepsie Journal*, May 1, June 5, 1798; June 11, 1805; May 25, 1808; July 1, 1818.

79. *Political Barometer*, November 16, 1808; *Poughkeepsie Journal*, April 25, 1810; *Poughkeepsie Journal*, July 14, 1789.

80. *Political Barometer*, May 14, 1805. See also *Poughkeepsie Journal*, August 18, 1789; *Republican Herald*, June 1, 1814; May 22, 1816.

81. *Poughkeepsie Journal*, November 17, 1789; October 21, 1795; November 23, 1802; June 11, 1805; *Political Barometer*, February 4, 1806.

82. *Political Barometer*, July 25, 1810.

83. Slaveholders surmised the destination of fugitives in only twenty-five cases.

84. *Poughkeepsie Journal*, August 20, 1799.

85. *American Farmer and Dutchess County Advertiser*, September 3, 1799; *Poughkeepsie Journal*, November 29, 1803. For similar examples, see *Poughkeepsie Journal*, October 8, 1805; October 27, 1813.

86. *Poughkeepsie Journal*, September 5, 1810; December 31, 1817. The Mid-Hudson Valley provided a destination for fugitives from outside of the

region. One fourteen-year-old servant boy named Gilbert supposedly left his master in New York City for the Poughkeepsie neighborhood of his former mistress. *Poughkeepsie Journal*, July 9, 1815. A slaveowner from Sussex County, New Jersey, went to the trouble of placing an advertisement in the *Poughkeepsie Journal* in 1808, suspecting that his slave Sam fled to his native Dutchess. *Poughkeepsie Journal*, October 19, 1808.

87. *Poughkeepsie Journal*, January 25, 1803.

88. *Political Barometer*, May 14, 1805.

89. *Poughkeepsie Journal*, June 5, 1798.

90. *Political Barometer*, August 9, 1809; *Poughkeepsie Journal*, August 16, 1809.

91. *Poughkeepsie Journal*, January 8, 1794. Similar warnings may be found in *Poughkeepsie Journal*, August 3, September 7, 1802; July 19, 1803.

92. *Dutchess Observer*, June 6, 1821; *Poughkeepsie Journal*, June 6, 1821.

93. *Dutchess Observer*, May 5, 1819.

94. For example, John Pinkney's slave Gin fled in May 1811, but Pinkney did not advertise for the runaway until the following January. *Poughkeepsie Journal*, January 15, 1812.

95. *Poughkeepsie Journal*, September 21, 1808.

96. *Poughkeepsie Journal*, August 3, 1802; August 27, 1805.

97. *Poughkeepsie Journal*, March 6, 1798.

98. *Poughkeepsie Journal*, August 4, 1789. In a similar case, Joe and Phillis, both twenty-three years of age, fled their master in Fishkill with their seventeen-month-old son in 1814. *Poughkeepsie Journal*, April 20, 1814.

99. *Political Barometer*, July 10, 1804.

100. *Poughkeepsie Journal*, August 2, 1803; October 8, 1805.

101. *Poughkeepsie Journal*, May 8, 1811.

102. Twenty runaways were identified as having knowledge of more than one language. For examples, see *Poughkeepsie Journal*, September 5, 1810; July 22, 1818.

103. *Dutchess Observer*, July 14, 1824.

104. *Poughkeepsie Journal*, January 20, 1808.

105. *Poughkeepsie Journal*, July 15, 1800.

106. See, for example, *Dutchess Observer*, April 2, 1823; *Poughkeepsie Journal*, November 20, 1797; July 15, 1800; August 2, 1803; October 16, 1816; April 19, 1820; *Republican Herald*, September 22, 1813; May 3, 1815.

107. *Poughkeepsie Journal*, November 18, 1800; September 7, 1802.

108. *Poughkeepsie Journal*, November 25, 1818. For similar examples, see *Poughkeepsie Journal*, January 8, January 15, 1794; and October 21, 1818.

109. Robert William Fogel and Stanley L. Engerman, "Philanthropy at Bargain Prices: Notes on the Economics of Gradual Emancipation," *Journal of Legal Studies* 3, no. 2 (June 1974): 392–93; Gellman, *Emancipating New York*, 162–65, 203–05; McManus, *History of Negro Slavery in New York*, 176–77. James Gigantino examines the robust trade in black bodies in New Jersey in *The Ragged Road to Abolition*, chap. 6. While Dutchess County's slave population dropped by 347 persons between 1800 and 1810, the free African American

population increased by only 193, merely twenty percent of the increase of the previous decade. Population Schedules of the Second Census of the United States, 1800, microcopy 32, roll 21, New York (Washington, DC: 1959); Population Schedules of the Third Census, 1810. The most famous case of a Hudson Valley slave illegally sold South is that of Sojourner Truth's son Peter, who was redeemed from bondage in Alabama after many agonizing months. Truth, *Narrative of Sojourner Truth*, 30–40; Mabee, *Sojourner Truth*, 16–19; Painter, *Sojourner Truth*, 32–37.

110. Berlin, "The Revolution in Black Life," 358, 365–68; Matison, "Manumission by Purchase," 161–62, 167; Whitman, *Price of Freedom*, 87–88, 98–108.

111. *Laws of the State of New York*, 40th Session, Chapter 137.

112. Rarely did fugitives in the Mid-Hudson region abscond with others. Merely seventeen advertisements in the Dutchess County press between 1785 and 1827 listed more than one runaway.

113. The age profile of runaways in the New York City region was comparable. See White, *Somewhat More Independent*, 122, 124, 143.

114. *Poughkeepsie Journal*, August 19, 1818. Jerome Scofield of Fishkill Plains complained that his servant girl Hager had a "disposition much averse to fidelity and truth." *Dutchess Observer*, March 6, 1822.

## Chapter 4. An Arduous Struggle: From Slavery to Freedom

1. Record of the Overseers of the Poor, Poughkeepsie, New York, 1807–1815, Adriance Memorial Library, Poughkeepsie, New York, 3, 43, 130, 271–72, 351, 364, 388.

2. Berlin, "The Revolution in Black Life," 349–82; Berlin and Harris, *Slavery in New York*, chaps. 5–7; Harris, *In the Shadow of Slavery*, chap. 3; Hodges, *Root and Branch*, chaps. 6–7; Horton and Horton, *In Hope of Liberty*; Nash, *Forging Freedom*; Reed, *Platform for Change*; White, *Somewhat More Independent*; White, *Stories of Freedom in Black New York*; Winch, *Between Slavery and Freedom*; Donald Wright, *African Americans in the Early Republic, 1789–1831* (Arlington Heights: Harlan Davidson, 1993).

3. *Laws of the State of New York*, 32nd Session, Chapter 44.

4. Such households dropped from 750 to only 699 during three decades between 1790 and 1820, a negligible decline from eleven to ten percent of all white families in the county. The proportion was skewed in part by the organization of Putnam County from Dutchess' southern towns in 1812. Putnam's African American population remained small.

5. The rate in New York City was one-third. White, *Somewhat More Independent*, 156.

6. Piersen, *Black Yankees*, 33–34; Wright, *African Americans in the Early Republic*, 148–49.

7. See Bruegel, *Farm, Shop, Landing*, chaps. 1 and 2; Bruegel, "Uncertainty,

Pluriactivity, and Neighborhood Exchange in the Rural Hudson Valley in the Late Eighteenth Century," *New York History* 77, no. 3 (July 1996): 245–72; Wermuth, *Rip Van Winkle's Neighbors*, chaps. 2 and 3.

8. Horatio Gates Spafford, *A Gazetteer of the State of New York* (Albany: H. C. Southwick, 1813), 74.

9. Bruegel, *Farm, Shop, Landing*, chaps. 3 and 4; David Maldwyn Ellis, *Landlords and Farmers in the Hudson-Mohawk Region, 1790–1850* (Ithaca: Cornell University Press, 1946); McDermott, *Dutchess County's Plain Folks*, chap. 4; Spafford, *Gazetteer of the State of New York* (1813); Horatio Gates Spafford, *A Gazetteer of the State of New York* (Albany: B. D. Packard, 1824); Thomas Wermuth, "New York Farmers and the Market Revolution: Economic Behavior in the Mid-Hudson Valley, 1780–1830," *Journal of Social History* 32, no. 1 (Fall 1998): 179–96; Wermuth, *Rip Van Winkle's Neighbors*, chap. 5.

10. Spafford, *Gazetteer* (1824), 149–50. Established in 1814, the Matteawan Cotton Manufactory located near Fishkill Landing was the largest of its kind in the state and warranted its own separate entry in Spafford's 1824 gazetteer. The extensive Barnegat lime works just southwest of the village of Poughkeepsie encompassed more than a dozen kilns and several buildings over an area of half a square mile.

11. Overseers of the Poor, 256.

12. Dutchess County Deeds, Liber 26, 580.

13. See Debra Eileen Lewis, "Walking Fredonia Lane," *Dutchess* (February 2002): 50–55.

14. Rates of black property holding in Dutchess were actually higher than elsewhere in the state. However small in number, the twenty-eight black residents comprised almost ten percent of black New Yorkers eligible to vote in 1825. *Journal of the Senate of the State of New York* (Albany: E. Croswell, 1826).

15. Ellis, *Landlords and Farmers in the Hudson-Mohawk Region*, 13, 27–28; James Smith, *History of Dutchess County, New York*, 214, 221; Spafford, *Gazetteer* (1813), 18, 281.

16. Overseers of the Poor, 184. For black tenancy in the rural North, see Berlin, *Many Thousands Gone*, 240–42; Hodges, *Slavery and Freedom in the Rural North*, 130–33, 159–65, 178–81; Nash and Soderlund, *Freedom by Degrees*, 188–92.

17. Overseers of the Poor, 131, 257.

18. Sambo also received a horse and bridle. Will Book C, Dutchess County Surrogate's Court, Poughkeepsie, New York, 232–33. Among fifty-five testators who emancipated at least one of their slaves during the latter half of the eighteenth and the beginning of the nineteenth centuries, only eighteen provided any form of compensation.

19. Melvin Patrick Ely provides a fascinating portrait of black labor in one rural Virginia community in *Israel on the Appomattox*.

20. Billy G. Smith, "Poverty and Economic Marginality in Eighteenth-Century America," *Proceedings of the American Philosophical Society* 132, no.

1 (1988): 108–15. See also Bruegel, *Farm, Shop, Landing*, chaps. 4 and 5; Mc Dermott, *Dutchess County's Plain Folks*, chap. 8.

21. *Dutchess Observer*, March 19, March 26, April 2, June 25, and September 17, 1817.

22. Overseers of the Poor, 399–400.

23. Overseers of the Poor, 267–68, 273, 290.

24. Overseers of the Poor, 1.

25. Overseers of the Poor, 167. Eleven of seventeen black men and women appearing in the Poughkeepsie poor record between 1807 and 1815 whose residential status was specified were transients who had lived in the town for fewer than two years.

26. Federal Writers' Project, *Dutchess County*, American Guide Series (Philadelphia: William Penn Association of Philadelphia, 1937), 128–29; Mid-Hudson Antislavery History Project, *Slavery, Antislavery, and the Underground Railroad: A Dutchess County Guide* (Poughkeepsie: Hudson House, 2010), 38–39; Frank Hasbrouck, *The History of Dutchess County, New York* (Poughkeepsie: S. A. Matthieu, 1909), 325; James Smith, *History of Dutchess County*, 534.

27. Lewis, "Walking Fredonia Lane," 50–55; Mid-Hudson Antislavery History Project, *Slavery, Antislavery, and the Underground Railroad*, 48–49; Henry T. Hackett, "The Hyde Park Patent," *Yearbook*, Dutchess County Historical Society, 24 (1939): 87.

28. Mid-Hudson Antislavery History Project, *Slavery, Antislavery, and the Underground Railroad*, 26–28; Philip Smith, *General History of Duchess County*, 135; Williams-Myers, "The Arduous Journey," 29.

29. Overseers of the Poor, 162.

30. Beekman's slave population declined by 81 persons between 1790 and 1820, but the town's free black population increased by 124. *Heads of Families at the First Census of the United States Taken in the Year 1790: New York*; Population Schedules of the First Census of the United States, 1790, microcopy 637, roll 6, New York, vol. 2 (Washington, DC: 1965); Population Schedules of the Fourth Census of the United States, 1820, roll 71, New York, vol. 10 (Washington, DC: 1959).

31. The African American population of the town of Washington increased from 72 in 1820 to 110 in 1830. The town of Stanford was set off from Washington in 1793. MacCracken, *Blithe Dutchess*, 105, 107; Mid-Hudson Antislavery History Project, *Slavery, Antislavery, and the Underground Railroad*, 32–34; "Remarks of Isaac S. Wheaton at Lithgow, September 21, 1921," *Yearbook*, Dutchess County Historical Society (1922): 22–24.

32. Overseers of the Poor, 81–82, 164–65, 192.

33. Overseers of the Poor, 292–93.

34. Overseers of the Poor, 260.

35. Overseers of the Poor, 184.

36. Overseers of the Poor, 150–51.

37. Abraham Schenck wrote that since her youth Hannah "deserved well of me and the family." Will Book B, 239. When making provision for Molly's "comfort and maintenance" in 1816, Nathaniel Pendleton of Clinton noted that he did so in accordance with the wishes of Molly's late mistress. Will Book F, 225–26. Reminiscing about his childhood in Fishkill, Henry Bailey recalled the alleged trials and tribulations of a former beloved family slave named Nanna, who supposedly left the Bailey homestead only to struggle in supporting herself as a free woman. According to Bailey, Nanna discovered that freedom was "far different than she expected" and "wished herself back again in the old kitchen, a slave under her old master." Bailey, *Local Tales and Historical Sketches*, 376–77.

38. Overseers of the Poor, 396.

39. Overseers of the Poor, 124.

40. Robert Cray calculated similar figures for rural areas surrounding New York City. Robert E. Cray, Jr., *Paupers and Poor Relief in New York City and Its Rural Environs, 1700–1830* (Philadelphia: Temple University Press, 1988), 148–52.

41. *Laws of the State of New York*, 7th Session, Chapter 35; 11th Session, Chapter 62; 24th Session, Chapter 184. Scholarship on poverty and poor relief during the late eighteenth and early nineteenth centuries includes John K. Alexander, *Render Them Submissive: Responses to Poverty in Philadelphia, 1760–1800* (Amherst: University of Massachusetts Press, 1980); Cray, *Paupers and Poor Relief*; Priscilla Ferguson Clement, *Welfare and the Poor in the Nineteenth-Century City: Philadelphia, 1800–1854* (Rutherford: Farleigh Dickinson University Press, 1985); Susan Grigg, *The Dependent Poor of Newburyport: Studies in Social History, 1800–1830* (Ann Arbor: UMI Research Press, 1984); Smith, *"The Lower Sort"*; Smith, "Poverty and Economic Marginality in Eighteenth-Century America"; Michael Katz, *In the Shadow of the Poorhouse: A Social History of Welfare in America* (New York: Basic Books, 1986); Katz, *Poverty and Public Policy in American History* (New York: Academic Press, 1983); Raymond Mohl, *Poverty in New York, 1783–1825* (New York: Oxford University Press, 1971); David J. Rothman, *The Discovery of the Asylum: Social Order and Disorder in the New Republic* (Boston: Little, Brown, 1971); Conrad Edick Wright, *The Transformation of Charity in Postrevolutionary New England* (Boston: Northeastern University Press, 1992).

42. Overseers of the Poor, 137.

43. Overseers of the Poor, 396.

44. Overseers of the Poor, 3, 43, 130, 271–72, 351, 364, 388.

45. Overseers of the Poor, 362.

46. Cray, *Paupers and Poor Relief*, 191–92; Cray, "White Welfare and Black Strategies: The Dynamics of Race and Poor Relief in New York, 1700–1825," *Slavery and Abolition* 7 (December 1986): 281–83; Smith, *"The Lower Sort,"* 174–75.

47. The motivations of 119 native-born whites, 30 African Americans, and 20 immigrants were specified. There were 90 cases in which there were multiple reasons for a deponent's appearance in the record or in which the reason was

unspecified. Reasons were coded as follows: sickness/injury, material need, widowhood, abandonment/orphaned, lame/blind, mental illness, pregnancy/childbirth, and advanced age.

48. Overseers of the Poor, 150–51, 212.

49. Overseers of the Poor, 362.

50. Overseers of the Poor, 182, 254, 258.

51. Overseers of the Poor, 41, 45. See also the case of Margaret Smith in Overseers of the Poor, 181.

52. Overseers of the Poor, 132, 182.

53. Overseers of the Poor, 256.

54. Overseers of the Poor, 207, 222, 233–34, 327–29, 362.

55. Overseers of the Poor, 17.

56. Overseers of the Poor, 218, 221.

57. Overseers of the Poor, 137.

58. Overseers of the Poor, 256.

59. Overseers of the Poor, 271–73.

60. Overseers of the Poor, 17.

61. Overseers of the Poor, 260–61.

62. Overseers of the Poor, 192, 202, 292–93.

63. Although the undercounting of absent husbands and fathers who worked away from home as seamen and transient laborers tended to inflate the number of female-headed households in New York City, the sex ratio was comparatively more skewed in the seaport, where females outnumbered males by as many as three to two. A similar ratio existed in the town of Poughkeepsie, where women comprised one in five heads of households in 1820. Countywide, however, women comprised just over half of Dutchess' black population. Figures for New York City are extracted from Gary B. Nash, "Forging Freedom: The Emancipation Experience in Northern Seaport Cities," in *Slavery and Freedom in the Age of the American Revolution*, ed. Ira Berlin and Ronald Hoffman (Charlottesville: University Press of Virginia, 1983), 30–35, and White, *Somewhat More Independent*, 154–56.

64. Augmented households included two parents with children or a conjugal unit without children plus kin or non-kin, as defined in Nash, "Forging Freedom," 34. Since the fourth federal census did not specify relationships among members of each household, the actual status of each household is admittedly conjectural. Ninety augmented households in Dutchess County included sixty-six families with children under fourteen years of age and twenty-four without children.

65. Overseers of the Poor, 137.

66. Overseers of the Poor, 43, 195. James Oliver Horton and Lois E. Horton explore the importance of kin networks and analyze the historical and cultural significance of boarding in *In Hope of Liberty*, 95–100.

67. *Dutchess Observer*, February 14, 1816.

68. Overseers of the Poor, 162.

69. *Poughkeepsie Journal*, August 11, 1824.

70. Harris, *The Long Shadow of Slavery*, 103–16; Horton, *Free People of Color*, 32–33; Melish, *Disowning Slavery*, 122–27. Shane White explores free black behavior in the wake of emancipation and black expressive culture in "Black Life in Freedom: Creating a Popular Culture," in *Slavery in New York*, ed. Ira Berlin and Leslie M. Harris (New York: New Press, 2005), chap. 5; *Somewhat More Independent*, chap. 7; and *Stories of Freedom in Black New York*.

## Chapter 5. Race and the Construction of a Free Community

1. *Colored American*, September, 28, 1839.

2. See White, "Black Life in Freedom," 147–80; White, *Stories of Freedom in Black New York*.

3. For an overview of racial construction in the Early Republic, see James Brewer Stewart, "The Emergence of Racial Modernity and the Rise of the White North, 1790–1840," with comments by Jean Soderlund, James Oliver Horton, and Ronald Walters, *Journal of the Early Republic* 18, no. 2 (Summer 1998): 181–236, and the Special Issue on Racial Consciousness and Nation-Building in the Early Republic, *Journal of the Early Republic* 19, no. 4 (Winter 1999). See also Bruce Dain, *A Hideous Monster of the Mind: American Race Theory in the Early Republic* (Cambridge: Harvard University Press, 2002); Melish, *Disowning Slavery*; and David R. Roediger, *The Wages of Whiteness: Race and the Making of the American Working Class* (New York: Verso, 1991). For a broader perspective of the construction of nationalism in post-revolutionary America, see Joyce Appleby, *Inheriting the Revolution: The First Generation of Americans* (Cambridge: Belknap Press of Harvard University Press, 2000), and David Waldstreicher, *In the Midst of Perpetual Fetes: The Making of American Nationalism, 1776–1820* (Chapel Hill: University of North Carolina Press, 1997), especially chap. 6.

4. James Gigantino uses the label "slaves for a term" to refer to children born of slaves under New Jersey's gradual abolition law. See Gigantino, *The Ragged Road to Abolition*, chap. 4. See also Melish, *Disowning Slavery*, chap. 3.

5. Joanne Pope Melish explores the distortion and reconstruction of historical memory among white New Englanders in *Disowning Slavery*. James Gigantino explains racial formation in New Jersey differently. In *The Ragged Road to Abolition*, Gigantino argues that the conservatism of abolition and construction of white supremacy stemmed not from a desire of white New Jerseyans to forget their slave past but from an attempt to perpetuate it in a different form. For New York, see Gellman, *Emancipating New York*, chap. 9; and Harris, *In the Shadow of Slavery*, chap. 4.

6. *Speech of the Hon. James Tallmadge, of Dutchess County, New York, in the*

*House of Representatives of the United States, on Slavery* (Boston: Ticknor & Company, 1849). See also John D. Gindele, "The Public Career of James Tallmadge," *Yearbook*, Dutchess County Historical Society, part 1, 45 (1960): 39–80, and part 2, 46 (1961): 52–93.

7. *Dutchess Observer*, May 19, 1819. See also *Dutchess Observer*, April 7, May 26, June 2, and November 24, 1819; *Poughkeepsie Journal*, February 23, March 8, May 17, 1820.

8. *Poughkeepsie Journal*, February 11, February 25, 1824; and *Seventh Annual Report of the American Society for Colonizing the Free People of Colour of the United States* (Washington, DC: Davis and Force, 1824), 170. See also *Dutchess Observer*, February 11, 1823.

9. Republican-dominated state legislatures imposed discriminatory registration requirements on black voters in 1811 and 1815. Gellman, *Emancipating New York*, 202–03; Christopher Malone, *Between Freedom and Bondage: Race, Party, and Voting Rights in the Antebellum North* (New York: Routledge, 2008), 43–44; Rael, "The Long Death of Slavery," 131.

10. Nathaniel H. Carter and William L. Stone, *Reports of the Proceedings and Debates of the Convention of 1821, Assembled for the Purpose of Amending the Constitution of the State of New York: Containing All the Official Documents, Relating to the Subject, and Other Valuable Matter* (Albany: E. & E. Howard, 1821), 198–99; David N. Gellman and David Quigley, eds., *Jim Crow New York: A Documentary History of Race and Citizenship, 1777–1877* (New York: New York University Press, 2003), 135–38.

11. The exemption from taxation for black New Yorkers who failed to meet the $250 threshold provided small consolation. Carter and Stone, *Reports of the Proceedings and Debates*, 38, 134–35, 178–202, 288–91, 370–78, 553–59, 643, 661. David Gellman and David Quigley provide excerpts of the debates with editorial comment in *Jim Crow New York*, 73–200. See also Malone, *Between Freedom and Bondage*, 45–53.

12. Tallmadge's Dutchess County colleague Peter Livingston warned that Tallmadge's proposal threatened to embroil the convention in the debates surrounding the Missouri Crisis. *Reports of the Proceedings and Debates*, 167, 171, 485–87, 497–98; Gellman and Quigley, *Jim Crow New York*, 100–02, 194–98.

13. Despite gradual decline, African Americans in Red Hook and Rhinebeck still comprised more than one of ten black county residents. The gradual migration from the countryside to larger villages is noted in Denise Love Johnson, "Black Migration Patterns: A Case Study of the Origin and Development of the Black Population of the City of Poughkeepsie, New York" (unpublished paper, Department of Geography, Vassar College, May 1973).

14. See Martha Collins Bayne, *County at Large* (Poughkeepsie: Women's City and County Club with Vassar College, 1937); Clyde Griffen and Sally Griffen, *Natives and Newcomers: The Ordering of Opportunity in Mid-Nineteenth-Century Poughkeepsie* (Cambridge: Harvard University Press, 1978); McCracken,

*Blithe Dutchess*; Edmund Platt, *The Eagle's History of Poughkeepsie, from the Earliest Settlements, 1683–1905* (Poughkeepsie: Dutchess County Historical Society, 1987; originally published 1905); James Smith, *History of Dutchess County, New York*; Philip Smith, *General History of Duchess County, from 1609 to 1876, Inclusive.*

15. Griffen and Griffen, *Natives and Newcomers*, 43–44; Joshua Gordon Hinerfeld, "The Fading Veneer of Equality: The Afro-American Experience in Poughkeepsie between 1840 and 1860," *Yearbook*, Dutchess County Historical Society 68 (1983): 95–96; Hinerfeld, "Putting Goat Hair on Sheep: A Case Study Approach Analyzing Northern Notions of Racial Equality during the Era of American Reconstruction" (unpublished paper, Vassar College, February 14, 1983), 21–22; Johnson, "Black Migration Patterns," 44–46; Lawrence H. Mamiya and Lorraine M. Roberts, "Invisible People, Untold Stories: A Historical Overview of the Black Community in Poughkeepsie," in *New Perspectives on Poughkeepsie's Past: Essays to Honor Edmund Platt*, ed. Clyde Griffen (Poughkeepsie: Dutchess County Historical Society, 1988), 78; *Poughkeepsie Journal*, August 5, 1835; *Poughkeepsie Telegraph*, August 5, 1835. Johnson identifies a small cluster on "Long Row" near the almshouse (now Pershing Avenue).

16. The number of black-headed households in the county increased from 315 in 1830 to 351 in 1840 and then dropped to 338 by 1850. The number of people in those households remained constant at just over 1,500 individuals throughout the two decades. At midcentury, only in Pine Plains on the county's northern border did a majority of black residents reside with white families; of the town's two dozen African American residents in 1850, nine lived in three black households.

17. Men headed approximately nine of every ten African American households in 1820, 1830, and 1840. The number of male-headed households dropped from 322 to 288 during the 1840s as the number of female-headed households increased from 29 to 50. There was little variability across the county; the proportion of male-headed households was smallest in Poughkeepsie, but even there, men headed as many as three-quarters of black households at midcentury. The sex ratio remained relatively balanced throughout the period; females comprised between fifty-one and fifty-three percent of the county's African American population between 1820 and 1850.

18. Albert J. Raboteau, *Canaan Land: A Religious History of African Americans* (New York: Oxford University Press, 2001). Nathan Hatch places African American Christianity in broader context in *The Democratization of American Christianity* (New Haven: Yale University Press, 1989).

19. Cornelius C. Cuyler, *A Narrative of the Revival of Religion in the Reformed Dutch Church at Poughkeepsie* (Poughkeepsie: P. & S. Potter, 1815), 3–5.

20. Local Episcopalians and members of the Dutch Reformed denomination originally worshipped together as members of the Stoutsburgh Religious Association but established separate churches early in the nineteenth century.

See Franklin Delano Roosevelt, ed., *Records of the Town of Hyde Park, Dutchess County*, Collections of the Dutchess County Historical Society, vol. 3 (Hyde Park: 1928). See also Mid-Hudson Antislavery History Project, *Slavery, Antislavery, and the Underground Railroad*, 48–49. Early records of the Dutch Reformed Church in Fishkill are transcribed in Jean D. Worden, comp., "First Reformed Church, Fishkill, Dutchess County, New York, and First Reformed Church, Hopewell, Dutchess County, New York" (Fishkill: First Reformed Church, 1981). Records of the Poughkeepsie Church are found in A. P. Gieson, comp., "Record of the First Reformed Dutch Church, Poughkeepsie, New York, 1716–1824" (1883).

21. James Brown's diaries contain numerous references to churches in Fishkill Landing, Fishkill Village, Matteawan, Glenham, Newburgh, and other communities. Myra B. Young Armstead discusses Brown's religious life in *Freedom's Gardener: James F. Brown, Horticulture, and the Hudson Valley in Antebellum America* (New York: New York University Press, 2012), 130–35.

22. Hatch, *Democratization of American Christianity*, 3–16, 102–13, 154–55. See also Harry V. Richardson, *Dark Salvation: The Story of Methodism as It Developed among Blacks in America* (Garden City: Doubleday, 1976).

23. The continuing appeal of Methodism in Poughkeepsie prompted the founding of a church on Cannon Street in 1840 and yet another congregation on South Clover Street in 1853. Platt, *Eagle's History of Poughkeepsie*, 90–91; James Smith, *History of Dutchess County*, 233, 276, 352, 422–23; Reverend L. M. Vincent, *Methodism in Poughkeepsie and Vicinity: Its Rise and Progress from 1780 to 1892* (Poughkeepsie: A.V. Haight, n.d.), 12–19.

24. *Emancipator*, April 29, 1834. Histories of the AMEZ Church include David Henry Bradley, *A History of the A.M.E. Zion Church*, part 1, 1796–1872 (Nashville: Parthenon Press, 1956); J. W. Hood, *One Hundred Years of the African Methodist Episcopal Zion Church* (New York: African Methodist Episcopal Zion Book Concern, 1895); John Jamison Moore, *History of the A.M.E. Zion Church in America* (York: Teachers' Journal Office, 1884); Richardson, *Dark Salvation*; William J. Walls, *The African Methodist Episcopal Zion Church: Reality of the Black Church* (Charlotte: A.M.E. Zion Publishing House, 1974). See also C. Eric Lincoln and Lawrence H. Mamiya, *The Black Church in the African American Experience* (Durham: Duke University Press, 1990), chap. 3.

25. Church Incorporations, vol. 1, 1797–1867, Dutchess County Archives, Poughkeepsie, New York, 124, 138. See also Gaius C. Bolin, Sr., "History of the AME Zion Church," in Rollin Howard Masten, "Dutchess County Churches," vol. 5 (unpublished, n.d.), Adriance Memorial Library, Poughkeepsie, New York; Mamiya and Roberts, "Invisible People, Untold Stories," 78–79; Mid-Hudson Antislavery History Project, *Slavery, Antislavery, and the Underground Railroad*, 42–44; Charles J. Sargent, Jr., "The Negro Church in Dutchess County, New York," (unpublished paper, September 30, 1955), Adriance Memorial Library, Poughkeepsie, New York, 1; James Smith, *History of*

*Dutchess County*, 426–27. I am grateful to Reverend McLaughlin of the Smith Metropolitan AMEZ Church for information he was able to provide.

26. *Colored American*, October 14; October 21, 1837.

27. *Census of the State of New York for 1855* (Albany: Charles Van Benthuysen, 1857), 461; Church Incorporations, 138, 140, 152; *Historical Sketch and Directory of the Town of Fishkill, with an Appendix and Much Useful Information* (Fishkill Landing: Dean & Spaight, 1866), 150; Hood, *One Hundred Years*, 65–67; Mamiya and Roberts, "Invisible People, Untold Stories," 79; Mid-Hudson Antislavery History Project, *Slavery, Antislavery, and the Underground Railroad*, 38–39; Moore, *History of the A.M.E. Zion Church*, 384–86; Walls, *African Methodist Episcopal Zion Church*, 94, 127, 334, 336, 460–461; James Smith, *History of Dutchess County*, 534. The Baxtertown church was likely established in 1847 or 1848.

28. Bolin, "History of AME Zion Church," 1.

29. The twelve Red Hook residents included Joseph Campbell, Prince Ellsworth, Tobias Grant, Joseph Harder, Joseph Herman, Peter Herman, Thomas Jefferson, Philip Johnson, William Jones, John Roe, Uriah St. Paul, and Isaac Thompson. Church Incorporations, vol. 1, 182–84. Black residents in Fishkill Landing purchased a lot for the burial ground in 1851. Armstead, *Freedom's Gardener*, 148–50; James F. Brown Diary, 1829–1866, New-York Historical Society, New York, New York, September 1, September 6, September 16, September 23, October 4, October 14, October 20, and October 31, 1851.

30. See Monroe Fordham, *Major Themes in Northern Black Religious Thought, 1800–1860* (Hicksville: Exposition Press, 1975); Eddie S. Glaude, *Exodus! Religion, Race, and Nation in Early Nineteenth-Century Black America* (Chicago: University of Chicago Press, 2000); Lincoln and Mamiya, *Black Church*; Benjamin E. Mays, *The Negro's God as Reflected in His Literature* (New York: Russell & Russell, 1968; originally published 1938); Raboteau, *Canaan Land*; Richardson, *Dark Salvation*; Joseph R. Washington, Jr., *Black Religion: The Negro and Christianity in the United States* (Boston: Beacon Press, 1964); and Gayraud S. Wilmore, *Black Religion and Black Radicalism* (Garden City: Doubleday, 1972).

31. See Glaude, *Exodus!*.

32. On September 28th, 1845, for example, James heard a sermon delivered by Episcopal minister Reverend Morgan in the morning and a second sermon delivered by AMEZ preacher William Bishop in the afternoon. Brown Diary, September 28, 1845.

33. Armstead, *Freedom's Gardener*, 142–45.

34. Brown Diary, May 28, September 8, 1844.

35. Bolin, "History of AME Zion Church," 1.

36. *Colored American*, September 9, 1837.

37. *Colored American*, September 26, 1840.

38. *Liberator*, July 20, 1833.

39. *Emancipator*, April 22, April 29, 1834.

40. *Poughkeepsie Telegraph*, November 8, 1837. Several individuals signed the

abstinence pledge at a "large" and "deeply interesting" meeting at the AMEZ Church in Newburgh in July 1841. *Colored American*, August 14, 1841; *The Black Abolitionist Papers*, microfilm, reel 4, no. 157.

41. Walls, *African Methodist Episcopal Zion Church*, 283.

42. *Poughkeepsie Telegraph*, January 18, 1837. See also *Poughkeepsie Telegraph*, November 8, 1837. The precise date of the school's founding is unknown. The *Telegraph* noted in January 1837 that the school had been established by Blount "two or three years" earlier.

43. *Colored American*, September 30, 1837. The Sunday School was to the mind what "the sun and rain" were "to the soil." *Colored American*, July 20, 1839. See also *Colored American*, June 30, 1838.

44. *Weekly Advocate*, February 25, 1837.

45. Carleton Mabee examines African American schooling in *Black Education in New York State from Colonial to Modern Times* (Syracuse: Syracuse University Press, 1979). For a broader perspective, see Curry, *The Free Black in Urban America, 1800–1850*, chap. 10; Litwack, *North of Slavery*, chap. 4; and Carter G. Woodson, *The Education of the Negro Prior to 1861* (New York: G. P. Putnam's Sons, 1915). Charles D. King, Jr., provides an overview of education in Dutchess County in "The Development of Public Education in Dutchess County," in *Transformation of an American County: Dutchess County, New York, 1683–1983*, ed. Joyce Ghee (Poughkeepsie: Dutchess County Historical Society, 1986), 123–30, and *History of Education in Dutchess County*.

46. Mamiya and Roberts, "Invisible People, Untold Stories," 81; Carleton Mabee, "Separate Black Education in Dutchess County," *Yearbook*, Dutchess County Historical Society 65 (1980): 5–6.

For an account of the New York school, see Charles C. Andrews, *The History of the New York African Free Schools* (New York: Negro Universities Press, 1969; originally published 1830). Gellman, *Emancipating New York*, and Harris, *In the Shadow of Slavery*, place the African Free Schools within the broader context of antislavery and reform.

47. *Liberator*, October 5, 1833.

48. Mid-Hudson Antislavery History Project, *Slavery, Antislavery, and the Underground Railroad*, 48.

49. Named after an English Quaker, the Lancaster system of education attempted to minimize costs and educate more children by utilizing older students to instruct younger pupils. Emphasis lay upon memorization rather than critical thought, and older students often lacked the competence to be effective teachers. As private institutions, the Lancaster Schools relied upon donations, but financial constraints often forced the schools to appeal for public funds. The society was organized in Poughkeepsie in 1814. Mabee, *Black Education*, 27–28.

50. *Colored American*, June 1, 1839.

51. *Poughkeepsie Telegraph*, August 23, 1843. Carleton Mabee attributes

tolerance of politically active black teachers to the comparatively small African American population, the difficulty school boards experienced in attracting qualified teachers for black schools, and the propensity of whites to ignore black protest. Mabee, *Black Education*, 119–32.

52. *Poughkeepsie Journal*, April 8, 1835. The original constitution and membership list of the society is at the Franklin Delano Roosevelt Library in Hyde Park, New York.

53. *Emancipator*, December 13, 1838; Dutchess County Anti-Slavery Society Executive Committee Minutes, Manuscripts and Archives Division, New York Public Library, March 9 and March 16, 1839. The project was "indefinitely postponed" and never materialized.

54. The *Telegraph* asked, "While citizens of our state are exhibiting intense anxiety for the abolition of *physical* slavery in other states, would it not be a matter of equal benevolence to use means for the abolition of *mental* slavery within our own doors?" *Poughkeepsie Telegraph*, January 18, 1837; Amy Pearce Ver Nooy, "The Anti-Slavery Movement in Dutchess County, 1835–1850," *Yearbook*, Dutchess County Historical Society 28 (1943): 59–61.

55. Herbert Aptheker, ed., *A Documentary History of the Negro People in the United States*, 6th ed., vol. 1 (New York: Citadel Press, 1968), 140–41; Curry, *The Free Black in Urban America*, 205–08; Harris, *In the Shadow of Slavery*, 185–87; Daniel Perlman, "Organizations of Free Negroes in New York City, 1800–1860," *Journal of Negro History* 56, no. 3 (July 1971): 191–93; Dorothy Porter, "The Organized Educational Activities of Negro Literary Societies, 1828–1846," in *The Making of Black America: Essays in Negro Life and History*, ed. August Meier and Elliot Rudwick, vol. 1 (New York: Athenaeum, 1969), 276–85. Across the river, black residents in Newburgh resolved to organize an auxiliary to the New York Society in August 1833. *Emancipator*, September 7, 1833.

56. *Colored American*, January 16, 1841.

57. *Poughkeepsie Telegraph*, January 18, 1837.

58. *Poughkeepsie Telegraph*, October 11, 1837. Noting the establishment of the literary association and library in an article printed four weeks later, the *Telegraph* concluded, "There is a spirit aroused among the coloured inhabitants of our village which has elevated them much, very much, and it is worthy of imitation every where." *Poughkeepsie Telegraph*, November 8, 1837.

59. *Poughkeepsie Telegraph*, May 9, November 8, 1837; Mabee, *Black Education*, 30; Ver Nooy, "Anti-Slavery in Dutchess County," 61. When announcing yet another exhibition on the second floor of the Lancaster School house in April 1839, the *Telegraph* encouraged all to attend, "particularly those who believe in the inferiority of the colored race." *Poughkeepsie Telegraph*, April 10, 1839.

60. *Colored American*, September 28, 1839. In early June, the *Poughkeepsie Journal* reported that forty-six students were attending Mr. Ward's school. *Poughkeepsie Journal*, June 5, 1839.

61. *Poughkeepsie Journal*, April 10, 1839; *Poughkeepsie Telegraph*, April 10, 1839.

62. *Poughkeepsie Journal*, March 31, 1841.

63. *Annual Report of the Superintendent of Common Schools, 1840* (Albany: 1841), 32–33. See also *Poughkeepsie Eagle*, May 13, 1843; *Poughkeepsie Journal*, March 31, 1841; *Poughkeepsie Telegraph*, March 29, May 10, 1843.

64. Adopted by the state legislature on April 18, "An Act to Establish Free Schools in Poughkeepsie" passed by a margin of 168 votes, 572 to 404. *Laws of the State of New York*, 66th Session, Chapter 211; *Poughkeepsie Eagle*, May 20, 1843; *Poughkeepsie Journal*, May 24, 1843; *Poughkeepsie Telegraph*, May 3, May 24, 1843; S. S. Randall, *A Digest of the Common School System in the State of New York* (Albany: C. Van Benthuysen & Co., 1844), 319–21. Despite their name, "free schools" were not completely free of charge for all students until the abolition of rate bills in 1867. King, *History of Education in Dutchess County*, 20–21.

65. Woodson, *Education of the Negro*, 307–08.

66. Record of the Proceedings of the Board of Education of Poughkeepsie, 1843–1854, Poughkeepsie City School District, Poughkeepsie, New York, 19, 21.

67. Board of Education, 19–21, 37, 39, 41, 43–44, 53, 57, 58, 60, 62, 99–100, 105; *Poughkeepsie Journal and Eagle*, February 24, 1844; February 22, 1850; *Poughkeepsie Telegraph*, August 23, December 14, 1843; February 21, March 13, May 29, August 26, 1844. In 1849, the Board of Education in Troy communicated their desire to hire Harriett as a teacher at a higher salary. Wishing to remain in Poughkeepsie, Harriett declined the offer. *Poughkeepsie Telegraph*, June 13, 1849.

68. An 1841 statute authorized but did not require municipalities to establish separate schools for black children. *Laws of the State of New York*, 1841, Chapter 260; *Annual Report of the Superintendent of Common Schools, 1844* (Albany: 1845), 145. The state superintendent of common schools recommended the establishment of separate schools for African American children as early as 1824. Mabee, *Black Education*, 71–73.

69. *Annual Report of the Superintendent of Common Schools, 1842* (Albany: 1843), 154–55; *Annual Report of the Superintendent of Common Schools, 1843* (Albany: 1844), 238–39.

70. *Annual Report, 1842*, 11, 25–26, 154–58; *Annual Report, 1843*, 237–46; *Annual Report of the Superintendent of Common Schools, 1844* (Albany: 1845), 22, 26, 142–55; *Annual Report of the Superintendent of Common Schools, 1845* (Albany: 1846), 44; *Poughkeepsie Telegraph*, June 6, 1849. Poughkeepsie newspapers printed the annual reports from the county's northern and southern districts and regularly published letters and articles on education.

71. *Annual Report, 1844*, 145.

72. *Annual Report, 1844*, 145. The county commissioner indicated that some black families were unable to lodge teachers in their scanty apartments. The boarding of white teachers with black families proved controversial. Mabee, *Black Education*, 70. The commissioner reported that several African American students in the county deserved "much credit for having made excellent progress" in the face of formidable obstacles.

73. *Annual Report of the Superintendent of Common Schools, 1846* (Albany: 1847), 20; See also *Annual Report of the Superintendent of Common Schools, 1848* (Albany: 1849), 10.

74. *Emancipator*, September 7, 1833.

75. *Poughkeepsie Telegraph*, July 27, August 17, and August 24, 1842. Paul Gilje puts such episodes into broader context in *The Road to Mobocracy: Popular Disorder in New York City, 1763–1834* (Chapel Hill: University of North Carolina Press, 1987), chap. 6.

76. *Poughkeepsie Eagle*, August 20, 1842, emphasis original.

77. *Poughkeepsie Telegraph*, October 11, 1837.

78. Citing Christian obligation and the importance of promoting the "public welfare," the authors of the notice reasoned that no "sober-minded" person could object to the enterprise. *Poughkeepsie Journal*, April 10, 1839; *Poughkeepsie Telegraph*, April 10, 1839. When appealing for public support for black education in November 1837, the *Telegraph* asserted that the only "abolitionism" associated with the movement was the "abolition of the mind from the thraldom [*sic*] of sin and ignorance." *Poughkeepsie Telegraph*, November 8, 1837. The paper went even farther to express its hope that readers would not be "deterred" from supporting such charitable efforts lest their failure to provide assistance actually *aid* radical abolitionism.

79. Men and women of the small free black middle class were hardly passive ideological victims of white cultural hegemony. Ball and Rael argue that rather than uncritically internalizing dominant bourgeois values of respectability, free people of color appropriated and adapted them for their own needs. Erica Ball, *To Live an Antislavery Life: Personal Politics and the Antebellum Black Middle Class* (Athens: University of Georgia Press, 2012); Rael, *Black Identity and Black Protest in the Antebellum North*.

80. While close to perfect during some months, attendance at other times fell as low as one-third or even one-quarter of the pupils whose names appeared on the roll. *Annual Report of the Superintendent of Common Schools, 1847* (Albany: 1848), 11–13; *Annual Report of the Superintendent of Common Schools, 1848* (Albany: 1849), 11–13; *Annual Report of the Superintendent of Common Schools, 1850* (Albany: 1851), 8; Board of Education,"146, 150.

81. Board of Education, 105, 108; *Poughkeepsie Telegraph*, September 20, 1848.

82. *Poughkeepsie Telegraph*, September 17, September 24, October 1, 1845.

## Chapter 6. Abolitionism, Protest, and Black Identity

1. *Colored American*, August 17, 1839. Accounts of a celebration in Catskill three years earlier appear in the *Emancipator*, August 11, 1836, and *Friend of Man*, August 18, 1836.

2. *Colored American*, July 25, 1840; August 21, 1841; *Poughkeepsie Journal*,

August 3, 1842. Studies of free black celebrations include William B. Gravely, "The Dialectic of Double-Consciousness in Black American Freedom Celebrations, 1808–1863," *Journal of Negro History* 67, no. 4 (Winter 1982): 302–17; Julie Roy Jeffrey, "'No Occurrence in Human History Is More Deserving of Commemoration Than This': Abolitionist Celebrations of Freedom," in *Prophets of Protest: Reconsidering the History of American Abolitionism*, ed. Timothy Patrick McCarthy and John Stauffer (New York: New Press, 2006), 200–19; John R. McKivigan and Jason H. Silverman, "Monarchial Liberty and Republican Slavery: West Indies Emancipation Celebrations in Upstate New York and Canada West," *Afro-Americans in New York Life and History* 10, no. 1 (January 1986): 7–18; and William H. Wiggins, *O Freedom! Afro-American Emancipation Celebrations* (Knoxville: University of Tennessee Press, 1987).

3. *Friend of Man*, March 8, 1837.

4. The clergyman's mother, who was present during the meeting, caustically suggested that the abolitionist should take a black wife. *Liberator*, October 5, 1833. Buffum's tour of Rhode Island, western Massachusetts, the Albany region, and the Hudson River Valley procured few donations, and Buffum enjoyed little success in establishing local antislavery organizations. John L. Myers examines early abolitionist organizing in "The Beginning of Anti-Slavery Agencies in New York State, 1833–1836," *New York History* 43, no. 2 (April 1962): 149–81.

5. *Emancipator*, April 15, April 29, 1834; January 13, 1835; Myers, "Beginning of Anti-Slavery Agencies," 155, 159.

6. Cited in the *Emancipator*, April 15, 1834.

7. The *Journal* expressed its hope that violent opposition to abolitionism would convince "advocates of equality between the negro and the white" to "pause in their mad career or else subject themselves to the fury of the ferocious mobs." *Poughkeepsie Journal*, July 16, 1834. The rival *Telegraph* acknowledged the evil of slavery but hoped that "no such madness as the abolitionists have displayed will again be shown." *Poughkeepsie Telegraph*, July 16, 1834. See also *Poughkeepsie Journal*, August 20, 1834.

8. *Emancipator*, March 31, 1835; *Poughkeepsie Journal*, April 8, 1835; Myers, "Beginning of Anti-Slavery Agencies," 163–64; Ver Nooy, "The Anti-Slavery Movement in Dutchess County, 1835–1850." The original constitution and list of 121 members is at the Franklin Delano Roosevelt Library in Hyde Park, New York.

9. *Poughkeepsie Journal*, August 5, August 12, 1835; *Poughkeepsie Telegraph*, July 29, August 12, August 19, 1835.

10. *Poughkeepsie Journal*, August 12, September 9, September 16, September 30, October 7, October 14, October 21, October 28, and November 4, 1835. The *Telegraph* defended the disruption of the convention as very "orderly." *Poughkeepsie Telegraph*, October 28, 1835. The Utica riot is examined in Howard Alexander Morrison, "Gentlemen of Proper Understanding: A Closer Look at Utica's Anti-Abolitionist Mob," *New York History* 62, no. 1 (January 1981): 61–82;

and Benjamin Sevitch, "The Well-Planned Riot of October 21, 1835: Utica's Answer to Abolitionism," *New York History* 50, no. 3 (July 1969): 251–63. More than a dozen local abolitionists reportedly attended the Utica convention. See *Liberator*, October 3, 1835.

The October 28 issue of the *Journal* also reported the mobbing of abolitionist William Lloyd Garrison in Boston, whose incendiary articles in the *Liberator* were "particularly offensive to the good people of that orderly city."

11. *Emancipator*, August 17, 1837; *Liberator*, August 4, 1837; *Friend of Man*, March 14, 1838. See also *Emancipator*, November 2, 1836; October 5, 1837; May 10, 1838; August 8, 1839; and *Friend of Man*, October 27, 1836.

12. *Emancipator*, March 16, 1837; *Friend of Man*, March 8, 1837; *Poughkeepsie Journal*, March 1, 1837; *Poughkeepsie Telegraph*, March 1, 1837.

13. Reprinted in the *Emancipator*, March 16, 1837.

14. *Poughkeepsie Telegraph*, March 1, 1837.

15. *Poughkeepsie Journal*, March 1, 1837.

16. "Open Letter to the Citizens of Poughkeepsie, March 4, 1837," in "Dutchess County Anti-Slavery Society Executive Committee Minutes," Manuscripts and Archives Division, New York Public Library, New York, New York.

17. Kathryn Kish Sklar, *Women's Rights Emerges within the Antislavery Movement, 1830–1870: A Brief History with Documents* (Boston/New York: Bedford/St. Martin's, 2000), 96–97.

18. *Emancipator*, April 20, 1837. The Dutchess County petitioners proved to be the exception to the rule; of the ninety-seven petitions listed from New York State, the Poughkeepsie petition was the only one from the Hudson Valley.

19. See, for example, *Poughkeepsie Journal*, March 2, 1836; August 16, December 6, 1837; January 3, 1838; *Poughkeepsie Telegraph*, January 27, March 2, March 23, 1836; January 18, November 22, November 29, 1837; *Poughkeepsie Eagle*, February 8, 1840.

20. Organizers invited abolitionists James G. Birney and Henry B. Stanton to speak for the occasion. The notice included 164 signatories from Poughkeepsie, 22 from Pawling, 21 from Amenia, 18 from LaGrange, 16 from Pleasant Valley, 6 from Fishkill, and 5 from Dover. All 252 individuals were men. *Emancipator*, April 12, 1838; *Poughkeepsie Journal*, April 18, 1838.

21. Defending the freedoms of opinion and speech to be the "inalienable prerogatives of every American," the paper expressed its hope that such a "scene of disorder so disgraceful and unjust" would never be repeated in the village. *Poughkeepsie Telegraph*, May 2, 1838.

22. *Poughkeepsie Journal*, July 4, July 18, July 25, 1838; *Poughkeepsie Telegraph*, July 18, July 25, August 1, 1838. Blakesly served as agent for Dutchess and Columbia Counties. *Friend of Man*, March 22, 1838.

23. Benjamin F. Wile, *Review of an Anti-Abolition Sermon, Preached at Pleasant Valley, New York* (Whitesboro: Press of the Oneida Institute, 1838).

24. *Emancipator*, December 13, 1838; *Poughkeepsie Journal and Eagle*, November 21, 1838; *Poughkeepsie Telegraph*, November 14, 1838.

25. For an overview of strategies and tactics within the abolitionist movement, see Aileen S. Kraditor, *Means and Ends in American Abolitionism: Garrison and His Critics on Strategy and Tactics, 1834–1850* (New York: Pantheon Books, 1969).

26. *Emancipator*, December 13, 1838; *Poughkeepsie Journal and Eagle*, November 21, 1838; Dutchess County Anti-Slavery Society Executive Committee Minutes, 2–10.

27. Newburgh sent five representatives and New Windsor one. New York City abolitionists accounted for approximately half of all participants. *Emancipator*, May 23, 1839.

28. *Emancipator*, October 17, November 7, 1839; *Poughkeepsie Journal*, October 30, 1839. See also *Emancipator*, January 23, 1840. Despite the "prevailing disposition" to form a separate political party, not all local activists endorsed political abolitionism. See *Emancipator*, October 17, 1839, and *National Anti-Slavery Standard*, August 20, 1840.

29. *Poughkeepsie Journal*, June 3, 1840, emphasis original.

30. *National Anti-Slavery Standard*, July 30, 1840.

31. Fergus Bordewich, *Bound for Canaan: The Underground Railroad and the War for the Soul of America* (New York: Harper Collins, 2005), chap. 9, especially 177–78; "The Underground Railroad in the New York Hudson Valley," July 28, 2005, accessed July 29, 2008, http://www.fergusbordewich.com/blog/archives/2005/07/the_underground_1.html#more; Mid-Hudson Antislavery History Project, *Slavery, Antislavery, and the Underground Railroad*. Henry Noble MacCracken identifies Joe Collis in *Blithe Dutchess*, 106. Rebecca Hitchcock Benton relates stories of her father's Underground Railroad activities in eastern Dutchess in "Reminiscenses," revised by William A. Benton, unpublished manuscript, Pleasant Valley Historical Society, 24–25.

32. For an overview of antislavery organizations in Dutchess, see Mid-Hudson Antislavery History Project, *Slavery, Antislavery, and the Underground Railroad*, 9–14. Several local abolitionists participated in meetings of the abolitionist Liberty Party during the spring and summer. Ira Armstrong of Poughkeepsie served as elector for Dutchess County in the 1840 presidential contest. A handful of local delegates attended the ill-fated meeting of the American Anti-Slavery Society in May 1840 that saw the fracturing of the national organization over goals, strategies, and tactics. See *Emancipator*, April 9, April 22, May 22, May 29, August 30, 1840; *Liberator*, June 12, 1840; *Poughkeepsie Telegraph*, August 26, 1840.

33. *Emancipator*, July 30, 1840.

34. *Emancipator*, August 20, 1840.

35. *Colored American*, December 12, 1840.

36. See David Grimsted, *American Mobbing, 1828–1861: Toward Civil War*

(New York: Oxford University Press, 1998), chaps. 1 and 2; Anthony Gronowicz, *Race and Class Politics in New York City before the Civil War* (Boston: Northeastern University Press, 1998); Leonard L. Richards, *"Gentlemen of Property and Standing": Anti-Abolition Mobs in Jacksonian America* (New York: Oxford University Press, 1970); and Lorman Ratner, *Powder Keg: Northern Opposition to the Antislavery Movement, 1831–1840* (New York: Basic Books, 1968).

37. Bordewich, *Bound for Canaan*, 151–52, 166–86, 194–95; Harris, *In the Shadow of Slavery*, 189–90; Craig Steven Wilder, *A Covenant with Color: Race and Social Power in Brooklyn* (New York: Columbia University Press, 2000), chaps. 3 and 4.

38. See Lee Benson, *The Concept of Jacksonian Democracy: New York as a Test Case* (New York: Athenaeum, 1964); Bruegel, *Farm, Shop, Landing*, chap. 7; John L. Brooke, *Columbia Rising: Civil Life on the Upper Hudson from the Revolution to the Age of Jackson* (Chapel Hill: University of North Carolina Press, 2010); and Phyllis F. Field, *The Politics of Race: The Struggle for Black Suffrage in the Civil War Era* (Ithaca: Cornell University Press, 1982).

39. Dutchess County Anti-Slavery Society Executive Committee Minutes, January 8, 1840. For a brief history of the antislavery First Congregational Church, see Mid-Hudson Antislavery History Project, *Slavery, Antislavery, and the Underground Railroad*, 40–41.

40. Witnesses claimed that it was difficult to discern "which party was the strongest." Alson Ward Diary (typescript), April 11, April 16, 1844; John Bower Diary (typescript), April 11, 1844, Dutchess County Historical Society, Poughkeepsie, New York; *Poughkeepsie Telegraph*, April 10, 1844. Barred from speaking in any of Newburgh's churches during a spring 1839 visit, Gerrit Smith managed only to engage a dozen local gentlemen in a discussion about antislavery and free speech in a small meetinghouse on the village outskirts before being forced to flee from an angry mob. *Liberator*, May 24, 1839.

41. The 1840 electoral returns from neighboring counties were comparable. *Emancipator*, December 10, 1840. Birney won 205 votes in Dutchess County in 1844, less than two percent of all ballots cast. *Poughkeepsie Journal and Eagle*, August 2, 1845. Returns for assembly elections are recorded in Election Book, 1835–1844, Dutchess County Archives, Poughkeepsie, New York. See also *Poughkeepsie Eagle*, October 28, 1843.

42. *Poughkeepsie Eagle*, September 18, 1841; *Emancipator*, September 9, 1841; *National Anti-Slavery Standard*, September 16, 1841; *Poughkeepsie Journal*, September 15, 1841; *Poughkeepsie Telegraph*, September 15, September 22, September 29, 1841.

43. Dutchess County Anti-Slavery Society Executive Committee Minutes, August 16, September 12, 1839; January 8, 1840. Perhaps the publisher himself entertained doubts about the journal's success when he noted in the inaugural issue, "In case this publication should not continue a whole year, the balance of the subscription money will be returned to the subscriber." *Bow of Promise*, August 29, 1839.

44. *National Anti-Slavery Standard*, October 12, 1843.

45. *Liberator*, October 5, 1833.

46. Blount evidently served as the sole representative from Dutchess County on the business committee of the fourth annual convention of the American Anti-Slavery Society in 1837, and he was among eight local delegates to the sixth annual meeting two years later. *Emancipator*, May 25, 1837; May 23, 1839; *Friend of Man*, May 31, 1837.

47. Mid-Hudson Antislavery History Project, *Slavery, Antislavery, and the Underground Railroad*, 41.

48. *Poughkeepsie Journal*, September 15, 1841; *Poughkeepsie Telegraph*, September 29, 1841.

49. Sklar, *Women's Rights Emerges within the Antislavery Movement*, 97.

50. For David Ruggles' association with Blount and links to Dutchess County, see Graham Russell Hodges, *David Ruggles: A Radical Black Abolitionist and the Underground Railroad in New York City* (Chapel Hill: University of North Carolina Press, 2010), 60, 110.

51. Minutes and Proceedings of the Third Annual Convention for the Improvement of the Free People of Color (New York: 1833), 4; and Minutes of the Fourth Annual Convention for the Improvement of the Free People of Colour (New York: 1834), 8, in Howard Holman Bell, ed., *Minutes of the Proceedings of the National Negro Conventions, 1830–1864* (New York: Arno Press, 1969).

52. *Emancipator*, September 7, 1833.

53. Ball, *To Live an Antislavery Life*.

54. *Emancipator*, April 22, 1834.

55. *Emancipator*, April 29, 1834. Donald Yacovone examines the politicization of the black temperance movement and its association with antislavery in "The Transformation of the Black Temperance Movement, 1827–1854: An Interpretation," *Journal of the Early Republic* 8, no. 3 (1988): 281–97. See also Benjamin Quarles, *Black Abolitionists* (New York: Oxford University Press, 1969), 90–100.

56. Classic studies of the African American abolitionist movement include Herbert Aptheker, *The Negro in the Abolitionist Movement* (New York: International, 1941); Jane and William Pease, *They Who Would Be Free: Blacks' Search for Freedom, 1830–1861* (New York: Athenaeum, 1974); and Quarles, *Black Abolitionists*. More recent scholarship places black abolitionism within broader contexts and examines how African Americans shaped the course of the national antislavery struggle. See Timothy Patrick McCarthy and John Stauffer, eds., *Prophets of Protest: Reconsidering the History of American Abolitionism* (New York: New Press, 2006).

57. Field, *Politics of Race*, 5–6.

58. Announcing his itinerary in the pages of the *Colored American*, Bell encouraged black residents of Fishkill, Hudson, and Catskill to organize meetings in anticipation of his visit. *Colored American*, August 19, August 26, 1837.

59. For a detailed examination of the contentious ideological debate within

the African American community about color and racial identification, see Rael, *Black Identity and Racial Protest in the Antebellum North*.

60. *Colored American*, May 2, 1840.

61. In endorsing separate black education, "A Friend" predicted, "We will see colored men arise from the state of gloomy despondency in which they have been, and come forth with joy and gladness." *Colored American*, May 23, 1840.

62. *Colored American*, June 6, 1840. "H. Johnson" was likely either Harry or Harmon Johnson.

63. *Colored American*, July 4, 1840. Blount remained active in Hudson Valley affairs even after he assumed a new pastorship in Connecticut.

64. *Colored American*, August 8, 1840.

65. While serving as a pastor in Stockbridge, Massachusetts, Reverend Mars traveled to Catskill, New York, in August 1836, where he played an active role in the spirited emancipation celebration in that community. *Emancipator*, August 11, 1836. Mars was reputedly "more an antislavery lecturer than a preacher." He left the Mid-Hudson Valley in 1842 or 1843 to labor in New England. Hood, *One Hundred Years*, 67, 83; Moore, *History of the A.M.E. Zion Church*, 218–19. See also *National Anti-Slavery Standard*, August 24, 1843.

66. Gaius C. Bolin, Sr., "History of the A.M.E. Zion Church," in Rollin Howard Masten, "Dutchess County Churches," vol. 5 (unpublished, n.d.), Adriance Memorial Library, Poughkeepsie, New York, 73–77.

67. *Colored American*, July 25, August 22, August 29, September 12, October 31, 1840; January 2, January 9, 1841; Philip Foner and George E. Walker, eds., *Proceedings of the Black State Conventions, 1840–1865*, vol. 1 (Philadelphia: Temple University Press), 9–15. Although local residents nominated John N. Gloucester to serve as a convention delegate, there is no record of Gloucester's attendance at the meeting.

68. *Colored American*, September 12, October 17, 1840; February 13, 1841. The number of signatures from the various communities were as follows: New York City 1,300, Rochester 107, Poughkeepsie 101, Flushing 100, Utica 84, Hudson 82, Troy 80, Syracuse 70, Newburgh 55, Schenectady 26, Windsor 21, St. Andrew's 20, Lansingburgh 13. Appearing on the convention's petition are 134 names, while 214 whites from Schenectady and 400 from New York City also signed petitions for equal suffrage. See also Field, *Politics of Race*, 45; Foner and Walker, *Proceedings of the Black State Conventions*, 13.

69. *Colored American*, October 2, 1841; *Black Abolitionist Papers*, reel 4, no. 231.

70. Phyllis Field examines the political context for the 1846 constitutional convention in *Politics of Race*, 43–52.

71. S. Croswell and R. Sutton, *Debates and Proceedings in the New York State Convention for the Revision of the Constitution* (Albany: Albany Argus, 1846), 68, 246, 775–78, 782–93, 795–99, 819–24, 828, 836. Phyllis Field summarizes convention debates and analyzes delegate votes in *Politics of Race*, 52–57, 231–35.

72. The committee included Uriah Boston, Jared Gray, D. Gordon, and William Jennings. *National Anti-Slavery Standard*, January 29, 1846.

73. *Poughkeepsie Telegraph*, April 29, May 17, 1846.

74. Statewide, the referendum was defeated by a vote of 224,336 to 85,406; Dutchess County voters rejected equal suffrage by a ratio of 6,523 to 858. The margin in most other Hudson Valley counties was even more overwhelming. While 11.6 percent of Dutchess County voters (and 11.2 percent in Columbia County) supported the amendment, only 6.9 percent in Orange, 5.3 in Greene, 4.4 in Ulster, 4.1 in Westchester, 3.6 in Rockland, and 2.3 percent in Putnam cast ballots for equal suffrage. Field, *Politics of Race*, 61–63, 236–37. The returns for Dutchess County by town appear in the *Poughkeepsie Telegraph*, November 25, 1846. Field notes that the lukewarm endorsement of the measure by the Whig *Poughkeepsie Journal and Eagle* called only for the equal rights and privileges of all citizens and avoided any reference to race. Field, *Politics of Race*, 50.

75. *Colored American*, July 4, 1840.

76. The committee included five men (Uriah Boston, William H. Noland, Mr. Jennings, A. Bradford, and Mr. Mitchell) and five women (Mrs. Boston, Mrs. Simmons, Mrs. Vermong, Miss J. E. Williams, and Miss A. M. Williams). *Colored American*, October 2, 1841.

77. *Colored American*, October 24, November 28, 1840; *Black Abolitionist Papers*, reel 3, no. 722. The cultural significance of the African American press and its impact on the freedom struggle are examined in Timothy Patrick McCarthy, "'To Plead Our Own Cause': Black Print Culture and the Origins of American Abolitionism," in *Pamphlets of Protest: Reconsidering the History of American Abolitionism*, ed. Timothy Patrick McCarthy and John Stauffer (New York: New Press, 2006), 114–44. See also Reed, *Platform for Change*, chap. 4.

78. *Colored American*, May 18, 1839; October 31, 1840. "A Friend" argued that votes for a third party were not only ineffectual but also ultimately detrimental to the abolitionist cause. A "scattering" of votes between the two major parties was more effective because it pressured both parties to adopt a more antislavery posture. References to additional communications from "A Friend" in Poughkeepsie appear in the *Colored American*, October 20, 1838.

79. *Colored American*, February 20, 1841. For an exploration of the so-called "names controversy," see Rael, *Black Identity and Black Protest*, chap. 3.

80. *Poughkeepsie Journal and Eagle*, July 11, 1846; *Poughkeepsie Telegraph*, June 17, July 8, July 15, 1846. See also the *Rhinebeck Gazette*, July 14, 1846.

81. The evening session reportedly degenerated into something of a "melee." *Poughkeepsie Journal and Eagle*, July 14, 1849; *Poughkeepsie Telegraph*, July 11, July 18, 1849. Poughkeepsie's Uriah Boston was elected president of the Delevan Temperance Union at the 1849 meeting.

82. *Poughkeepsie Journal and Eagle*, July 11, 1846. The *Poughkeepsie Telegraph* similarly described the proceedings as a "gala day." See *Poughkeepsie Telegraph*, June 17, July 8, July 15, 1846. The equally impressive meeting three years later evoked a similar response. Considering it a "finger mark of the age" that such a large throng of colored people should assemble unmolested and deliberate

peacefully, the *Journal and Eagle* patronizingly expressed gratification that "a class of persons so far depressed, should have learned that elevation in the scale of being depended upon self-exertion." *Poughkeepsie Journal and Eagle*, July 14, 1849.

83. See Bethel, *The Roots of African-American Identity*; Glaude, *Exodus!*, chap. 5; Gravely, "Dialectic of Double-Consciousness"; Jeffrey, "'No Occurrence in Human History Is More Deserving of Commemoration Than This'"; McKivigan and Silverman, "Monarchial Liberty and Republican Slavery"; Rael, *Black Identity and Black Protest*; and Wiggins, *O Freedom!*.

## Chapter 7. Black Dutchess County at Midcentury

1. *Poughkeepsie Eagle*, January 25, 1851.

2. "John A. Bolding, Fugitive Slave," *Yearbook*, Dutchess County Historical Society 20 (1935): 51–55; Mid-Hudson Antislavery History Project, *Slavery, Antislavery, and the Underground Railroad: A Dutchess County Guide*, 46–47; *Poughkeepsie Journal and Eagle*, August 30, September 6, September 13, 1851; *Poughkeepsie Telegraph*, September 2, September 9, September 16, 1851. The *Poughkeepsie Journal and Eagle* reprinted the report of the proceedings originally published in the *New York Commercial Advertiser*.

3. The *Eagle* dismissed Green's fears, suggesting that Green, who had been arrested for an assault and battery allegedly committed when he was intoxicated, demonstrated "symptoms of insanity." *Poughkeepsie Eagle*, April 25, 1855.

4. As for Douglass himself, the *Telegraph* conceded that the eloquent speaker was "an extraordinary man" who "far exceeded anything we expected of him." *Poughkeepsie Telegraph*, October 13, 1847. See also *Poughkeepsie Journal and Eagle*, October 9, 1847.

5. *Poughkeepsie Journal and Eagle*, October 30, 1847.

6. *National Anti-Slavery Standard*, November 1, November 8, November 22, November 29, 1849; *Poughkeepsie Journal and Eagle*, November 3, November 10, November 17, November 24, 1849. Lucretia Mott returned to Dutchess County a year later and addressed a large audience in Poughkeepsie in October. *Poughkeepsie Eagle*, October 26, 1850.

7. The classic examination of free labor ideology is Eric Foner, *Free Soil, Free Labor, Free Men: The Ideology of the Republican Party before the Civil War* (New York: Oxford University Press, 1970). See also Foner, *Politics and Ideology in the Age of the Civil War* (New York: Oxford University Press, 1980).

8. *Poughkeepsie Telegraph*, September 13, 1848.

9. Those present decided not to bother sending delegates to the state political convention. *Poughkeepsie Journal and Eagle*, September 1, 1849.

10. *National Anti-Slavery Standard*, November 22, 1849.

11. *National Anti-Slavery Standard*, December 27, 1849. See also February 14 and March 7, 1850.

12. *Poughkeepsie Journal and Eagle*, August 31, 1850; *Poughkeepsie Telegraph*, August 28, 1850. Reporting on a "sort of abolition convention" in Syracuse in early 1851 that drew only "a baker's dozen" and "amounted to nothing," the *Eagle* reassured its readers, "There never was less abolitionism in this state than at the present." *Poughkeepsie Eagle*, March 15, 1851.

13. *Rhinebeck Gazette*, May 25, 1850.

14. *Poughkeepsie Telegraph*, September 2, 1851.

15. *Poughkeepsie Journal and Eagle*, August 30, 1851.

16. Bruegel, *Farm, Shop, Landing*, chap. 4; Ellis, *Landlords and Farmers in the Hudson-Mohawk Region, 1790–1850*; Wermuth, *Rip Van Winkle's Neighbors*, chap. 6._

17. The owner of an estate valued at $1,500, Heady ranked as the county's second-largest African American farmer. Population Schedules of the Seventh Census of the United States, 1850, New York, Dutchess County, microcopy 432, roll 496 (Washington, DC: 1963), 136, 285.

18. Only five farmers were listed as owning real estate. Census records provide a poor measure of property ownership, but returns are suggestive. See Curry, *The Free Black in Urban America, 1800–1850*, 267–69.

19. The imprecise label of "farmer" designated tenants and agricultural laborers as well as freeholders. Eight black or mulatto "farmers" in the census, for example, resided in white-headed households. "Farmer" was the only occupation for African American men in Pine Plains. All nine black "farmers" in the town—five of whom resided in white households and none of whom were identified as owning real estate—were likely farm laborers. Seventh Census, roll 496, 185–97.

20. Seventh Census, roll 496, 142. The twelve boatmen hailed from Red Hook, Milan, Stanford, Poughkeepsie, and Fishkill.

21. Black residents living and working in white households were dispersed across the county, but those explicitly identified as coachmen, cooks, servants, and waiters came overwhelmingly from western river towns, especially Poughkeepsie.

22. Seventh Census, roll 496, 150, 178.

23. Seventh Census, roll 497, 53, 99, 115, 117, 125, 126, 180, 189, 341.

24. Seventh Census, roll 496, 7, 9, 12, 22, 66, 106, 178.

25. See Armstead, *Freedom's Gardener*, especially chaps. 3–6; and A. J. Williams-Myers, *On the Morning Tide: African Americans, History, and Methodology in the Historical Ebb and Flow of Hudson River Society* (Trenton: Africana World Press, 2003), chap. 4.

26. *C. P. Luyster's Directory for the Village of Poughkeepsie*, 1843, 4, 11, 13; *Directory*, 1844, 4, 11, 13; *Directory*, 1845, 5, 10; *Directory*, 1847, 3, 9, 11; *Directory*, 1849, 4, 9; Mid-Hudson Antislavery History Project, *Slavery, Antislavery, and the Underground Railroad*, 42.

27. Seventh Census, roll 496, 177.

28. The absence of occupational differentiation in the countryside is

particularly striking. Returns for ten county towns—Beekman, Hyde Park, LaGrange, Northeast, Pawling, Pine Plains, Pleasant Valley, Rhinebeck, Union Vale, and Washington—listed only three different occupational categories for black men: laborers, domestics, and farmers. Martin Bruegel discovered a similarly narrow spectrum of occupations in Columbia and Greene Counties. See Bruegel, *Farm, Shop, and Landing*, 144–45.

29. Most holdings were small, typically valued at a few hundred dollars, but eight laborers managed to acquire larger estates. Robert Dewitt and Isaac Adkins, two Fishkill laborers, owned property valued at $1,000 and $900, respectively.

30. Seventh Census, roll 496, 7, 101; roll 497, 103, 110, 135, 260. Thomas held $700 in property; Sacket $500; Abraham Bradford $300; Thomas Bradford $600.

31. Bruegel, *Farm, Shop, Landing*, chap. 4, especially 105–14; McDermott, *Dutchess County's Plain Folks*, chaps. 3 and 9.

32. Bruegel, *Farm, Shop, Landing*, chap. 5; Griffen and Griffen, *Natives and Newcomers*, chap. 7; McDermott, *Dutchess County's Plain Folks*, chap. 10; Wermuth, *Rip Van Winkle's Neighbors*, chap. 6 and conclusion.

33. Seventh Census, roll 496, 12, 178; roll 497, 341.

34. Armstead, *Freedom's Gardener*, 65; Williams-Myers, *On the Morning Tide*, 89–90.

35. The number of black county residents on assessment rolls rose from 80 in 1825 to 379 30 years later, but that increase lagged far behind that for the state as a whole; the number of black taxpayers statewide increased by almost five times between 1845 and 1855 alone. *Journal of the Senate of the State of New York, Forty-Ninth Session* (Albany: E. Croswell, 1826); *Census of the State of New York for 1835* (Albany: Croswell, Benthuysen, and Burt, 1836); *Census of the State of New York for 1845* (Albany: Carroll and Cook, 1846); *Census of the State of New York* (Albany: Charles Van Benthuysen, 1857). State censuses were linked to federal manuscript censuses. In 1839 Poughkeepsie, twelve African American taxpayers—comprising fifteen percent of black household heads—collectively held real estate valued at $3,550, accounting for a miniscule 0.1 percent of all assessed property in the town. Five years later, twelve black residents owned fourteen different properties with an aggregate assessed value of $4,450, but the largest property did not exceed $700. No African Americans can be positively identified in assessment rolls for 1829 or 1834. See also Griffen and Griffen, *Natives and Newcomers*, 79–80.

36. Griffen and Griffen, *Natives and Newcomers*, 123. In citing credit reports made by the R. G. Dun & Company, the Griffens maintained the anonymity of their subjects, identifying individuals by their initials rather than their full names. I am very grateful to Clyde Griffen for graciously sharing their research.

37. Griffen and Griffen, *Natives and Newcomers*, 214.

38. Griffen and Griffen, *Natives and Newcomers*, chap. 11.

39. Assessment Roll, Town of Poughkeepsie, 1844, Adriance Memorial

Library, Poughkeepsie, New York. In addition to Nathaniel and Elisabeth, the Townsend household in 1850 included Jane and William, each twenty-nine years of age, and their infant child Judith. Seventh Census, roll 497, 125.

40. James Smith, *History of Dutchess County, New York*, 534; Williams-Myers, "The Arduous Journey," 29.

41. Tracing the path of the epidemic across the nation in 1832 and anticipating its arrival in the region, the *Telegraph* observed, "This epidemic appears to operate as a scourge upon the filthy and intemperate. It strikes down the drunkard as with a strong arm; and searches out the dwellings of the filthy, and the haunts of the polluted, as if it delighted to show its power there." *Poughkeepsie Telegraph*, July 25, 1832. For the 1832 outbreak, see *Poughkeepsie Journal*, August 1, August 8, August 15, August 22, August 29, and September 5, 1832; *Poughkeepsie Telegraph*, August 1, August 8, August 15, August 22, August 29, 1832. In one report during the 1849 outbreak, the Board of Health noted that four of eight victims who succumbed to the disease during a particular week in July were African Americans who had not received proper medical attention because authorities "could not for a time induce any people to care for them." See *Poughkeepsie Journal and Eagle*, July 21, July 28, August 4, August 11, August 18, August 25, September 1, September 8, September 15, 1849; *Poughkeepsie Telegraph*, July 18, July 25, August 1, August 8, August 15, August 22, August 29, September 5, September 12, 1849.

42. The *Poughkeepsie Journal and Eagle* noted the building's destruction would not be regretted had the loss not fallen "upon the name of a worthy colored man named Townsend, who had no insurance." *Poughkeepsie Journal and Eagle*, August 31, 1850.

43. *Poughkeepsie Telegraph*, November 13, 1850.

44. James Brown recorded "great excitement" in Fishkill Landing precipitated by rioting among Irish workmen in early 1849. The sheriff and Poughkeepsie Guards arrived to restore order. James F. Brown Diary, New-York Historical Society, New York, New York, January 4, January 6, January 9, January 10, 1849.

45. *Poughkeepsie Journal and Eagle*, February 2, February 9, February 16, February 23, 1850; *Poughkeepsie Telegraph*, January 30, February 6, February 13, 1850.

46. As late as 1845, more than nine of ten Dutchess County residents were native-born. Ten years later, foreign-born immigrants—almost two-thirds of whom were Irish—comprised one-sixth of the county's population. More than four of ten Poughkeepsie residents were foreign-born in 1855. McDermott, *Dutchess County's Plain Folks*, 172–73.

47. See Griffen and Griffen, *Natives and Newcomers*, and Hinerfeld, "The Fading Veneer of Equality."

48. James Brown Diary, January 21, 1846; Armstead, *Freedom's Gardener*, 114–15. Brown also promoted abolitionist Gerrit Smith's scheme to establish a free black colony in northern New York.

49. Douglas Walter Bristol, Jr., provides a comprehensive history of African American barbers in *Knights of the Razor: Black Barbers in Slavery and Freedom* (Baltimore: Johns Hopkins University Press, 2009).

50. Failure to do so was "selfish," "short-sighted," "mean," and "cruelly unjust." *Frederick Douglass' Paper*, March 4, March 11, March 18, 1853.

51. *Frederick Douglass' Paper*, April 1, 1853.

52. Douglass continued to deny having attacked barbers but agreed to publish the subsequent letter wherein Boston had "quite redeemed his penmanship." *Frederick Douglass' Paper*, April 15, April 22, 1853. The exchange between Boston and Douglass is examined in Bristol, *Knights of the Razor*, 114–19, and Harris, *In the Shadow of Slavery*, 232–34, 240–42.

53. Out of a total of fifty-six candidates from across the state, the Poughkeepsie abolitionist received the fourth-highest number of votes from the convention's delegates. *Frederick Douglass Paper*, December 9 and December 23, 1853.

54. Although he was not present in Troy, Boston was among those who assembled in a meeting of "colored citizens" in Poughkeepsie just days after the close of the convention to hear the convention's report and organize a local suffrage association. *Frederick Douglass' Paper*; July 20, September 14, October 5, 1855.

55. *Frederick Douglass' Paper*, June 24, 1853; *Black Abolitionist Papers*, reel 8, number 314.

56. *Frederick Douglass' Paper*; January 19, 1855; *Black Abolitionist Papers*, reel 9, number 393. Religious imagery and jeremiad characterized much of African American nationalist thought during the decade preceding the Civil War. See Glaude, *Exodus!*, and Rael, *Black Identity and Black Protest in the Antebellum North*, chap. 7, especially 266–71.

57. *Frederick Douglass' Paper*, April 22, 1855; *Black Abolitionist Papers*, reel 9, number 546; C. Peter Ripley, ed., *The Black Abolitionist Papers*, vol. 4 (Chapel Hill: University of North Carolina Press, 1991), 278–80. Patrick Rael explores the ideological debate between Boston and black nationalists like Smith, Wilson, and Martin Delany in *Black Identity and Black Protest*, chap. 7, especially 237–41.

58. In closing his letter, Boston asked, "Why should citizens of the free States shudder at the oft-repeated threat of dissolutions?" *Frederick Douglass' Paper*, August 31, 1855; *Black Abolitionist Papers*, reel 9, no. 817. See also Rael, *Black Identity and Black Protest*, 261–66.

59. *Frederick Douglass' Paper*, September 28, 1855; *Black Abolitionist Papers*, reel 9, number 849; and Ripley, *Black Abolitionist Papers*, vol. 4, 304–09. Later in the year, Boston added his voice to the chorus of abolitionists who engaged in rigorous debates with proslavery theorists. *Frederick Douglass' Paper*, December 14, 1855; *Black Abolitionist Papers*, reel 9, number 981; Ripley, *Black Abolitionist Papers*, vol. 4, 323–25.

60. Audiences were small for the most part, but the final meeting in Pleasant Valley drew a "large and specially [*sic*] intelligent audience." The tour also

included a stop across the river in Milton. *Poughkeepsie Eagle*, March 14, May 9, May 30, 1857. A similar tour the following spring that included William Lloyd Garrison himself was disrupted by Garrison's illness. *Poughkeepsie Eagle*, February 6, February 13, March 6, 1858.

61. *Poughkeepsie Eagle*, January 9, January 16, 1858.

62. The 1859 celebration included a well-attended ball. *Poughkeepsie Eagle*, July 17, July 31, August 7, 1858; *Poughkeepsie Eagle*, July 30, August 6, 1859; *Weekly Anglo-African*, August 13, 1859. The full text of Douglass' oration appears in John W. Blassingame, ed., *The Frederick Douglass Papers, Series One: Speeches, Debates, and Interviews*, vol. 3 (New Haven: Yale University Press, 1985), 214–42.

63. *Weekly Anglo-African*, August 13, 1859.

64. *Weekly Anglo-African*, December 31, 1859; March 31, 1860.

65. The rift in the larger church was healed in 1860, and the cornerstone of a new building for Poughkeepsie's reunited congregation was laid early that fall. Charles J. Sargent, Jr., "The Negro Church in Dutchess County, New York" (unpublished paper, September 30, 1955) Adriance Memorial Library, Poughkeepsie, New York, 1. "Romeo's" otherwise positive assessment of the Poughkeepsie community noted lagging church attendance and low school enrollments. The report was also marred by news of the tragic death of Lydia Freeman by poisoning and the subsequent trial of her husband Ishmael for murder. *Weekly Anglo-African*, December 31, 1859; March 31, 1860.

66. *Frederick Douglass' Paper*, October 19, 1855.

67. See Quarles, *Black Abolitionists*, 56–58.

68. *Colored American*, August 21, 1841.

# Bibliography


## Primary Sources

### *A. Unpublished Collections and Archival Materials*

Adriance Memorial Library, Poughkeepsie, New York
Assessment Rolls, Town of Poughkeepsie, 1829, 1834, 1839, 1844.
Record of the Overseers of the Poor, Town of Poughkeepsie, 1807–1815.
Records of the Town Clerk of Amenia Precinct, 1749–1868.
Records of the Town of Poughkeepsie Precinct, 1769–1831.

Dutchess County Archives, Poughkeepsie, New York
Ancient Documents Collection, 1732–1800.
Church Incorporations, 2 vols.
Election Book, 1835–1844.
Record of Roads, 1744–1788.
Town of Beekman Record Book, 1772–1827.

Dutchess County Historical Society, Poughkeepsie, New York
Alson Ward Diary, 1843–1847 (typescript).
John Bower Diary, 1842–1845 (typescript).
Petition of Slaveholders of Ulster County to the Legislature of the State of New York, December 28, 1791.

Dutchess County Surrogate's Court, Poughkeepsie, New York
Will Books AA–H.

*Hudson River Valley Heritage*. Southeastern New York Library Research Council http://hrvh.org/.

New-York Historical Society, New York, New York
James F. Brown Diary, 1829–1866, 8 vols. (microfilm).

Manuscript and Archives Division, New York Public Library, New York, New York

Dutchess County Anti-Slavery Society Executive Committee Minutes, 1837–1840.

New York State Archives, Albany, New York
Eighteenth-Century Wills Collection.

Pleasant Valley Historical Society, Pleasant Valley, New York
Rebecca Hitchcock Benton "Reminiscences," revised by William A. Benton

Poughkeepsie City School District, Poughkeepsie, New York
Record of the Proceedings of the Board of Education of Poughkeepsie, 1843–1854.

Rhinebeck Historical Society, Rhinebeck, New York
Record of Slaves.

Franklin Delano Roosevelt Library, Hyde Park, New York
Constitution and Names of the Members of the Poughkeepsie Anti-Slavery Society.
Smith Thompson File.

Stanford Public Library, Stanfordville, New York
Town of Stanford Records, 1793–1824 (microfilm).

Starr Library, Rhinebeck, New York
Rhinebeck Town Documents, 1718–1842.
Rhinebeck Town Records, 1748–1863 (microfilm).

State Senate House, Kingston, New York
Petition of the Subscribers, Freeholders, and Inhabitants of the Townships of Rochester, Marble, and Hurley, in the County of Ulster, 1785.
Speech of John Addison in the Committee of the Whole House, Against the Bill for the Gradual Abolition of Slavery.

Microfilm
*Black Abolitionist Papers*, 17 reels.
Federal Manuscript Censuses of Dutchess County, 1790–1860.
Nine Partners Monthly Meeting, Men's Minutes, 1769–1799, vol. 1153. LDS 17307.
Nine Partners Vital Records, 1769–1798, vol. 2005. LDS 0017311.
Oblong Monthly Meeting, Men's Minutes, vol. 1141, 1757–1781; vol. 1142, 1781–1788. LDS 0017315.

### *B. Antislavery and African-American Newspapers*

*Colored American*
*Emancipator*
*Frederick Douglass' Paper*
*Freedom's Journal*

*Friend of Man*
*Liberator*
*National Anti-Slavery Standard*
*North Star*
*Northern Star and Freeman's Advocate*
*Rights of All*
*Weekly Advocate*
*Weekly Anglo-African*

### *C. Dutchess County Newspapers*

*American Farmer and Dutchess County Advertiser*
*Country Journal and Poughkeepsie Advertiser*
*Dutchess Observer*
*Free Press*
*Herald of Reason and Common Sense*
*New York Journal and General Advertiser* (1777–1782)
*New York Packet and American Advertiser* (1777–1783)
*Political Barometer*
*Poughkeepsie Eagle*
*Poughkeepsie Journal*
*Poughkeepsie Journal and Constitutional Republican*
*Poughkeepsie Journal and Eagle*
*Poughkeepsie Telegraph*
*Republican Herald*
*Republican Telegraph*
*Republican Telegraph and Observer*
*Rhinebeck Gazette*
*Safeguard and General Temperance Advocate*

### *D. Published Primary Sources*

"Abstracts of Wills." *Collections of the New-York Historical Society*, vols. 1–18. New York: The Society, 1893–1909.

Allinson, William J. *Memoir of Quamino Buccau, A Pious Methodist*. Philadelphia: Henry Longstreth, 1851.

Andrews, Charles C. *The History of the New York African Free Schools*. New York: Negro Universities Press, 1969; originally published 1830.

*Annual Reports of the Superintendent of Common Schools*, 1814–1851.

Aptheker, Herbert, ed. *A Documentary History of the Negro People in the United States*, 6th edition, vol. 1. New York: Citadel Press, 1968.

Bailey, Henry D. B. *Local Tales and Historical Sketches*. Fishkill Landing: J. W. Spaight, 1874.

Bell, Howard H., ed. *Minutes of the Proceedings of the National Negro Conventions, 1830–1834*. New York: Arno Press, 1969.

Blassingame, John W., ed. *The Frederick Douglass Papers, Series One: Speeches, Debates, and Interviews*, vol. 3. New Haven: Yale University Press, 1985.

Bureau of Census. *A Century of Population Growth: From the First Census of the United States to the Twelfth, 1790–1900*. Washington, DC: Government Printing Office, 1909.

———. *Negro Population, 1790–1915*. New York: Arno Press and New York Times, 1968; originally published 1918.

*C. P. Luyster's Directory for the Village of Poughkeepsie*, 1843–1850.

*Calendar of Historical Manuscripts Relating to the War of the Revolution*, 2 vols. Albany: Weed, Parsons, & Company, 1868.

Carter, Nathaniel H., and William L. Stone. *Reports of the Proceedings and Debates of the Convention of 1821, Assembled for the Purpose of Amending the Constitution of the State of New York: Containing All the Official Documents, Relating to the Subject, and Other Valuable Matter.* Albany: E. & E. Howard, 1821.

Catterall, Helen T., ed. *Judicial Cases Concerning American Slavery and the Negro*, vol. 4. New York: Octagon Books, 1968.

*Census of the State of New York for 1835*. Albany: Croswell, Benthuysen, and Burt, 1836.

*Census of the State of New York for 1845*. Albany: Carroll and Cook, 1846.

*Census of the State of New York for 1855*. Albany: Charles Van Benthuysen, 1857.

*Colonial Laws of New York from the Year 1664 to the Revolution*, 5 vols. Albany: James B. Lyon, 1894.

Croswell, S., and R. Sutton. *Debates and Proceedings in the New York State Convention for the Revision of the Constitution*. Albany: Albany Argus, 1846.

Cuyler, Cornelius C. *A Narrative of the Revival of Religion in the Reformed Dutch Church at Poughkeepsie*. Poughkeepsie: P. & S. Potter, 1815.

De Crevecoeur, J. Hector St. John. *Letters from an American Farmer.* New York: E. P. Dutton & Company, 1912.

———. *Sketches of Eighteenth-Century America*, ed. Henri L. Bordin, Ralph H. Gabriel, and Stanley T. Williams. New Haven: Yale University Press, 1925.

Foner, Philip, and George E. Walker, eds. *Proceedings of the Black State Conventions, 1840–1865*, vol. 1. Philadelphia: Temple University Press, 1979.

Force, Peter, comp. *American Archives, Fourth Series*, 6 vols. Washington, DC: M. St. Clair Clarke and Peter Force, 1837–1846.

———. *American Archives, Fifth Series*, 3 vols. Washington, DC: M. St. Clair Clarke and Peter Force, 1848–1853.

Frost, Josephine C., comp. *Quaker Marriages, Births, Deaths, and Slaves, Nine Partners Monthly Meeting, Dutchess County, New York*. Brooklyn: 1910.

Gellman, David N., and David Quigley, eds. *Jim Crow New York: A Documentary History of Race and Citizenship, 1777–1877*. New York: New York University Press, 2003.

Gieson, A. P., comp. "Record of the First Reformed Church, Poughkeepsie, New York, 1716–1824." 1883.

Greene, Evarts B., and Virginia D. Harrington. *American Population before the Federal Census of 1790*. New York: Columbia University Press, 1932.

Greene, Marilyn Cole, comp. *Town Minutes, Town of Carmel, Putnam County, New York, 1795–1839*. Rhinebeck: Kinship Press, 1990.

*Heads of Families at the First Census of the United States Taken in the Year 1790: New York*. Baltimore: Genealogical Publishing Company, 1976.

*Historical Sketch and Directory of the Town of Fishkill, with an Appendix of Much Useful Information*. Fishkill Landing: Dean & Spaight, 1866.

Hodges, Graham, ed. *The Black Loyalist Directory: African Americans in Exile after the American Revolution*. New York: Garland, 1996.

Hurd, John C. *The Law of Freedom and Bondage in the United States*, vol. 2. New York: Negro Universities Press, 1968; originally published 1862.

*Journal of the Assembly of the State of New York.*

*Journal of the Senate of the State of New York.*

*Journals of the Provincial Congress, Provincial Convention, Committee of Safety, and Council of Safety of the State of New York, 1775–1777*, 2 vols. Albany: Thurlow Reed, 1842.

*Laws of the State of New York.*

"Manumissions in Dutchess County, New York." *Journal of the Afro-American Historical and Genealogical Society* 2, no. 2 (Summer 1981): 75–78.

McDermott, William, ed. *Eighteenth-Century Documents of the Nine Partners Patent*, comp. Clifford Buck and William McDermott. Collections of the Dutchess County Historical Society, vol. 10. Baltimore: Gateway Press, 1979.

"Minutes of the Committee and of the First Commission for Detecting and Defeating Conspiracies in the State of New York, December 11, 1776–September 23, 1778." In *Collections of the New-York Historical Society*, vols. 57 and 58. New York: 1924, 1925.

Nell, William C. *The Colored Patriots of the American Revolution*, with an introduction by Harriet Beecher Stowe. Boston: Robert F. Wallcut, 1855.

*New York in the Revolution as Colony and State*, 2 vols. Albany: J. B. Lyon & Company, 1904.

O'Callaghan, E. B. *The Documentary History of the State of New York*, 4 vols. Albany: Weed, Parsons, & Company, 1849–1851.

———. *Documents Relative to the Colonial History of the State of New York*, 15 vols. Albany: Weed, Parsons, & Company, 1853–1887.

Randall, S. S. *A Digest of the Common School System of the State of New York.* Albany: C. Van Benthuysen & Company, 1844.

Reynolds, Helen Wilkinson, ed. *Eighteenth-Century Records of the Portion of Dutchess County, New York That Was Included in Rombout Precinct and the Original Town of Fishkill*. Collections of the Dutchess County Historical Society, vol. 6. Albany: J. B. Lyon, 1938.

Ripley, C. Peter, ed. *The Black Abolitionist Papers*, vols. 3 and 4. Chapel Hill: University of North Carolina Press, 1991.

Roosevelt, Franklin Delano, ed. *Records of Crum Elbow Precinct, Dutchess County, New York 1738–1761, Together with Records of Charlotte Precinct, 1762–1785, Records of Clinton Precinct 1786–1788, and Records of the Town of Clinton, 1789–1799*. Collections of the Dutchess County Historical Society, vol. 7. Poughkeepsie: 1940.

———. *Records of the Town of Hyde Park, Dutchess County*. Collections of the Dutchess County Historical Society, vol. 3. Hyde Park: 1928.

*Seventh Annual Report of the American Society for Colonizing the Free People of Colour of the United States*. Washington, DC: Davis and Force, 1824.

*The Seventh Census of the United States: 1850*. Washington, DC: Robert Armstrong, 1853.

*The Sixth Census or Enumeration of the Inhabitants of the United States*. Washington, DC: 1841.

Spafford, Horatio Gates. *A Gazetteer of the State of New York*. Albany: H. C. Southwick, 1813.

———. *A Gazetteer of the State of New York*. Albany: B. D. Packard, 1824.

*Speech of the Hon. James Tallmadge, of Dutchess County, New York, in the House of Representatives of the United States, on Slavery*. Boston: Ticknor & Company, 1849.

Truth, Sojourner. *Narrative of Sojourner Truth*, ed. and intro. Margaret Washington. New York: Vintage Books, 1993.

Wile, Benjamin F. *Review of an Anti-Abolitionist Sermon, Preached at Pleasant Valley, New York*. Whitesboro: Press of the Oneida Institute, 1838.

Woolman, John. *The Journal of John Woolman*. London: Headley Brothers, 1903.

Worden, Jean D., comp. "First Reformed Church, Fishkill, Dutchess County, New York, and First Reformed Church, Hopewell, Dutchess County, New York." Fishkill: First Reformed Church, 1981.

———, comp. "Quaker Manumission, Nine Partners, Dutchess County, New York." *Journal of the Afro-American Historical and Genealogical Society* 3, no. 3 (Fall 1982).

## Secondary Sources

Alexander, John K. *Render Them Submissive: Responses to Poverty in Philadelphia, 1760–1800*. Amherst: University of Massachusetts Press, 1980.

Alexander, Leslie M. *African or American? Black Identity and Political Activism in New York City, 1784–1861*. Urbana: University of Illinois Press, 2008.

Appleby, Joyce. *Inheriting the Revolution: The First Generation of Americans*. Cambridge: Belknap Press of Harvard University Press, 2000.

Aptheker, Herbert. *Abolitionism: A Revolutionary Movement*. Boston: Twayne, 1989.

———. *American Negro Slave Revolts*. 5th ed. New York: International, 1983; originally published 1943.

———. *The Negro in the Abolitionist Movement*. New York: International, 1941.
———. *The Negro in the American Revolution*. New York: International, 1940.
———. *To Be Free: Studies in American Negro History*. New York: International, 1969; originally published 1948.

Armstead, Myra B. Young. *Freedom's Gardener: James F. Brown, Horticulture, and the Hudson Valley in Antebellum America*. New York: New York University Press, 2012.

Ball, Erica L. *To Live an Antislavery Life: Personal Politics and the Antebellum Black Middle Class*. Athens: University of Georgia Press, 2012.

Bayne, Martha Collins. *County at Large*. Poughkeepsie: Women's City and County Club with Vassar College, 1937.

Beers, J. H. *Commemorative Biographical Record of Dutchess County, New York*. Chicago: 1897.

Bell, Howard H. "Expressions of Negro Militancy in the North." *Journal of Negro History* 45, no. 1 (January 1960): 11–20.

———. "National Negro Conventions of the Middle 1840s: Moral Suasion vs. Political Action." *Journal of Negro History* 42, no. 4 (October 1957): 247–60.

———. *A Survey of the Negro Convention Movement, 1830–1861*. New York: Arno Press, 1969; originally published 1953.

Benson, Lee. *The Concept of Jacksonian Democracy: New York as a Test Case*. New York: Athenaeum, 1964.

Berlin, Ira. *Many Thousands Gone: The First Two Centuries of Slavery in North America*. Cambridge: Belknap Press of Harvard University Press, 1998.

———. "The Revolution in Black Life." In *The American Revolution: Explorations in the History of American Radicalism*, ed. Alfred Young, 349–82. DeKalb: Northern Illinois University Press, 1976.

———. *Slaves without Masters: The Free Negro in the Antebellum South*. New York: Pantheon Books, 1974.

———. "The Structure of the Free Negro Caste in the Antebellum United States." *Journal of Social History* 9, no. 3 (September 1976): 297–318.

Berlin, Ira, and Leslie M. Harris, eds. *Slavery in New York*. New York: New Press, 2005.

Berlin, Ira, and Ronald Hoffman, eds. *Slavery and Freedom in the Age of the American Revolution*. Charlottesville: University Press of Virginia, 1983.

Berlin, Ira, and Philip D. Morgan, eds. *Cultivation and Culture: Labor and the Shaping of Slave Life in the Americas*. Charlottesville: University Press of Virginia, 1993.

———. *The Slaves' Economy: Independent Production by Slaves in the Americas*. London: Frank Cass, 1991.

Bethel, Elizabeth Rauh. *The Roots of African-American Identity: Memory and History in Free Antebellum Communities*. New York: St. Martin's Press, 1999.

Blackburn, Robin. *The Overthrow of Colonial Slavery, 1776–1848*. New York: Verso, 1988.

Blackett, R. J. M. *Building an Antislavery Wall: Black Americans in the Atlantic Abolitionist Movement, 1830–1860*. Baton Rouge: Louisiana State University Press, 1983.

Bloch, Herman D. "The New York Negro's Battle for Political Rights, 1777–1865." *International Review of Social History* 9 (1964): 63–80.

Bolin, Gaius, Sr. "History of the AME Zion Church." In Rollin Howard Masten, Dutchess County Churches, vol. 5. Unpublished paper, Adriance Memorial Library, Poughkeepsie, n.d.

Bonomi, Patricia. *A Factious People: Politics and Society in Colonial New York*. New York: Columbia University Press, 1971.

Bordewich, Fergus M. *Bound for Canaan: The Underground Railroad and the War for the Soul of America*. New York: Harper Collins, 2005.

———. "The Underground Railroad in the New York Hudson Valley," July 28, 2005. http://www.fergusbordewich.com/blog/archives/2005/07/the_underground_1.html#more.

Bracey, John H., August Meier, and Elliott Rudwick, eds. *Blacks in the Abolition Movement*. Belmont: Wadsworth, 1971.

Brackett, Jeffrey R. "The Status of the Slave, 1775–1789." In *Essays in the Constitutional History of the United States in the Formative Period, 1775–1789*, ed. J. Franklin Jameson, 263–311. New York: DaCapo Press, 1970; originally published 1889.

Bradley, David Henry. *A History of the A.M.E. Zion Church, Part I, 1796–1872*. Nashville: Parthenon Press, 1956.

Breen, T. H. "Making History: The Force of Public Opinion and the Last Years of Slavery in Revolutionary Massachusetts." In *Through a Glass Darkly: Reflections on Personal Identity in Early America*, ed. Ronald Hoffman, Mechal Sobel, and Frederika Teute, 67–95. Chapel Hill: University of North Carolina Press, 1997.

Breyfogle, William. *Make Free: The Story of the Underground Railroad*. Philadelphia: Lippincott, 1958.

Brink, Benjamin Myer. *The Early History of Saugerties, 1660–1825*. Kingston: R. W. Anderson & Son, 1902.

Bristol, Douglas Walter, Jr. *Knight of the Razor: Black Barbers in Slavery and Freedom*. Baltimore: Johns Hopkins University Press, 2009.

Brooke, John L. *Columbia Rising: Civil Life on the Upper Hudson from the Revolution to the Age of Jackson*. Chapel Hill: University of North Carolina Press, 2010.

Bruegel, Martin. *Farm, Shop, Landing: The Rise of a Market Society in the Hudson Valley, 1780–1860*. Durham: Duke University Press, 2002.

———. "Uncertainty, Pluriactivity, and Neighborhood Exchange in the Rural Hudson Valley in the Late Eighteenth Century." *New York History* 77, no. 3 (July 1996): 245–72.

———. "Unrest: Manorial Society and the Market in the Hudson Valley, 1780–1850." *Journal of American History* 82, no. 4 (March 1996): 1393–1424.

Butler, Reginald Dennin. "Evolution of a Rural Free Black Community: Goochland County, Virginia, 1728–1832." PhD dissertation, Johns Hopkins University, 1989.

Caro, Edythe Quinn. *"The Hills" in the Mid-Nineteenth Century: The History of a Rural Afro-American Community in Westchester County, New York.* Valhalla: Westchester County Historical Society, 1988.

Castle, Musette S. "A Survey of the History of African Americans in Rochester, New York, 1800–1860." *Afro-Americans in New York Life and History* 13, no. 2 (July 1989): 7–32.

Clark, Jonathan C. "A Government to Form: The Story of Dutchess County and the Political Upheaval in Revolutionary New York." In *From English Colony to Sovereign State: Essays on the American Revolution in Dutchess County, Province of New York*, ed. Richard B. Morris, Jonathan C. Clark, and Charlotte Cunningham Finkel, 50–88. Millbrook: Dutchess County American Revolution Bicentennial Commission, 1983.

———. "The Problem of Allegiance in Revolutionary Poughkeepsie." In *Saints and Revolutionaries: Essays on Early American History*, ed. David D. Hall, John M. Murrin, and Thad W. Tate, 285–317. New York: W.W. Norton & Company, 1984.

Clay, Robert E., Jr. "Poverty and Poor Relief: New York City and Its Rural Environs, 1700–1790." In *Authority and Resistance in Early New York*, ed. William Pencak and Conrad Edick. New York: New-York Historical Society, 1988.

Clearwater, Alphonso T., ed. *The History of Ulster County, New York.* Kingston: W. J. Van Deusen, 1907.

Clement, Priscilla Ferguson. *Welfare and the Poor in the Nineteenth-Century City: Philadelphia, 1800–1854.* Rutherford: Farleigh Dickinson University Press, 1985.

Cohen, David Steven. "In Search of Carolus Africanus Rex: Afro-Dutch Folklore in New York and New Jersey." *Journal of the Afro-American Historical and Genealogical Society* 5, nos. 3–4 (1984): 148–68.

Cooper, Frederick. "Elevating the Race: The Social Thought of Black Leaders, 1827–1850." *American Quarterly* 24, no. 5 (December 1972): 604–25.

Cottrol, Robert J. *The Afro-Yankees: Providence's Black Community in the Antebellum Era.* Westport: Greenwood Press, 1982.

Countryman, Edward. *A People in Revolution: The American Revolution and Political Society in New York, 1760–1790.* Baltimore: Johns Hopkins University Press, 1981.

Cramer, George E. *Historical Sketch of the Poughkeepsie Public Schools and Public Library from 1843 to 1893.* Poughkeepsie: 1894.

Crane, Susan J. "Antebellum Dutchess County's Struggle against Slavery." *Yearbook*, Dutchess County Historical Society 65 (1980): 35–43.

Cray, Robert E., Jr. *Paupers and Poor Relief in New York City and Its Rural Environs, 1700–1830.* Philadelphia: Temple University Press, 1988.

———. "Poverty and Poor Relief: New York City and Its Rural Environs." In *Authority and Resistance in Early New York*, ed. William Pencak and Conrad Edick Wright, 173–201. New York: New-York Historical Society, 1988.

———. "White Welfare and Black Strategies: The Dynamics of Race and Poor Relief in Early New York, 1700–1825." *Slavery and Abolition* 7 (December 1986): 273–89.

Curry, Leonard P. *The Free Black in Urban America, 1800–1850: The Shadow of a Dream*. Chicago: University of Chicago Press, 1981.

Dain, Bruce. *A Hideous Monster of the Mind: American Race Theory in the Early Republic*. Cambridge: Harvard University Press, 2002.

Davis, David Brion. *The Problem of Slavery in the Age of Revolution, 1770–1823*. Ithaca: Cornell University Press, 1975.

———. *The Problem of Slavery in Western Culture*. Ithaca: Cornell University Press, 1966.

———. *Slavery and Human Progress*. New York: Oxford University Press, 1984.

Davis, Thomas J. "New York's Black Line: A Note on the Growing Slave Population." *Afro-Americans in New York Life and History* 2, no. 1 (January 1978): 41–59.

———. *A Rumor of Revolt: The "Great Negro Plot" in Colonial New York*. New York: Free Press, 1985.

Diamant, Lincoln. *Chaining the Hudson: The Fight for the River in the American Revolution*. New York: Fordham University Press, 2004.

Dick, Robert C. "Rhetoric of Ante-Bellum Black Separatism." *Negro History Bulletin* 34, no. 6 (October 1971): 133–37.

Dillon, Merton L. *The Abolitionists: The Growth of a Dissenting Minority*. DeKalb: Northern Illinois University Press, 1974.

Drake, Thomas E. *Quakers and Slavery in America*. Gloucester: P. Smith, 1965; originally published 1950.

Duberman, Martin, ed. *The Antislavery Vanguard: New Essays on the Abolitionists*. Princeton: Princeton University Press, 1965.

Du Bois, W. E. B. *The Souls of Black Folk*, ed. David W. Blight and Robert Gooding-Williams. Boston/New York: Bedford Books, 1997; originally published 1903.

Dumond, Dwight Lowell. *Antislavery: The Crusade for Freedom in America*. Ann Arbor: University of Michigan Press, 1961.

East, Robert, and Jacob Judd, eds. *The Loyalist Americans: A Focus on Greater New York*. Tarrytown: Sleepy Hollow Restorations, 1975.

Egerton, Douglas R. *Death or Liberty: African Americans and Revolutionary America*. New York: Oxford University Press, 2009.

Ellis, David Maldwyn. *Landlords and Farmers in the Hudson-Mohawk Region, 1790–1850*. Ithaca: Cornell University Press, 1946.

Ellis, David M., James A. Frost, Harold C. Syrett, and Harry J. Carman.

*A History of New York State*, revised ed. Ithaca: Cornell University Press, 1967.

Ely, Melvin Patrick. *Israel on the Appomattox: A Southern Experiment in Black Freedom from the 1790s through the Civil War*. New York: Alfred A. Knopf, 2004.

Farley, Ena L. "The African-American Presence in the History of Western New York." *Afro-Americans in New York Life and History* 14, no. 1 (January 1990): 27–89.

Federal Writers' Project. *Dutchess County, American Guide Series*. Philadelphia: William Penn Association of Philadelphia, 1937.

Field, Phyllis F. *The Politics of Race in New York: The Struggle for Black Suffrage in the Civil War Era*. Ithaca: Cornell University Press, 1982.

Filler, Louis. *The Crusade Against Slavery, 1830–1860*. New York: Harper & Row, 1960.

Flick, Alexander C. *The American Revolution in New York: Its Political, Social, and Economic Significance*. Albany: State University of New York, 1926.

Fogel, Robert William, and Stanley L. Engerman. "Philanthropy at Bargain Prices: Notes on the Economics of Gradual Emancipation." *Journal of Legal Studies* 3, no. 2 (June 1974): 377–401.

Foner, Eric. *Free Soil, Free Labor, Free Men: The Ideology of the Republican Party before the Civil War*. New York: Oxford University Press, 1970.

———. *Politics and Ideology in the Age of the Civil War*. New York: Oxford University Press, 1980.

Foner, Philip S. *Blacks in the American Revolution*. Westport: Greenwood Press, 1975.

Foote, Thelma Louise. *Black and White Manhattan: The History of Racial Formation in Colonial New York City*. New York: Oxford University Press, 2004.

Fordham, Monroe. *The African-American Presence in New York State History: Four Regional History Surveys*. Albany: State University of New York Press, 1990.

———. *Major Themes in Northern Black Religious Thought, 1800–1860*. Hicksville: Exposition Press, 1975.

Franklin, John Hope, and Loren Schweninger. *Runaway Slaves: Rebels on the Plantation*. New York: Oxford University Press, 1999.

Frazier, E. Franklin. *The Free Negro Family: A Study of Family Origins before the Civil War*. New York: Arno Press, 1968; originally published 1932.

———. *The Negro Church in America*. New York: Schocken Books, 1974; originally published 1963.

———. *The Negro Family in the United States*, revised ed. Chicago: University of Chicago Press, 1966; originally published 1939.

Fredriksen, Beatrice, comp. *The Role of Dutchess County during the American Revolution*. Dutchess County American Revolution Bicentennial Project, 1976.

Freeman, Rhonda Golden. "The Free Negro in New York City in the Era before the Civil War." PhD dissertation, Columbia University, 1966.

Frey, Sylvia. *Water from the Rock: Black Resistance in a Revolutionary Age*. Princeton: Princeton University Press, 1991.

Gara, Larry. *The Liberty Line: The Legend of the Underground Railroad*. Lexington: University of Kentucky Press, 1961.

Geismar, Joan H. *The Archaeology of Social Disintegration in Skunk Hollow: A Nineteenth-Century Rural Black Community*. New York: Academic Press, 1982.

Gellman, David N. *Emancipating New York: The Politics of Slavery and Freedom, 1777–1827*. Baton Rouge: Louisiana State University Press, 2006.

———. "Race, the Public Sphere, and Abolition in Late Eighteenth-Century New York." *Journal of the Early Republic* 20, no. 4 (Winter 2000): 607–36.

Genovese, Eugene D. *From Rebellion to Revolution: Afro-American Slave Revolts in the Making of the Modern World*. Baton Rouge: Louisiana State University Press, 1979.

George, Carol V. R. *Segregated Sabbaths: Richard Allen and the Emergence of Independent Black Churches, 1760–1840*. New York: Oxford University Press, 1973.

———. "Widening the Circle: The Black Church and the Abolitionist Crusade, 1830–1860." In *Antislavery Reconsidered: New Perspectives on the Abolitionists*, ed. Lewis Perry and Michael Fellman, 75–95. Baton Rouge: Louisiana State University Press, 1979.

Gerzina, Gretchen Holbrook. *Mr. and Mrs. Prince: How an Extraordinary Eighteenth-Century Family Moved Out of Slavery and into Legend*. New York: Amistad/ Harper Collins, 2008.

Ghee, Joyce C., ed. *Transformations of an American County: Dutchess County, New York, 1683–1983*. Poughkeepsie: Dutchess County Historical Society, 1986.

Gigantino II, James J. *The Ragged Road to Abolition: Slavery and Freedom in New Jersey, 1775–1865*. Philadelphia: University of Pennsylvania Press, 2015.

———. "'The Whole Nation Is Not Abolitionized': Slavery's Slow Death in New Jersey, 1830–1860." *Journal of the Early Republic* 34, no. 3 (Fall 2014): 411–37.

Gilbert, Alan. *Black Patriots and Loyalists: Fighting for Emancipation in the War for Independence*. Chicago: University of Chicago Press, 2012.

Gilje, Paul. *Rioting in America*. Bloomington: Indiana University Press, 1996.

———. *The Road to Mobocracy: Popular Disorder in New York City, 1763–1834*. Chapel Hill: University of North Carolina Press, 1987.

Gindele, John D. "The Public Career of James Tallmadge." *Yearbook*, Dutchess County Historical Society, part 1 45 (1960): 39–80, part 2 46 (1961): 52–93.

Glaude, Eddie S. *Exodus! Religion, Race, and Nation in Early Nineteenth-Century Black America*. Chicago: University of Chicago Press, 2000.

Goodfriend, Joyce D. *Before the Melting Pot: Society and Culture in Colonial New York City, 1664–1730*. Princeton: Princeton University Press, 1992.

———. "Burghers and Blacks: The Evolution of a Slave Society at New Amsterdam." *New York History* 59, no. 2 (April 1978): 125–44.

———. "Merging the Two Streams of Migration to New Netherland." In *The Worlds of the Seventeenth-Century Hudson Valley*, ed. Japp Jacobs and L. H. Roper, 237–52. Albany: State University of New York Press, 2014.

———. "Slavery in Colonial New York City." *Urban History* 35, no. 3 (2008): 485–96.

Gravely, William B. "The Dialectic of Double-Consciousness in Black American Freedom Celebrations, 1808–1863." *Journal of Negro History* 67, no. 4 (Winter 1982): 302–17.

———. "The Rise of African Churches in America, 1786–1822: Re-examining the Contexts." *Journal of Religious Thought* 41, no. 1 (Spring/Summer 1984): 58–73.

Greene, Jack P. *Understanding the American Revolution: Issues and Actors*. Charlottesville: University Press of Virginia, 1995.

Griffen, Clyde, and Sally Griffen. *Natives and Newcomers: The Ordering of Opportunity in Mid-Nineteenth-Century Poughkeepsie*. Cambridge: Harvard University Press, 1978.

Grigg, Susan. *The Dependent Poor of Newburyport: Studies in Social History, 1800–1830*. Ann Arbor: UMI Research Press, 1984.

Grimsted, David. *American Mobbing, 1828–1861: Toward Civil War*. New York: Oxford University Press, 1998.

Gronowicz, Anthony. *Race and Class Politics in New York City before the Civil War*. Boston: Northeastern University Press, 1998.

Grover, Kathryn. *Make a Way Somehow: African-American Life in a Northern Community, 1790–1865*. Syracuse: Syracuse University Press, 1994.

Hackett, Henry T. "The Hyde Park Patent." *Yearbook*, Dutchess County Historical Society 24 (1939): 75–90.

Harding, Vincent. "Religion and Resistance among Antebellum Negroes." In *The Making of Black America*, ed. August Meier and Elliott Rudwick, vol. 1, 179–97. New York: Athenaeum, 1969.

Harris, Leslie M. *In the Shadow of Slavery: African Americans in New York City, 1626–1863*. Chicago: University of Chicago Press, 2003.

Hartgrove, W. B. "The Negro Soldier in the American Revolution." *Journal of Negro History* 1, no. 2 (April 1916): 110–31.

Hasbrouck, Frank. *The History of Dutchess County, New York*. Poughkeepsie: S. A. Matthieu, 1909.

Hatch, Nathan, O. *The Democratization of American Christianity*. New Haven: Yale University Press, 1989.

Hershberg, Theodore, ed. *Philadelphia: Work, Space, Family, and Group Experience in the Nineteenth Century*. New York: Oxford University Press, 1981.

Hesslink, George K. *Black Neighbors: Negroes in a Northern Rural Community*, 2nd ed. Indianapolis: Bobbs-Merrill, 1974.

Higginbotham, A. Leon, Jr. *In the Matter of Color: Race and the American Legal Process: The Colonial Period*. New York: Oxford University Press, 1978.

Hine, Darlene Clark, ed. *The State of Afro-American History: Past, Present, and Future*. Baton Rouge: Louisiana State University Press, 1986.

Hinerfeld, Joshua Gordon. "The Fading Veneer of Equality: The Afro-American Experience in Poughkeepsie Between 1840 and 1860." *Yearbook*, Dutchess County Historical Society 68 (1983): 83–100.

———. "Putting Goat Hair on Sheep: A Case Study Approach Analyzing Northern Notions of Racial Equality during the Era of American Reconstruction." Unpublished paper, Department of History, Vassar College, February 14, 1983.

Hirsch, Leo. "New York and the Negro from 1783 to 1865." *Journal of Negro History* 16, no. 4 (October 1931): 382–473.

*Historical and Genealogical Record, Dutchess and Putnam Counties*. Poughkeepsie: Oxford/A. V. Haight, 1912.

Hodges, Graham Russell. "Black Revolt in New York City and the Neutral Zone: 1775–1783." In *New York in the Age of the Constitution, 1775–1800*, ed. Paul A. Gilje and William Pencak, 20–47. Rutherford: Farleigh Dickinson University Press, 1992.

———. *David Ruggles: A Radical Black Abolitionist and the Underground Railroad in New York City*. Chapel Hill: University of North Carolina Press, 2010.

———. *Root and Branch: African Americans in New York and East Jersey, 1613–1863*. Chapel Hill: University of North Carolina Press, 1999.

———. *Slavery and Freedom in the Rural North: African Americans in Monmouth County, New Jersey, 1665–1865*. Madison: Madison House, 1997.

Hoffman, Ronald, and Peter J. Albert, eds. *The Transforming Hand of Revolution: Reconsidering the American Revolution as a Social Movement*. Charlottesville: University Press of Virginia, 1995.

Holton, Woody. *Forced Founders: Indians, Debtors, Slaves, and the Making of the American Revolution in Virginia*. Chapel Hill: University of North Carolina Press, 1999.

Hood, J. W. *One Hundred Years of the African Methodist Episcopal Zion Church*. New York: African Methodist Episcopal Zion Book Concern, 1895.

Horton, James Oliver. *Free People of Color: Inside the African-American Community*. Washington, DC: Smithsonian Institution Press, 1993.

Horton, James Oliver, and Lois E. Horton. *Black Bostonians: Family Life and Community Struggle in the Antebellum North*. New York: Holmes and Meier, 1979.

———. *In Hope of Liberty: Culture, Community, and Protest among Northern Free Blacks, 1700–1860*. New York: Oxford University Press, 1997.

Hudson, Larry E., Jr. *To Have and to Hold: Slave Work and Family Life in Antebellum South Carolina*. Athens: University of Georgia Press, 1997.

———, ed. *Working Toward Freedom: Slave Society and Domestic Economy in the American South*. Rochester: University of Rochester Press, 1994.

Humphrey, Thomas J. *Land and Liberty: Hudson Valley Riots in the Age of Revolution*. DeKalb: Northern Illinois University Press, 2004.

Huntington, Isaac. *History of Little Nine Partners of Northeast Precinct, and Pine Plains, New York, Dutchess County*. Amenia: Charles Walsh & Company, 1897.

Ignatiev, Noel. *How the Irish Became White*. New York: Routledge, 1995.

Jeffrey, Julie Roy. "'No Occurrence in Human History Is More Deserving Than This': Abolitionist Celebrations of Freedom." In *Prophets of Protest: Reconsidering the History of American Abolitionism*, ed. Timothy Patrick McCarthy and John Stauffer, 200–19. New York: New Press, 2006.

"John A. Bolding, Fugitive Slave." *Yearbook*, Dutchess County Historical Society 20 (1935): 51–55.

Johnson, Denise Love. "Black Migration Patterns: A Case Study of the Origin and Development of the Black Population in the City of Poughkeepsie, New York." Unpublished paper, Department of Geography, Vassar College, May 1973.

Johnson, Franklin. *The Development of State Legislation Concerning the Free Negro*. Westport: Greenwood Press, 1979; originally published 1918.

Johnson, James M., Christopher Pryslopski, and Andrew Villani, eds. *Key to the North Country: The Hudson River Valley in the American Revolution*. Albany: State University of New York Press, 2013.

Johnson, James Weldon. *Black Manhattan*. New York: Alfred A. Knopf, 1940; originally published 1930.

Jones, Douglas Lamar. "The Strolling Poor: Transiency in Eighteenth-Century Massachusetts." *Journal of Social History* 8 (1975): 28–54.

Kammen, Michael. "The American Revolution as a *Crise de Conscience*: The Case of New York." In *Society, Freedom, and Conscience: The American Revolution in Virginia, Massachusetts, and New York*, ed. Richard M. Jellison. New York: W.W. Norton & Company, 1976.

———. *Colonial New York: A History*. New York: Oxford University Press, 1975.

Kaplan, Sidney, and Emma Nogrady Kaplan. *The Black Presence in the Era of the American Revolution*, revised edition. Amherst: University of Massachusetts Press, 1989.

Kates, Don B. "Abolition, Deportation, Integration: Attitudes toward Slavery in the Early Republic." *Journal of Negro History* 53, no. 1 (January 1968): 33–47.

Katz, Michael B. *In the Shadow of the Poorhouse: A Social History of Welfare in America*. New York: Basic Books, 1986.

———. *Poverty and Policy in American History*. New York: Academic Press, 1983.

Katzman, David M. *Before the Ghetto: Black Detroit in the Nineteenth Century*. Urbana: University of Illinois Press, 1973.

Kerber, Linda. "Abolitionists and Amalgamators: The New York City Race Riots of 1834." *New York History* 48, no. 1 (January 1967): 28–39.

Kierner, Cynthia A. "Landlord and Tenant in Revolutionary New York: The Case of Livingston Manor." *New York History* 70, no. 1 (April 1989): 133–52.

Kim, Sung Bok. "Impact of Class Relations and Warfare in the American Revolution: The New York Experience." *Journal of American History* 69, no. 2 (September 1982): 326–46.

———. *Landlord and Tenant in Colonial New York: Manorial Society, 1664–1775*. Chapel Hill: University of North Carolina Press, 1978.

———. "The Limits of Politicization in the American Revolution: The Experience of Westchester County, New York." *Journal of American History* 80, no. 3 (December 1993): 868–89.

King, Charles Donald, Jr. "The Development of Education in Dutchess County." In *Transformations of an American County: Dutchess County, New York, 1683–1983*, ed. Joyce C. Ghee, 123–30. Poughkeepsie: Dutchess County Historical Society, 1986.

———. *History of Education in Dutchess County*. Cape May: The Author, 1959.

Klein, Milton M., ed. *The Empire State: A History of New York*. Ithaca: Cornell University Press, 2001.

Kobrin, David. *The Black Minority in Early New York*. Albany: University of the State of New York, 1971.

Kraditor, Aileen S. *Means and Ends in American Abolitionism: Garrison and His Critics on Strategy and Tactics, 1834–1850*. New York: Pantheon Books, 1969.

Kruger, Vivienne L. "Born to Run: The Slave Family in Early New York, 1626 to 1827." PhD dissertation, Columbia University, 1985.

Kwasney, Mark V. *Washington's Partisan War, 1775–1783*. Kent: Kent State University Press, 1996.

Lepore, Jill. *New York Burning: Liberty, Slavery, and Conspiracy in Eighteenth-Century Manhattan*. New York: Alfred A. Knopf, 2005.

———. "The Tightening Vise: Slavery and Freedom in British New York." In *Slavery in New York*, ed. Ira Berlin and Leslie M. Harris, chap. 2. New York: New Press, 2005.

Levine, Lawrence. *Black Culture and Black Consciousness*. New York: Oxford University Press, 1977.

Lewis, Debra Eileen. "Walking Fredonia Lane." *Dutchess*, February 2002.

Lincoln, C. Eric. *The Black Church since Frazier*. New York: Schocken Books, 1974.

Lincoln, C. Eric, and Lawrence H. Mamiya. *The Black Church in the African-American Experience*. Durham: Duke University Press, 1990.

Lindsay, Arnett G. "The Economic Condition of the Negroes of New York Prior to 1861." *Journal of Negro History* 6, no. 2 (April 1921): 190–99.

Littlefield, Daniel C. *Revolutionary Citizens: African Americans, 1776–1804*. New York: Oxford University Press, 1997.

Litwack, Leon F. "The Abolitionist Dilemma: The Antislavery Movement and the Northern Negro." *New England Quarterly* 34, no. 1 (March 1961): 50–73.

———. *North of Slavery: The Negro in the Free States, 1790–1860*. Chicago: University of Chicago Press, 1961.

Lydon, James G. "New York and the Slave Trade." *William and Mary Quarterly*, Third Series, 35, no. 2 (April 1978): 375–94.

Lynd, Staughton. *Anti-Federalism in Dutchess County, New York: A Study of Democracy and Class Conflict in the Revolutionary Era*. Chicago: Loyola University Press, 1962.

———. *Class Conflict, Slavery, and the United States Constitution*. New York: Bobbs-Merrill Company, 1967.

Mabee, Carlton. *Black Education in New York State from Colonial to Modern Times*. Syracuse: Syracuse University Press, 1979.

———. *Black Freedom: The Nonviolent Abolitionists from 1830 through the Civil War*. Toronto: Macmillan, 1970.

———. "Separate Black Education in Dutchess County." *Yearbook*, Dutchess County Historical Society 65 (1980): 5–20.

———. *Sojourner Truth: Slave, Prophet, Legend*. New York: New York University Press, 1993.

MacCracken, Henry Noble. *Blithe Dutchess: The Flowering of an American Community from 1812*. New York: Hastings House, 1958.

———. *Old Dutchess Forever! The Story of an American County*. New York: Hastings House, 1956.

MacEacheren, Elaine. "Emancipation of Slavery in Massachusetts: A Reexamination, 1770–1790." *Journal of Negro History* 55, no. 4 (October 1970): 289–308.

MacLeod, Duncan J. *Slavery, Race, and the American Revolution*. New York: Cambridge University Press, 1974.

Magdol, Edward. *The Antislavery Rank and File: A Social Profile of the Abolitionists' Constituency*. Westport: Greenwood Press, 1986.

Maika, Dennis. "Encounters: Slavery and the Philipse Family: 1680–1751." In *Dutch New York: The Roots of Hudson Valley Culture*, ed. Roger Panetta. Yonkers: Hudson River Museum/Fordham University Press, 2009.

Malone, Christopher. *Between Freedom and Bondage: Race, Party, and Voting Rights in the Antebellum North*. New York: Routledge, 2008.

Mamiya, Lawrence, and Patricia Kaurouma. "You Never Hear About Their Struggles: Black Oral History in Poughkeepsie, New York." *Afro-Americans in New York Life and History* 4, no. 2 (July 1980): 55-70.

Mamiya, Lawrence H., and Lorraine M. Roberts. "Invisible People, Untold Stories: A Historical Overview of the Black Community in Poughkeepsie." In *New Perspectives on Poughkeepsie's Past: Essays to Honor Edmund Platt*, ed. Clyde Griffen. Poughkeepsie: Dutchess County Historical Society, 1988.

Matison, Sumner Eliot. "Manumission by Purchase." *Journal of Negro History* 33, no. 2 (April 1948): 146–67.

Mays, Benjamin E. *The Negro's God as Reflected in His Literature*. New York: Russell & Russell, 1968; originally published 1938.

McCarthy, Timothy Patrick. "'To Plead Our Own Cause': Black Print Culture and the Origins of American Abolitionism." In *Prophets of Protest: Reconsidering the History of American Abolitionism*, ed. Timothy Patrick McCarthy and John Stauffer, 114–44. New York: New Press, 2006.

McCarthy, Timothy Patrick, and John Stauffer, eds. *Prophets of Protest: Reconsidering the History of American Abolitionism*. New York: New Press, 2006.

McDermott, William P., ed. *Clinton, Dutchess County, New York: A History of a Town*. Clinton Corners: Clinton Historical Society, 1987.

———. *Dutchess County's Plain Folks: Enduring Uncertainty, Inequality, and Uneven Prosperity, 1725–1875*. Tolland: Kerleen Press, 2004.

———. "Slaves and Slaveowners in Dutchess County." *Afro-Americans in New York Life and History* 19 (January 1995): 17–41.

McKee, Samuel. "A Century of Labor." In *History of the State of New York*, ed. Alexander C. Flick, vol. 2. New York: Columbia University, 1933.

———. "The Economic Pattern of Colonial New York." In *History of the State of New York*, ed. Alexander C. Flick, vol. 2. New York: Columbia University, 1933.

———. *Labor in Colonial New York, 1664–1776*. Port Washington: Ira J. Friedman, 1963; originally published 1935.

McKivigan, John R., and Jason H. Silverman. "Monarchial Liberty and Republican Slavery: West Indies Emancipation Day Celebrations in Upstate New York and Canada West." *Afro-Americans in New York Life and History* 10, no. 1 (January 1986): 7–18.

McManus, Edgar. *A History of Negro Slavery in New York*. Syracuse: Syracuse University Press, 1966.

Medford, Edna Greene. "'It Was a Very Comfortable Place for Poor Folks': Subsistence in a Rural Antebellum Free Black Community." *Locus* 5, no. 2 (Spring 1993): 131–44.

Melish, Joanne Pope. *Disowning Slavery: Gradual Emancipation and "Race" in New England, 1780–1860*. Ithaca: Cornell University Press, 1998.

Mid-Hudson Antislavery History Project. *Slavery, Antislavery, and the Underground Railroad: A Dutchess County Guide*. Poughkeepsie: Hudson House, 2010.

Middlekauf, Robert. *The Glorious Cause: The American Revolution, 1763–1789*. New York: Oxford University Press, 1982.

Mohl, Raymond. *Poverty in New York, 1783–1825*. New York: Oxford University Press, 1971.

Moore, Christopher. "A World of Possibilities: Slavery and Freedom in Dutch New Amsterdam." In *Slavery in New York*, ed. Ira Berlin and Leslie M. Harris, chap. 1. New York: New Press, 2005.

Moore, John Jamison. *History of the A.M.E. Zion Church in America*. York: Teachers' Journal Office, 1884.

Morgan, Edmund. *American Slavery, American Freedom*. New York: W.W. Norton & Company, 1975.

Morgan, Edmund V. "Slavery in New York: The Status of the Slave under the English Colonial Government." *Papers of the American Historical Association* 5, no. 4 (October 1891): 3–16.

Morrison, Howard Alexander. "Gentlemen of Proper Understanding: A Closer Look at Utica's Anti-Abolitionist Mob." *New York History* 62, no. 1 (January 1981): 61–82.

Moss, Richard Shannon. *Slavery on Long Island: A Study in Local Institutional and Early African-American Community Life*. New York: Garland, 1993.

Moss, Simeon F. "The Persistence of Slavery and Involuntary Servitude in a Free State, 1685–1866." *Journal of Negro History* 35, no. 3 (July 1950): 289–314.

Myers, John L. "The Beginning of Anti-Slavery Agencies in New York State, 1833–1836." *New York History* 43, no. 2 (April 1962): 149–81.

———. "The Major Effort of National Anti-Slavery Agents in New York State, 1836–1837." *New York History* 46, no. 2 (April 1965): 162–86.

Nash, Gary B. "Forging Freedom: The Emancipation Experience in Northern Seaport Cities." In *Slavery and Freedom in the Age of the American Revolution*, ed. Ira Berlin and Ronald Hoffman, 3–48. Charlottesville: University Press of Virginia, 1983.

———. *Forging Freedom: The Formation of Philadelphia's Black Community, 1720–1840*. Cambridge: Harvard University Press, 1988.

———. "Poverty and Poor Relief in Pre-Revolutionary Philadelphia." *William and Mary Quarterly*, Third Series 33, no. 1 (January 1976): 3–30.

———. *Race and Revolution*. Madison: Madison House, 1990.

———. *The Unknown American Revolution: The Unruly Birth of Democracy and the Struggle to Create America*. New York: Viking, 2005.

———. *The Urban Crucible: Social Change, Political Consciousness, and the Origins of the American Revolution*. Cambridge: Harvard University Press, 1979.

Nash, Gary B., and Jean R. Soderlund. *Freedom by Degrees: Emancipation in Pennsylvania and Its Aftermath*. New York: Oxford University Press, 1991.

Newman, Richard S. *The Transformation of American Abolitionism: Fighting Slavery in the Early Republic*. Chapel Hill: University of North Carolina Press, 2002.

Nordstrom, Carl. "The New York Slave Code." *Afro-Americans in New York Life and History* 4, no. 1 (January 1980): 7–26.

Northrup, A. Judd. *Slavery in New York*. Albany: University of the State of New York, 1900.

Norton, Mary Beth. "The Fate of Some Black Loyalists of the American Revolution." *Journal of Negro History* 58, no.4 (October 1973): 402–26.

Nye, Russell B. *Fettered Freedom: Civil Liberties and the Slavery Controversy, 1830–1860*. Urbana: University of Illinois Press, 1972; originally published 1948.

Oblinger, Carl D. "Alms for Oblivion: The Making of a Black Underclass in Southeastern Pennsylvania, 1780–1860." In *The Ethnic Experience in Pennsylvania*, ed. John E. Bodnar, 94–119. Lewisburg: Bucknell University Press, 1973.

———. "Freedom's Foundations: Black Communities in Southeastern Pennsylvania Towns, 1780–1860." *The Northwest Missouri State University Press* 33, no. 4 (November 1972): 3–23.

———. "In Recognition of Their Prominence: A Case Study of the Economic and Social Backgrounds of an Antebellum Negro Business and Farming Class in Lancaster County." *Journal of the Lancaster County Historical Society* 72 (1968): 65–83.

———. "New Freedoms, Old Miseries: The Emergence and Disruption of Black Communities in Southeastern Pennsylvania, 1780–1860." PhD dissertation, Lehigh University, 1988.

O'Callaghan, E. B. *History of New Netherland*, 2 vols. New York: D. Appleton & Company, 1846.

Olson, Edwin. "The Slave Code in Colonial New York." *Journal of Negro History* 29, no. 2 (April 1944): 147–65.

———. "Social Aspects of the Slave in New York." *Journal of Negro History* 27, no. 1 (January 1941): 66–77.

Ottley, Roi, and William J. Weatherby. *The Negro in New York: An Informal Social History, 1626–1940*. New York: New York Public Library, 1967.

Painter, Nell Irvin. *Sojourner Truth: A Life, a Symbol*. New York: W.W. Norton and Company, 1996.

Pease, Jane, and William Pease. "Antislavery Ambivalence: Immediatism, Expediency, Race." *American Quarterly* 17, no. 4 (Winter 1965): 682–95.

———. "Confrontation and Abolitionism in the 1850s." *Journal of American History* 58, no. 4 (March 1972): 923–37.

———. "Ends, Means, and Attitudes: Black-White Conflict in the Anti-Slavery Movement." *Civil War History* 18, no. 2 (June 1972): 117–28.

———. "Negro Conventions and the Problem of Black Leadership." *Journal of Black Studies* 2, no. 1 (September 1971): 29–44.

———. *They Who Would Be Free: Blacks' Search for Freedom, 1830–1861*. New York: Athenaeum, 1974.

Perlman, Daniel. "Organizations of the Free Negroes in New York City, 1800–1860." *Journal of Negro History* 56, no. 3 (July 1971): 181–97.

Piersen, William D. *Black Yankees: The Development of an Afro-American Subculture in Eighteenth-Century New England*. Amherst: University of Massachusetts Press, 1988.

Platt, Edmund. *The Eagle's History of Poughkeepsie, From the Earliest Settlements, 1683–1905*. Poughkeepsie: Dutchess County Historical Society, 1987; originally published 1905.

Poillucci, Richard. "Historical Directory of Religion in Poughkeepsie, New

York, 1810–1976." Unpublished paper, Adriance Memorial Library, January 1977.

Porter, Dorothy. "The Organized Educational Activities of Negro Literary Societies, 1828–1846." In *The Making of Black America: Essays in Negro Life and History*, ed. August Meier and Elliott Rudwick, vol. 1, 276–88. New York: Athenaeum, 1969.

Pybus, Cassandra. *Epic Journeys of Freedom: Runaway Slaves of the American Revolution and Their Global Quest for Liberty*. Boston: Beacon Press, 2006.

Quarles, Benjamin. *Black Abolitionists*. New York: Oxford University Press, 1969.

———. *Black Mosaic: Essays in Afro-American History and Historiography*. Amherst: University of Massachusetts Press, 1988.

———. *The Negro in the American Revolution*. Chapel Hill: University of North Carolina Press, 1961.

Quigley, David. "Southern Slavery in a Free City: Economy, Politics, and Culture." In *Slavery in New York*, ed. Ira Berlin and Leslie M. Harris, chap. 9. New York: New Press, 2005.

Quinn, Edythe Ann. *Freedom Journey: Black Civil War Soldiers and the Hills Community, Westchester County, New York*. Albany: State University of New York Press, 2015.

———. "'The Hills' in the Mid-Nineteenth Century: The History of a Rural Afro-American Community in Westchester County, New York." *Afro-Americans in New York Life and History* 14, no. 2 (July 1990): 35–50.

Raboteau, Albert. *Canaan Land: A Religious History of African Americans*. New York: Oxford University Press, 2001.

Rael, Patrick, ed. *African-American Activism before the Civil War*. New York: Routledge, 2008.

———. *Black Identity and Black Protest in the Antebellum North*. Chapel Hill: University of North Carolina Press, 2002.

———. "The Long Death of Slavery." In *Slavery in New York*, ed. Ira Berlin and Leslie M. Harris, chap. 4. New York: New Press, 2005.

Raphael, Ray. *A People's History of the American Revolution: How Common People Shaped the Fight for Independence*. New York: Harper Collins, 2002.

Ratner, Lorman. *Powder Keg: Northern Opposition to the Antislavery Movement, 1831–1840*. New York: Basic Books, 1968.

Reed, Harry. *Platform for Change: The Foundations of the Northern Free Black Community, 1775–1865*. East Lansing: Michigan State University Press, 1994.

Reed, Newton. *Early History of Amenia*. Amenia: DeLacey and Wiley, 1875.

"Remarks of Isaac S. Wheaton at Lithgow, September 21, 1921." *Yearbook*, Dutchess County Historical Society (1922): 22–24.

Reynolds, Helen Wilkinson. "The Negro in Dutchess County in the Eighteenth Century." *Yearbook*, Dutchess County Historical Society 26 (1941): 89–100.

Richards, Leonard L. *"Gentlemen of Property and Standing": Anti-Abolition Mobs in Jacksonian America*. New York: Oxford University Press, 1970.

Richardson, Harry V. *Dark Salvation: The Story of Methodism as It Developed Among Blacks in America*. Garden City: Doubleday, 1976.

Riddell, William Renwick. "The Slave in Early New York." *Journal of Negro History* 13 (1928): 53–86.

Robinson, Donald L. *Slavery in the Structure of American Politics, 1765–1820*. New York: Harcourt, Brace, Jovanovich, 1971.

Roediger, David R. *The Wages of Whiteness: Race and the Making of the American Working Class*. New York: Verso, 1991.

Rogers, Eleanor. "Mills of the Old Clinton Precinct." In *Clinton, Dutchess County, New York: A History of a Town*, ed. William P. McDermott, 57–69. Clinton Corners: Clinton Historical Society, 1987.

Rose, Willie Lee. "The Impact of the American Revolution on the Black Population." In Willie Lee Rose, *Slavery and Freedom*, expanded edition, ed. William W. Freehling, 3–17. New York: Oxford University Press, 1982.

Roth, Eric J. "'The Society of Negroes Unsettled': A History of Slavery in New Paltz, New York." *Afro-Americans in New York Life and History* 27, no. 1 (January 2003): 27–54.

Rothman, David J. *The Discovery of the Asylum: Social Order and Disorder in the New Republic*. Boston: Little, Brown, 1971.

Sargent, Charles J., Jr. "The Negro Church in Dutchess County, New York." Unpublished paper, Adriance Memorial Library, September 30, 1955.

Scott, Kenneth. "The Slave Insurrection in New York in 1712." *New-York Historical Society Quarterly* 45, no. 1 (January 1961): 43–74.

Sernett, Milton C. *North Star Country: Upstate New York and the Crusade for African-American Freedom*. Syracuse: Syracuse University Press, 2001.

Sevitch, Benjamin. "The Well-Planned Riot of October 21, 1835: Utica's Answer to Abolitionism." *New York History* 50, no. 3 (July 1969): 251–63.

Sewell, Richard H. *Ballots for Freedom: Antislavery Politics in the United States, 1837–1860*. New York: Oxford University Press, 1976.

Singer, Roberta. "The Livingstons as Slave Owners: The 'Peculiar Institution' on Livingston Manor and Clermont." In *The Livingston Legacy: Three Centuries of American History*, ed. Richard Wiles. Annandale-on-Hudson: Bard College, 1987.

Sklar, Kathryn Kish. *Women's Rights Emerges within the Antislavery Movement, 1830–1870: A Brief History with Documents*. Boston/New York: Bedford St. Martin's, 2000.

Smith, Billy G. "Black Family Life in Philadelphia from Slavery to Freedom." In *Shaping a National Culture: The Philadelphia Experience, 1750–1800*, ed. Catherine E. Hutchins, 77–97. Winterthur: Henry Francis du Pont Winterthur Museum, 1994.

———. *The "Lower Sort": Philadelphia's Laboring People, 1750–1800*. Ithaca: Cornell University Press, 1990.

———. "Poverty and Economic Marginality in Eighteenth-Century America." *Proceedings of the American Philosophical Society* 132, no. 1 (1988): 85–118.

———. "Runaway Slaves in the Mid-Atlantic Region during the Revolutionary Era." In *The Transforming Hand of Revolution: Reconsidering the American Revolution as a Social Movement.* Charlottesville: University Press of Virginia, 1995.

Smith, Edward D. *Climbing Jacob's Ladder: The Rise of Black Churches in Eastern American Cities, 1740–1877.* Washington, DC: Smithsonian Institution, 1988.

Smith, Edward M. *Documentary History of Rhinebeck, in Dutchess County, New York.* Rhinebeck, Dutchess County: 1881.

Smith, James H. *History of Dutchess County, New York.* Syracuse: D. Mason & Company, 1882.

Smith, Philip H. *General History of Duchess County, from 1609 to 1876, Inclusive.* Pawling: The Author, 1877.

Soderlund, Jean R. *Quakers and Slavery: A Divided Spirit.* Princeton: Princeton University Press, 1985.

Sorin, Gerald. *The New York Abolitionists: A Case Study of Political Radicalism.* Westport: Greenwood, 1971.

"Special Issue on Racial Consciousness and Nation-Building in the Early Republic." *Journal of the Early Republic* 19, no. 4 (Winter 1999).

Stauffer, John. *The Black Hearts of Men: Radical Abolitionists and the Transformation of Race.* Cambridge: Harvard University Press, 2002.

Stewart, James Brewer. "The Emergence of Racial Modernity and the Rise of the White North," with comments by Joan Soderlund, James Oliver Horton, and Ronald G. Walters. *Journal of the Early Republic* 18, no. 2 (Summer 1998): 181–236.

———. *Holy Warriors: The Abolitionists and American Slavery.* New York: Hill & Wang, 1976.

Stuckey, Sterling. *The Ideological Origins of Black Nationalism.* Boston: Beacon Press, 1972.

———. *Slave Culture: Nationalist Theory and the Foundations of Black America.* New York: Oxford University Press 1987.

Sutherland, Cara, ed. *A Heritage Uncovered: The Black Experience in Upstate New York, 1800–1925.* Elmira: Chemung County Historical Society, 1988.

Tiedemann, Joseph. "Loyalists and Conflict Resolution in Post-Revolutionary New York: Queens County as a Test Case." *New York History* 68, no.1 (January 1987): 27–43.

———. "Patriots by Default: Queens County, New York, and the British Army, 1776–1783." *William and Mary Quarterly*, Third Series, 43, no. 1 (January 1986): 35–63.

———. "A Revolution Foiled: Queens County, New York, 1775–1776." *Journal of American History* 75, no. 2 (September 1988): 417–44.

Tise, Larry E. *The American Counterrevolution: A Retreat from Liberty, 1783–1800*. Mechanicsburg: Stockpole Books, 1998.

———. *Proslavery: A History of the Defense of Slavery in America, 1701–1840*. Athens: University of Georgia Press, 1987.

Upton, Dell. "Dutchess County Quakers and Slavery, 1750–1830." *Yearbook*, Dutchess County Historical Society 55 (1970): 55– 60.

Van Buskirk, Judith L. *Generous Enemies: Patriots and Loyalists in Revolutionary New York*. Philadelphia: University of Pennsylvania Press, 2002.

Ver Nooy, Amy Pearce. "The Anti-Slavery Movement in Dutchess County, 1835–1850." *Yearbook*, Dutchess County Historical Society 28 (1943): 57–66.

Vincent, Reverend L. M. *Methodism in Poughkeepsie and Its Vicinity: Its Rise and Progress from 1780 to 1892*. Poughkeepsie: A. V. Haight, n.d.

Vincent, Stephen A. *Southern Seed, Northern Soil: African-American Farm Communities in the Midwest, 1765–1900*. Bloomington: Indiana University Press, 1999.

Waldstreicher, David. *In the Midst of Perpetual Fetes: The Making of American Nationalism, 1776–1820*. Chapel Hill: University of North Carolina Press, 1997.

———. "Reading the Runaways: Self-Fashioning Print Culture, and Confidence in Slavery in the Eighteenth-Century Mid-Atlantic." *William and Mary Quarterly*, Third Series, 56, no. 2 (April 1999): 243–72.

Walker, Clarence E. *Deromanticizing Black History: Critical Essays and Reappraisals*. Knoxville: University of Tennessee, 1991.

Walker, George. "The Afro-American in New York City, 1827–1860." PhD dissertation, Columbia University, 1975.

Walker, James W. St. G. *The Black Loyalists: The Search for a Promised Land in Nova Scotia and Sierra Leone, 1783–1870*. New York: Dalhousie University Press, 1976.

Walls, William J. *The African Methodist Episcopal Zion Church: Reality of the Black Church*. Charlotte: A.M.E. Zion Publishing House, 1974.

Washington, Joseph R. *Black Religion: The Negro and Christianity in the United States*. Boston: Beacon Press, 1964.

Watkins, Ralph. "A Survey of the African-American Presence in the History of the Downstate New York Area." *Afro-Americans in New York Life and History* 15, no. 1 (January 1991): 53–79.

Wermuth, Thomas. "The Central Hudson Valley: Dutchess, Orange, and Ulster Counties." In *The Other New York: The American Revolution beyond New York City, 1763–1787*, ed. Joseph S. Tiedemann and Eugene R. Fingerhut, 127–54. Albany: State University of New York Press, 2005.

———. "New York Farmers and the Market Revolution: Economic Behavior in the Mid-Hudson Valley, 1780–1830." *Journal of Social History* 32, no. 1 (Fall 1998): 179–96.

———. *Rip Van Winkle's Neighbors: The Transformation of Rural Society in the Hudson River Valley, 1720–1850*. Albany: State University of New York Press, 2001.

Wesley, Charles H. "The Negroes of New York in the Emancipation Movement." *Journal of Negro History* 24, no. 1 (January 1939): 65–103.

———. "The Participation of Negroes in Anti-Slavery Political Parties." *Journal of Negro History* 29, no. 1 (January 1944): 32–74.

White, Shane. "Black Life in Freedom: Creating a Popular Culture." In *Slavery in New York*, ed. Ira Berlin and Leslie M. Harris, chap. 5. New York: New Press, 2005.

———. "Impious Prayers: Elite and Popular Attitudes Toward Blacks and Slavery in the Middle Atlantic States, 1783–1810." *New York History* 67, no. 3 (July 1986): 261–83.

———. "Pinkster: Afro-Dutch Syncretization in New York City and the Hudson Valley." *Journal of American Folklore* 102, no. 403 (January–March 1989): 68–75.

———. "Pinkster in Albany, 1803: A Contemporary Description." *New York History* 70 (1989): 191–99.

———. *Somewhat More Independent: The End of Slavery in New York City, 1770–1810*. Athens: University of Georgia Press, 1991.

———. *Stories of Freedom in Black New York*. Cambridge: Harvard University Press, 2002.

White, Shane, and Graham White. *Stylin': African-American Expressive Culture from Its Beginnings to the Zoot Suit*. Ithaca: Cornell University Press, 1998.

Whitman, T. Stephen. *The Price of Freedom: Slavery and Manumission in Baltimore and Early National Maryland*. Lexington: University of Kentucky Press, 1997.

Wiggins, William H. *O Freedom! Afro-American Emancipation Celebrations*. Knoxville: University of Tennessee Press, 1987.

Wilder, Craig Steven. *A Covenant with Color: Race and Social Power in Brooklyn*. New York: Columbia University Press, 2000.

———. *In the Company of Black Men: The African Influence on African-American Culture in New York City*. New York: New York University Press, 2001.

Williams-Myers, A. J. "The African (American) in the Mid-Hudson Valley before 1800: Some Historiographical Clues." In *Transformations of an American County: Dutchess County, New York, 1683–1983*, ed. Joyce C. Ghee, 107–16. Poughkeepsie: Dutchess County Historical Society, 1986.

———. "The African Presence in the Hudson River Valley: The Defining of Relationships between the Masters and the Slaves." *Afro-Americans in New York Life and History* 12, no. 1 (January 1988): 81–98.

———. "The African Presence in the Mid-Hudson Valley before 1800: A Preliminary Historiographical Sketch." *Afro-Americans in New York Life and History* 8, no. 1 (January 1984): 31–39.

———. "The Arduous Journey: The African-American Presence in the Mid-Hudson Region." In *The African-American Presence in New York State History: Four Regional History Surveys*, ed. Monroe Fordham, 19–49. Albany: State University of New York Press, 1990.

———. "Hands That Picked No Cotton: An Exploratory Examination of African Slave Labor in the Colonial Economy of the Hudson River Valley to 1800." *Afro-Americans in New York Life and History* 11, no. 2 (July 1987): 25–51.

———. *Long Hammering: Essays on the Forging of an African-American Presence in the Hudson River Valley to the Early Twentieth Century*. Trenton: Africana World Press, 1994.

———. *On the Morning Tide: African Americans, History, and Methodology in the Historical Ebb and Flow of Hudson River Society*. Trenton: Africana World Press, 2003.

———. "Pinkster Carnival: Africanisms in the Hudson River Valley." *Afro-Americans in New York Life and History* 9, no. 1 (January 1985): 7–17.

Wilmore, Gayraud S. *Black Religion and Black Radicalism*. Garden City: Doubleday, 1972.

Wilson, Ellen Gibson. *The Loyal Blacks*. New York: G. P. Putnam's Sons, 1976.

Wilson, Warren H. *Quaker Hill: A Sociological Study*. New York, 1907.

———. *Quaker Hill in the Eighteenth Century*, 2nd ed. Quaker Hill: Quaker Hill Conference Association, 1905.

Winch, Julie. *Between Slavery and Freedom: Free People of Color in America from Settlement to the Civil War*. New York: Rowman & Littlefield, 2014.

Wood, Gordon S. *The Radicalism of the American Revolution*. New York: Alfred A. Knopf, 1992.

Wood, Peter H. "'The Dream Deferred': Black Freedom Struggles on the Eve of White Independence." In *In Resistance: Studies in African, Caribbean, and Afro-American History*, ed. Gary Y. Okihiro, 166–87. Amherst: University of Massachusetts Press, 1986.

———. "'Liberty Is Sweet': African-American Freedom Struggles in the Years before White Independence." In *Beyond the American Revolution: Explorations in the History of American Radicalism*, ed. Alfred Young. DeKalb: Northern Illinois University Press, 1993.

Woodson, Carter G. *The Education of the Negro Prior to 1861*. New York: G. P. Putnam's Sons, 1915.

———. *The History of the Negro Church*. Washington, DC: Associated Publishers, 1945; originally published 1921.

Wright, Conrad Edick. *The Transformation of Charity in Postrevolutionary New England*. Boston: Northeastern University Press, 1992.

Wright, Donald. *African Americans in the Colonial Era: From African Origins Through the American Revolution*. Arlington Heights: Harlan Davidson, 1990.

———. *African Americans in the Early Republic, 1789–1831*. Arlington Heights: Harlan Davidson, 1993.

Yacovone, Donald. "The Transformation of the Black Temperance Movement, 1827–1854: An Interpretation." *Journal of the Early Republic* 8, no. 3 (1988): 281–97.

Young, Alfred F., ed. *The American Revolution: Explorations in the History of American Radicalism*. DeKalb: Northern Illinois University Press, 1976.

———. *Beyond the American Revolution: Explorations in the History of American Radicalism.* DeKalb: Northern Illinois University Press, 1993.

Zilversmit, Arthur. *The First Emancipation: The Abolition of Slavery in the North.* Chicago: University of Chicago Press, 1967.

Zimm, Louise Hasbrouck, Rev. A. Elwood Corning, Joseph W. Emsley, and Willitt C. Jewell, eds. *Southeastern New York: A History of the Counties of Ulster, Dutchess, Orange, Rockland, and Putnam*, vol. 1. New York: Lewis Historical Publishing Company, 1946.

# Index